The Challenge of
Liberation Theology:
A First World Response

The Challenge of
Liberation Theology:
A First World Response

Edited by
BRIAN MAHAN
and
L. DALE RICHESIN

ORBIS BOOKS
Maryknoll, New York 10545

The Catholic Foreign Mission Society of America (Maryknoll) recruits and trains people for overseas missionary service. Through Orbis Books Maryknoll aims to foster the international dialogue that is essential to mission. The books published, however, reflect the opinions of their authors and are not meant to represent the official position of the society.

Library of Congress Cataloging in Publication Data

Main entry under title:

The Challenge of liberation theology.

   Includes bibliographical references and index.
   1. Liberation theology—Addresses, essays,
lectures. I. Richesin, L. Dale. II. Mahan, Brian.
BT83.57.C46   261.8   81-9527
ISBN 0-88344-092X (pbk.)   AACR2

Contents

Introduction   *David Tracy*   1

1. "Thou Shalt Have No Other Jeans Before Me" (Levi's Advertisement, Early Seventies): The Need for Liberation in a Consumerist Society
    Dorothee Soelle   4

Response   *Schubert M. Ogden*   17

2. Liberation and Salvation: A First World View
    Lee Cormie   21

Response   *Brian Mahan*   48

3. Christian Faith and Political Praxis
    James H. Cone   52

Response   *Robin W. Lovin*   65

4. Black Theologies of Liberation: A Structural-Developmental Analysis
    James W. Fowler   69

5. Toward a Feminist Biblical Hermeneutics: Biblical Interpretation and Liberation Theology
    Elisabeth Schüssler Fiorenza   91

6. The Political Dimensions of Theology
    Langdon Gilkey   113

7. The Concept of a Theology of Liberation: Must a Christian Theology Today Be So Conceived?
    Schubert M. Ogden   127

Index   141

Acknowledgments

In May of 1979 a group of theologians gathered to address the challenge of liberation theology at a student conference at the Divinity School of the University of Chicago. L. Dale Richesin, Joe Colombo, and Emilie Townes were the student facilitators of that conference. With the exceptions of James Fowler and Langdon Gilkey, all the articles in this volume are based on papers from the conference in 1979. James Fowler's article is included because it brings a unique perspective to bear on the basic questions of liberation. Langdon Gilkey originally gave a response to Lee Cormie's paper at the conference. Gilkey's article is presented as a fuller exposition of his thought.

The editors wish to express their gratitude to the contributors to this volume as well as to those who participated in the conference. We also wish to acknowledge the support of the administration and faculty of the Divinity School of the University of Chicago, particularly Dean Joseph Kitagawa, Dean of Students Larry Greenfield, Associate Dean Anne Carr, David Tracy, Robin Lovin, Bernard O. Brown, David Bartlett, and Langdon Gilkey. Thanks also to the Divinity School Association, Joe Colombo, Emilie Townes, Ismael Garcia, Jim Bohman, Mary Patrick, David Booth, Janet Summers, Terrence Martin, Jr., Larry Bouchard, Ruth Bedell, and Merle Lufen for their valuable assistance.

Introduction

It is now clear that the major breakthrough in Christian theology in the last decade has been the explosive emergence of political and liberation theologies. From Latin American, African, and Asian liberation theologies through Euro-American political theologies to North American black theologies and feminist theologies, the theological landscape has been irretrievably changed. As this volume makes clear, this multifaceted challenge to theology-as-usual cannot be ignored. One of the singular virtues of this present collection is that the challenge of liberation and political theologies is discussed both by major representatives of those traditions and by several representatives of other forms of theology. As the reader soon learns, there is no lack of conflict in the conversation which liberation theologies have posed for all theologians. But what serious conversation (as distinct from vague attempts at "dialogue") has ever lacked such conflict?

Liberation and political theologians have provided persuasive evidence on several issues crucial to all theology. Among those issues are: first, the concept and the reality of full liberation is indeed a central, irreplaceable demand of any Christian theology; second, earlier existentialist and transcendental theologies were so concerned with the "authentic individual" that they were in constant danger of a kind of apolitical individualism that betrayed the socio-political insistence of all prophetic Christianity. Behind both these obvious gains—gains, let us note, that every form of theology *should* be open to recognizing—are some situational factors worth noting. Every form of theology is, in fact, the development of some mutually critical correlations between an interpretation of the Christian tradition and an interpretation of the contemporary situation. The moves forward (and backward) in theology occur principally when one of these three factors is challenged: either through some new interpretation of the contemporary situation; or some new interpretation of the Christian tradition; or some new mode of correlation.

On each of these counts, the political and liberation theologians have advanced the discussion of the options available. On the interpretation of the Christian tradition, they have shown, once and for all, that any purely individualist and any apolitical understanding of Christian salvation is a betrayal of the prophetic heritage of both Testaments. By their emphasis on the Exodus tradition and the prophetic and apocalyptic strands in both Testaments, they have exposed the crypto-Marcionism of much Christian theology. By their retrieval of often half-forgotten, even repressed move-

1

ments in the Christian tradition—especially the underground radical apocalyptic movements in every age—they have recovered a major strand of the tradition. By their insistence on hearing and speaking for those groups—living and dead—whose voices have not been heard by mainline Christian theology, they have forced us all to face the prophetic demand in the tradition itself. That demand was and is the prophetic and Jesuanic insistence on the oppressed as God's own privileged ones. That demand insists that no Christian can dare to ignore the memory of the suffering of the oppressed throughout the centuries—a memory that must instill action for liberation, never fatalism for the oppressed nor complacency for the oppressors.

Precisely by their hermeneutic of retrieval of these prophetic and apocalyptic traditions, the liberation and political theologians have released as well a profound hermeneutics of suspicion upon both the Christian tradition and the contemporary situation. By their development of genuine forms of Christian ideology-critique, these theologians have exposed the sexism, racism, classism, and economic, political, and cultural oppressions present in both the Christian tradition and the wider Western secular culture. Like their secular counterparts in the great secular liberation movements of our day, these theologians have shown, on both secular and inner-Christian grounds (i.e., prophetic and eschatological) the actualities of systemic oppression and even cognitive illusion in both Christianity and culture.

With that move to ideology-critique, the liberation and political theologians have also shifted the main focus of the contemporary theological discussion away from the "crisis of cognitive claims" provided by the Enlightenment and the rise of historical consciousness to a recognition of the crisis of massive global suffering, indeed of systemic oppression for whole groups, peoples, and cultures. It is not the case, of course, that the crisis of cognitive claims for Christianity will simply evaporate once this second and more radical crisis for an emerging global humanity is faced. Indeed, a good case could be made that even the crisis of cognitive claims has now been intensified through the work of these theologians (sometimes, despite their own protestations to the contrary). At any rate, that cognitive crisis can no longer simply dominate the theological agenda.

More exactly, it is interesting to note that precisely these new interpretations of both the tradition and the contemporary situation have forced these theologians into developing a Christian theological form of ideology-critique of all cognitive claims. That theological critique of ideology functions as a hermeneutics of suspicion directly related to their earlier hermeneutics of the retrieval of the prophetic and apocalyptic strands of Christianity itself. Insofar as this twofold move occurs, the particular form of "correlation" that liberation and political theologies take will ordinarily prove to be a form not of liberal identity nor one of the several forms of analogy or similarity but rather one of sheer confrontation. The confrontation will take place on every major ideological illusion—sexism, racism, classism, economic, political, and cultural oppression—that systemically affects both tradition and situation. The confrontations will be demanded by both the retrieval of the prophetic tradition's stand for the oppressed and by the suspicions released by the prophetic ideology-critique embedded in that retrieval. These correlations as confrontations will become the major liberation-theological form of establishing mutually critical correlations between the tradition and contemporary situation.

This emphasis on illusion, not error, on "ideology," not mistaken opinion will drive these theologians to emphasize praxis more than theory and "witness" more than other contemporary forms of critical reflection on the issues. And just this insistence, as the reader of the different positions represented in this volume will soon see, provokes a serious, even sharp exchange between Schubert Ogden's formulations and those of Dorothee Soelle, Elisabeth Schüssler Fiorenza, and James Cone. The major question at issue is nothing less than how to formulate criteria for truth in theology and thereby the very nature of theology as theology. The issue is inevitable and pressing for all forms of theology. What emerges with great clarity and sharpness in the discussions in this volume is how disagreement occurs even (perhaps especially) among conversation partners who fundamentally agree on the substantive centrality of the theme of "liberation" or contemporary theology. Just this conflict-within-more-fundamental-agreements makes this volume unique, to my knowledge, among collections on political and liberation theology.

To repeat: it is a sign of every serious conversation that the issue of truth and the conflicts on its proper formulation will soon take over. For every serious conversation (as distinct from either debates or "friendly" dialogues) must allow the subject-matter itself, not the subjects, to take over. It is to the credit of the organizers of the original conference, the editors of the volume itself, and the participants and authors that here authentic theological conversation does happen. For here the subject-matter and its attendant conflicts do genuinely take over.

I have given my own judgments on this conflict over "witness" and "critical reflection" and on "theory and praxis" elsewhere. A preface to a conversation is obviously not the place to repeat those personal judgments and their appropriate warrants. It is the place, however, to thank the editors and authors for provoking the central issues in new and sharply formulated ways for us all. For in this collection the major contemporary theological issues gripping every theologian are not only joined but clarified and intensified in ways that could bear profound consequences for all theology.

—*David Tracy*

1

"Thou Shalt Have No Other Jeans Before Me" (Levi's Advertisement, Early Seventies): The Need for Liberation in a Consumerist Society

Dorothee Soelle

About halfway through her essay Dorothee Soelle writes, "I want my theology to become a prayer." Although it is misleading to infer from this that she wishes to redefine theology as prayer, her impatience with abstract methodological canons which would preclude that possibility ipso facto is evident. Soelle believes that religious language has lost its power to give expression to the human need for self-renewal and to challenge individuals to embrace life "in the emphatic sense." This failure is symptomatic of a culture-wide indifference to integral human values and thus to the spiritual dimension of experience. Unaware of the awesome significance of this process of deconversion, inhabitants of First World nations have become hopelessly ensnarled in a culture system that perceives value almost entirely in quantitative terms—a system which demands an ultimate commitment to having rather than to being and that consumes plastic as if it were the bread of life.

Soelle contends that if theology is to challenge the enslaving ethic of "hedonistic consumerism," it must move beyond debilitating distinctions between spiritual salvation and the process of liberation and evolve into a language of "existential interpretation" which fuses Christian witness and critical reflection.

Dorothy Soelle is a German Protestant theologian and writer. She is presently teaching at Union Theological Seminary in New York. She is the author of many books and essays including Christ the Representative *(Philadelphia: Fortress, 1967),* Political Theology, *trans. John Shelley (Philadelphia:*

Fortress, 1974), Suffering, *trans. R. Everett (Philadelphia: Fortress, 1975),* Death by Bread Alone, *trans. David L. Scherdt (Philadelphia: Fortress Press, 1978), and* Revolutionary Patience, *trans. Rita and Robert Kimber (Maryknoll, N.Y.: Orbis Books, 1977). The Response by Schubert Ogden is an edited version of Ogden's verbal response to Soelle given at the conference in Chicago.*

Exile

"The real exile of Israel in Egypt was that they had learned to endure it."[1] The real exile of Christians in the First World is that we have learned to endure it. We do not consider our living in the affluent societies as being in captivity. We rather have adjusted ourselves so much to Egypt that we feel at home. We have adjusted ourselves to the Egyptian lifestyle. We have adopted the basic beliefs of the Egyptians. We see individualism as the measure of human development, and we share assumptions of history's caprice—sometimes this group on top, sometimes another group. We have learned to endure the exile so well that we no longer see ourselves as exiled people—as strangers in a strange land. Quite the contrary, we attempt to Egyptize the whole world. We see countries that have not yet adjusted to the capitalistic lifestyle and value-system as "not yet" developed. Rather than take the historical context of our present-day Egypt seriously, we have ontologized it. We say that the things we find distasteful are due to the sinful nature of humanity. We have come to understand idiosyncratic human qualities like competitiveness, greed, and possessiveness as essential elements of human nature.

The Egyptian way of life, to put it simply, conforms to the way things are. We have forgotten that some people prefer the desert to our cities, the struggle to our peace, and would choose hunger before eating our meat produced from the grain the starving lack. To learn to endure the exile is to suppress even our thirst for justice. It means we have become one with the objective cynicism of the prevailing culture. We sometimes pray for political prisoners in foreign countries, but we conveniently forget to ask who supports those oppressive governments. Neither do we ask where these countries get their weapons or who trains their torturers. Within our mainstream culture, we see no need for liberation. Our whole education is aimed at rooting out remnants of this need.

> If I forget you, O Jerusalem,
> let my right hand wither away;
> let my tongue cling to the roof of my mouth
> if I do not remember you,
> if I do not set Jerusalem
> above my highest joy [Ps. 137:5-6 NEB].

To remember Jerusalem means to define our need for liberation. It means to denounce the Egypt in which we live.

Pier Paolo Pasolini,[2] director of *The Gospel According to Matthew*, was a member of the Communist Party of Italy until he was kicked out because of his sexual preference. He has given an analysis of what has occurred in Italy since the onset of the 1970s. This analysis is informed by both a cultural conservatism and a Marxist understanding of political economy. He speaks of a "revolution from the right," the effects of which have been more devastating than any political overthrow in this century. In his opinion this revolution has been able to destroy or to redefine previously subsisting institutions such as the family, culture, language, and the Church. Pasolini calls this new state of affairs *consumismo*. He claims that where historic fascism failed to touch the soul of the Italian people, this new consumerism represents a total and relentless repression of what once had been called soul. Pasolini lived in a time which he calls the end of the "age of bread." Plastic had not yet become the basic food, and although religion was going to die out, the need for meaning was still acute. During the age of bread, religion had provided a language to talk about the need for meaning *(das Sinnbeduerfnis)*, about the human capacity for truth *(Wahrheitsfaehigkeit)*, and about existential unconditionality *(existenzielle Unbedingtheit)*. Religious language was the reservoir of a general language utilized to express the general consciousness that life was less a given than it was a tenuous gift. Pasolini was one who was not ashamed of talking about the holiness of life.

The Lost Age of Bread

In the age of bread life could be experienced as meaningless, and human anxieties about losing the self and losing the meaning of life could still be addressed by the language of religion. "Save us from hell" used to be a prayer for centuries. The anxiety over the possible loss of a meaningful existence seems obsolete in today's world. People with such feelings about life in our culture today are considered mad.

Humanity's deepest needs once found their expression in the language of religion. There was a need to be different; not different from others, but from the old self. "Create a pure heart in me, O God, and give me a new and steadfast spirit" (Ps. 51:10). A prayer like this presupposed certain human needs for renewal and change that have been destroyed. In the time of hedonism, all wishes and needs that would move toward existential unconditionality have been manipulated and exchanged. All the needs that once had reference to being have now been exchanged for new ones which have reference to more having. Further, the language of existential unconditionality presupposed the possible wholeness of our lives. "Set your mind on God's kingdom and his justice before anything else, and all the rest will come to you as well" (Matt. 6:33). There are still situations in our lives in which we may experience ourselves as whole and unseparated—as being one and being aware of being alive in the emphatic sense of the word. All our capacities and dimensions—our past and our future—are to be experienced. The oil in the lamps of the virgins who expect the bridegroom served as an image for this wholeness. If they lack the oil, everything is lacking. They are "foolish" and not ready for eternal life. They are distracted by a thousand things.

Existential unconditionality constitutes itself in the indivisible wholeness in favor of which I should decide. There is an integrative and a voluntary component in the concept. Wholeness and decision are constitutive. The biblical demand "Choose life!" presupposes that there is life in the emphatic and unconditioned sense of the word, and that life can be chosen and grasped, or abandoned and missed. "I summon heaven and earth to witness against you this day: I offer you the choice of life or death, blessing or curse. Choose life and then you and your descendants will live" (Deut. 30:19). Religious tradition has developed a language that reminds us of the emphasis on life. This represents to us life's threats as well as the possibilities of being rescued. As long as this language still communicates, it gives emphasis to a life which is both possible and tangible.

This language, however, has been stripped of its meaning in the new age of hedonistic fascism, as Pasolini sees it. "Fascism" in this concept refers to the totalitarian character of the new culture which permeates every thought and every feeling, every action, passion, and omission. It is omnipresent and omnipotent. Pasolini talks of the ideal image of a young couple in love and its mythic quality in the old culture. An "aura" surrounded the pair. There was a promise of happiness and a fear of fragility surrounding the two young people. The two of them were more than just two young people. It is precisely this "more" which has been lost. What I am trying to say may sound vague, but without an understanding of this mythic quality of life that transcends the given, it is impossible to understand even a line of Dante, Shakespeare, or Goethe, or to appreciate any of the works of Rembrandt or Chagall.

The fragile quality of this relationship in which two people participate was once a part of the promise of life. The point I want to make, however, is not primarily concerned with high culture, but it has reference to ordinary people who once were able to touch the mythic quality of life in their day-to-day existence. No matter how vigorously religion was rejected as being oppressive to the individual, the religious was the mediator between this emphasis on life and the world of everyday existence. But the young couple that we now see on television has no aura. They seem removed from any form of transcendence. Their life is entirely expressed within the culture of consumerism. They no longer have a need for a language which might speak about their pain and their hopes. Life is no longer at stake; it is indeed worth as much as one can buy. I have often heard American tourists who traveled in countries behind the Iron Curtain say, "Look at those empty show windows. There are no colors. Life isn't worthwhile here." In the age of bread show windows were not considered to be the criterion of life's worth. But this age ended in the mid-1950s in West Germany. In Italy it ended in the early 1970s. Pasolini rightly calls the prevailing consumerism a new fascism because it simply destroys all human values softly without physical violence. It does this by employing new means of communication and information.

When the age of bread is gone it no longer makes sense to share bread and wine. The emphatic understanding of life affirmed by the Judeo-Christian tradition was precisely this being-at-stake. Life was addressed as the tension between the possibility of authenticity and the omnipresent threat of death. Existential unconditionality goes hand in hand with existential anxiety. The emphatic understanding of life, seen as developing new qualities and threatened by eternal loss—this whole emphatic concept of life includes an emphatic-traumatic relationship to death. We are killable! To know this is more important than to repeat that we are mortals. To be killable means that this emphatic meaning of life can be taken away from us. It may be that nobody knows as much about what I am trying to say with awkward words like unconditionality, capacity for truth, and need for meaning, than the psychically disturbed. People in mental institutions know that one may lose one's life before death.

Consumerism

In the age of bread happiness was defined differently from the way it is defined in the culture of consumerism. The young man and the young woman on the television show who have no aura around them are merciless and graceless. They no longer need grace and they no longer expect it. Nobody even entertains the idea of saying to them, "God be with you." But it is precisely this wish to bestow a blessing upon the couple which was reflected in our old culture. The aura of fragile happiness which rendered them into moving, touching people is completely absent. The ideal television couple does not touch us; there is no need to wish for them, to pray for them. Pray for what? They will buy what they wish. Thus our prayer for them freezes on our lips.

The blasphemous use of language is a language free from memories, threats, and wounds. The slogan for Levi jeans, "Thou shalt have no other jeans before me," captures the spirit of the second industrial revolution and the mutation of values that is accrued from it. The rotation of production and consumption runs smoothly and efficiently. People are cut off from the rhythm of nature. Our need for a renewal of life also disappears, and we forget our need for rest after working, for night after day, for cleansing after pollution, and for stillness after noise. Without this sustaining rhythm we find ourselves caught up in the false rhythm of incessant and meaningless activity. Everything just continues. The pill as well as the machine-like bleeding which occurs when we refrain from taking it once a month are powerful symbols of the replacement of natural rhythm by one that is totally independent from bodily and physcic conditions.

As surely as we have severed our relationship with experienced nature, we have severed ourselves from experienced history that transcends us. Consumerism has changed our conversational culture totally. The most seriously discussed questions are now concerned with how to save taxes and where to get what at a better price. The sense of living in a particular epoch is no longer a framework of speech. The point of reference in historical suffering which was the kingdom of God and its new justice is now an obsolete concept, unthinkable, and not to be mentioned. The cyclical understanding of history has triumphed over the eschatological one with its accompanying goals and hopes. Lack of natural continuity and planned obsolescence of memory are necessary for hedonistic consumerism, because to remember is to be less determined by consumerism. The loss of history as a human horizon of meaning brings with it the absence of a future and an undramatic hopelessness.

It is not only the slogan that uses the first commandment which is blasphemy, but any advertising. This attempt to focus our interests and life-priorities on hairspray, cat food, and traveling to the Virgin Islands represents an assault on the One in whose image I am created. It is an assault on human dignity. Consumerism means that my eyes are offended, my ears are obstructed, and my hands are robbed of their creativity. My relationships with other people now fall under laws of which earlier generations could not even dream. My longings for absoluteness, for life in an emphatic sense, are stolen from me. Marx spoke about "universal salability," but its devastating consequences for the individual and day-to-day life are apparent only now.

The age of bread was also a time when it was possible to communicate about our expectations, wishes, and dreams. Religious language transmits a sharing of hope with others, as well as what I call the emphatic understanding of life. The public death of this language and its replacement by the public language of advertising is a major cultural event. The limits of our language are the limits of our world. What is not spoken does not exist, at least not in the emphatic sense of existence described to us by the existentialist philosophers. We no longer talk about the kingdom and its justice, about our prayers for the young couple, or about the possibility of going to hell while living comfortably in a nice house. If this whole language dies out, it follows that we have experienced a major shift in the nature of our needs as well. The need for liberation itself will die if we cease to communicate it to others. It may be more precise to say that the limits of our language are the limits of our needs. To transcend the limits of a given language then means to clarify and to intensify our need to liberate ourselves from our present situation.

There is a root experience which grounds a liberation theology for First World citizens. The point of departure is the world in which thou shalt have no other jeans before me. This root experience is the totalitarianism of the hedonistic culture. The voice of Levi's is the voice of God. To grow up in this culture is to listen to the voice of this God. Our father in heaven is the hedonistic fascistic beast. Our need for liberation has a different starting point than the struggle for economic justice. Our being exploited is different from the exploitation of the Third World. Still, it is one beast that rules over us,

Third World and First World people, but we in the affluent societies tend to overlook its fascist dimensions. Our immediate experience of the beast is of its hedonistic side rather than of its oppressive side. As Marx pointed out, the ruling and the exploited classes represent two sides of the same alienation from life.

As we become aware of our situation, our need for a new language grows. The lack of expressiveness in the language of the dominant culture is a phenomenon which has often been described. Expressiveness is seen as an idiosyncratic quality which characterizes the language of the lower classes, of women, and of the inhabitants of certain particular locations. Its destruction is an ongoing process. The capacities for self-expression which were strongly developed in the regional dialects in Italy, for example, have been extirpated. The language of television is now the dominant language which eliminates all regional, professional, and group languages. This bringing-into-line *(Gleichschaltung)* of the language of nondominant cultures means the loss of expressiveness in languages of the dominating media. Scientific language, in particular, has suppressed the expressiveness of nondominant cultures for a long time. It is difficult for women to communicate in scientific language because it conflicts with their societal role as carriers of expressiveness. Speaking a normal male phrase often seems to me like saying nothing at all, and this saying nothing seems to be the educational goal of the prevailing languages of science and television.

Liberation Theology

Schubert Ogden has recently presented his understanding of language in theology in the context of his criticisms of liberation theology. Ogden's description of the use of language by liberationists claims that they tend "to obscure any distinction between theology and witness." Rather than obscuring the distinction, liberationists lift up witness as a return to a first-hand theological language capable of a norm of self-expression filled with passion and struggle. The language of testimony, witness, and confession is considered by liberation theologians as *the* theological language. They feel no need to transcend this type of God talk by systematization into a doctrinal and/or metaphysical language.

Liberation theologians are skeptical about the usefulness of the distinction between the witness and the theologian; between the language of prayer and sermons on the one hand, and the language of theological reflection on the other. A theological language that has turned its back on praying and preaching and tries to define itself as independent of piety seems inadequate. At the very least we should expect that the deepest reflection will lead us back to its source, namely, the language of prayer. I conceive of the language of prayer as a union of thought, emotion, and will. To pray means to wish, to be open to the transcendent expressively, thoughtfully, and in an unlimited way.

I want my theology to become a prayer, and in light of this the distinction between witnessing and doing theology is neither adequate nor useful. This distinction seems to be related to the more basic distinction which bourgeois liberalism has made between private and public life. To liberalism, religion is a private affair. Thus, to bear witness becomes a private matter. Public talk, it is thought, must have the qualities of generalization and systematization. To bear witness already has a public quality where the language of true prayer is understandable. If praxis and faith are seen as essential, and theory and theology are seen as handmaidens of faith without any value in themselves separate from these, then this distinction concerning modes of language loses relevance.

Concepts of God must be evaluated according to a functional criterion. We must ask whether they are liberating or oppressive. We have no interest in a metaphysical truth claim about God's being in itself. Truth in the understanding of liberation theologians is essentially "concrete": any metaphysical or revelational doctrine of God makes truth abstract. Lenin, after reading Hegel, coined the phrase "truth is concrete."[3] It was also written on Bertolt Brecht's desk when he was a political refugee in Denmark. The phrase has a meaning which can be understood in both existentialist and Marxist terms. Truth cannot be said to occur apart from us. Truth is not timeless, but it happens among us. Truth is essentially related to our making it come true. Talking about our capacity for truth is talking about our being enabled to love effectively in a way that changes this world. Which language then is adequate to talk about truth? Returning to the discussion among existentialist theologians in the 1950s, one may ask the question in this way: Is existential interpretation possible? Is there a possible third way between a theoretical objective talk that excludes passion, self-expression, and the call to struggle, and a merely personal immediate talk which excludes rationality and objectivity?

Bultmann, following the early Heidegger, made a three-fold distinction pertaining to theological languages. First, there is the theoretical objective talk of the theologian, a language without fear and trembling that is strictly opposed to the language of the existing thinker. Second, there is the practical-existential talk of the witness, which often lacks intelligibility, but has the qualities of immediacy and personalism—close to what Buber describes as the I-thou relationship. But in Bultmann's understanding there is an alternative to objectivism and subjectivism, which he and Heidegger called "existential interpretation." They made an almost untranslatable distinction between existential immediacy[4] and existential interpretation.[5] Bultmann claimed that there was a third possibility which moved beyond both the language of the uncommitted objective philosopher and the language of witness born of a specific *kairos*. The whole concept of existential interpretation includes a certain tension. It is "existential" in the sense that it is committed, impassioned, and praxis-oriented. It is "interpretative" in the sense that it is reflective, reasonable, and theory-oriented. The Bultmannians who set out to find this third language may have failed. Some of them returned to neo-orthodoxy and its objective talk about the kerygma as the salvation event. Others, outsiders like Fritz Buri, went back to the existential thinker Soren Kierkegaard (who if he had to choose would more likely situate himself in the category of witness rather than theology). In any case, most of those who entertained this dream of an existential interpretation never reached this promised land of a new common language.

Today's liberation theologians share many of these same problems. They have made progress in their attempts to relate faith and theology in a new way. They emphasize praxis over theory, action over reflection, people's exegesis over academic exegesis, and political struggle over solitary contemplation. They have also redefined the goals of theological education. It is considered better by many liberation theologians to become a militant organizer for the kingdom than a Harvard professor of theology. But what does this tendency reveal about the use of languages? Which language is adequate for liberation theology? Is the confessional language sufficient or do we need a universal language? Ogden has suggested the use of two criteria for theological God talk: (1) appropriateness to the Christian witness and its tradition, and (2) intelligibility to human existence, especially to the nonbeliever. Confessional talk, in his opinion, lacks the quality of critical reflection that would render it adequate relative to both criteria.

I agree with Schubert Ogden in his use of these two criteria, but I disagree with his judgment that existential talk cannot satisfy these criteria. In reading the texts of liberation theology, I do not miss the presence of critical reflection on the tradition or its intelligibility to the non-Christian world. It is necessary at this juncture to give some examples of a liberating theology in the form of confession or witnessing.

In one of the few debates of historical relevance in the German Bundestag, Gustav Heinemann, who later became state president, made an unforgettable remark during the time of the German rearmament and integration into the Western coalition. In the interest of a peace-seeking policy he said, "Jesus Christ did not die against Karl Marx but for all of us." This statement had a political-theological quality. It was polemical in that it was opposed to those who used Christ to justify German rearmament. It was a confessional statement, unprecedented in the Bundestag. Yet, it was understandable for everybody in that culture, and it was, indeed, faithful to former witnesses of the Church, especially to members of the Confessing Church.

Let me give you another example of what I would call liberation theology. It is a text written on the wall of a harbor in Mar del Plata by unknown people. According to Eduardo Galeano, an exiled writer from Uruguay, it says, "I am seeking Christ, but I don't find him. I am seeking myself, but I do not find me. But I do find my neighbor and the three of us get started on our way."[6] Notice that these words are not written on a church wall or in a book, but on the wall of a harbor. They are not written by a well-known theologian, but by unknown hands. It is not I, the seeker, and Christ who communicate inside of a church religiously, but we, the three of us, who are marching on in the communication of the struggle.

Let me present another text that further obscures the line of distinction between theological reflection and immediate existential language, and that demonstrates once more that liberation theology in Latin America is not primarily the invention of some well-read theologians, but indeed emerges from the struggle. This example is a catechism picture that is used for religious education. On the lower part of the sheet there is a hill on which there are many crosses. On the crosses there are words written that indicate the meaning of the cross for the people: hunger, alienation, oppression, illiteracy, torture, *favella*. On the upper part of the sheet there is the resurrected Christ, and on his side it reads: peace, love, freedom, progress, conscientization, life.

When I attempt to understand this theological textbook, I am all the more skeptical about another criticism of Schubert Ogden's which has reference to the distinction between liberation and emancipation. Ogden reproached liberation theologians for confusing God the redeemer with God the emancipator. The little catechism picture is a good example of what I would call the oneness of the process of liberation, and what Schubert Ogden would call the confusion of two liberation events which must be distinguished. The one, in his view, has to do with the redemption from death, transience, and sin, in other words, liberation in a theological-spiritual sense. The other, the worldly one, concerns the emancipation from the diverse forms of oppression, as economic, political, racial, and sexual.

I find that the better texts of liberation theology do have this specific quality that renders the distinction between reflective theological and immediate witness-talk as purely technical. The claim of liberation theologians to do theology with the people, by the people, and for the people is not necessarily anti-intellectualist. It rejects, however, the hierarchical order which places theory over praxis, and which has been the dominant pattern in Western culture. To hang up a poster from Latin America which says "Evangelio es lucha" (the gospel is the struggle), or to listen to the *campesinos* and fisherfolk in Solentiname at Bible study makes theology relevant in a new way.[7] The distinction between witness and reflection, in terms of a sociology of knowledge that mirrors the labor and power division between laypeople and theologians, no longer has any specific productive function. It stabilizes class distinctions that should be and could be reduced through the language of liberation. The poster, the prayer, and the catechism do not lack, in my perspective, critical reflection or intelligibility.

Ogden's thesis is indeed a frontal attack from the right on any form of liberation theology. It is essential for us to decide whether we understand emancipation/liberation as one historical process that allows us to talk about God the liberator who operates in, with, and among us in a liberating way, or whether we must distinguish God's activities into two sets of actions which can be separated within a nonclassical, yet dualistic scheme. The question is this: Are the reasons we need liberation twofold, one set bound to our mortal, frail, and guilty being, and another set defined by historical conditions like slavery, patriarchy, and class domination? Do we need liberation in the emphatic and wholistic sense that liberation theology has tried to develop, or do we fragment our liberation needs by receiving one form of liberation from God who is the redeemer and another form of liberation from an agent such as a liberation army?

"Choose Life"

Let us return to the starting point, the world in which I must live, and which shall have no other jeans before God than Levi's. Let us go back to a text of Paul in Romans 8 where he talks about the sufferings we now endure.

> For the created universe waits with eager expectation for God's sons [and daughters] to be revealed. It was made the victim of frustration, not by its own choice, but because of him who made it so; yet always there was hope, because the universe itself is to be freed from the shackles of mortality and enter upon the liberty and splendor of the children of God. Up to the present, we know, the whole created universe groans in all its parts as if in the pangs of childbirth [Rom. 8:19–22].

I find three things in this text: (1) the groaning of the universe, which I take in both dimensions of nature and history; (2) the need for liberation in a wholistic understanding; and (3) God as the liberator who needs our participation.

There is a groaning of the universe born of the need to be free. Earlier times might have heard this text with a certain ironic distance because it seems to naively anthropologize nature. The exploitation of the ecological environment may have made us more open to the message of this text; a message that is indeed a unifying one, its groaning is everywhere. Nature and history are together in what Allen Ginsberg has named in his famous poem "Howl." They are present in the words of the German writer, Hans Magnus Enzensberger, when he describes the "whimpering" *(das Gewimmer)* he hears in the streets, the houses, and the nights.[8] The frustration of Paul's universe needs humanity. The first task of those who understand themselves as the sons and daughters of God, therefore, is to listen to the cry, to hear the groaning and the howl. But how can we listen if our ears are offended from one hour to the next by the noise of hedonistic fascism? To listen to the howl, to its rage, its despair, its revenge, to listen to the offended and raped earth, and to listen to the cry in ourselves and in our brothers and sisters is the first step in doing theology. To listen to the cry means to remember human dignity, which is our capacity for truth. It means to insist upon the possible meaning of life and upon the necessity of a language to communicate that meaning even to those who we cannot hear crying. Once the howling, the whimpering, and the groaning are heard, the next step is to name them. Paul does this when he speaks of "the pangs of childbirth." He might as easily have called it a death rattle. It often sounds like that. Still he gives a birth-name to the cry.

In our context, it is important to keep in mind the wholeness of the need for liberation. The distinction between God's work as redemption and God's work as emancipation causes problems because it presupposes a double set of needs which can be separated by imposing a classical framework which includes the distinctions between the mind and body, spirit and praxis, and other such hierarchical designations. Liberation theology neither negates the multi-dimensionality of the need for liberation, nor does it deny the situational emphasis of liberation, be it political, economic, spiritual, cultural, or educational. But we must keep in mind that any deep political struggle is a spiritual struggle at the same time. The school kids in Soweto with their slogan, "Afrikaans the language of the Oppressor" are fighting for cultural self-determination as well as for better housing, water, and electricity. To classify our needs into lower and higher orders is reactionary. We do not need first to be redeemed by an act of God, and only then go about the task of constructing a better world. The struggle is one because the need is one. "Choose life" is a single imperative and posits no special religious dimension which separates the imperative from other dimensions of liberation. Liberation is emancipation. Our need is to be redeemed for humanity's struggles; to abandon ourselves in a day-to-day betrayal of the class in which we were born, as Sartre puts it. Our social, political, and cultural needs for liberation are themselves spiritual needs. To distinguish or separate our need to be emancipated from our oppressors from our need to be reconciled with nature is dangerous because it decries the spiritual identity of the struggle itself.

Nicolai Berdyaev says that one's own hunger is a materialistic problem, while the hunger of one's neighbor is a spiritual one. In light of this the struggles for liberation do have their spiritual dimension. If one denies this spiritual quality immanent in the struggle, it becomes impossible to understand such recent events as the victory of the Vietnamese people over the strongest war machine of history or the Iranian revolution.

The third message I hear in Paul's text has reference to God and God's work. The basic assumption is that God needs us and will not liberate us without our participation. Liberation theology makes sense only if we understand this participatory quality of all liberation. Objects cannot be liberated; they can only be moved from a bad place to a better one. The concept of salvation through a God who sets us in a better place, and who is the agent of our liberation (our being the objects of the same action) is a concept which is plainly inadequate. Such a concept mirrors the oppression of the people, and reaffirms their powerlessness by celebrating the opium-like character of the bourgeois interpretation of the gospel.

Redemption is "the ever new event of God's own self-creation in response to the free self-creation of all his creatures."[9] This way of defining the liberation event is derived from process thought, and indeed solves the problem of the subject-object split that plagued existentialist theologians. But this same responsive process is at work within both redemption and emancipation. Both are unthinkable if we are mere objects. If this is the case, I see little reason to emphasize the distinction between emancipation and redemption. Both respond to the one need for liberation.

What we need is a life before death and not a life after death. We need to be free from the coercion to sin in our collective life. If forty-eight cents of one tax dollar goes to the military, then this socio-economic fact defines our need to seek liberation from this implicit coercion to sin. But should I talk to God the redeemer or to God the emancipator about that? God is one. We know of redemption and liberation only through our participation. There is nothing that God could give us without our involvement. To live means to participate. The groaning of the created universe causes us to be opened to participation in what has been called creation. If we realize the revelation of being as participating sons and daughters, then we become one with the liberating force in history as well as in nature. Our context calls upon us in a threefold sense. We are to listen to the cry, to name the need, and to participate in the struggle.

Notes

1. Martin Buber, *Tales of the Hassidim,* vol. 2 (New York: Schocken, 1947), p. 315.

2. Pier Paolo Pasolini, "Die Zerstoerung der Kultur des Enzelnen durch die konsumgesellschaft" (Berlin: Friedbeuterschriften, 1978).

3. Vladimir Ilych Lenin, *Selected Works,* vol. 2: *Notes to Hegel* (London: Lawrence and Wishart, 1960), p. 412.

4. Rudolf Bultmann, "Neues Testament und Mythologie," in *Kerygma und Mythos,* I, ed. H. W. Bartsch, 2nd ed. (Hamburg: Herbert Reich-Evangelischer Verlag, 1951), pp. 14–48.

5. Rudolf Bultmann, "Zum Problem der Entmythologisierung," in *Kerygma und Mythos,* II (Hamburg: Herbert Reich-Evangelischer Verlag, 1952), pp. 179–208.

6. Eduardo Galeano, *Schlachtnof der Worte* (Wuppertal, 1977).

7. Ernesto Cardenal, *The Gospel in Solentiname,* I, II, and III (Maryknoll, N.Y.: Orbis Books, 1976, 1978, 1979).

8. Hans Magnus Enzensberger, *Landessprache* (Frankfurt am Main: Suhrkamp, 1960).

9. Schubert M. Ogden, *Faith and Freedom: Toward a Theology of Liberation* (Nashville: Abingdon, 1979), p. 83.

Response to Dorothee Soelle

Schubert M. Ogden

The following comments, which I have been invited to make by the editors, are not intended as a balanced response to Dorothee Soelle's contribution to our discussion. With what I take to be the burden of her argument concerning "the need for liberation in a consumerist society," as with her positive theological intentions generally, I find myself in substantial agreement. But she has taken issue with me at a couple of points, and in the interests of avoiding misunderstanding and locating the real issues between us, I have agreed simply to comment on each of these two points.

The first is the distinction I make in *Faith and Freedom* between "witness" and "theology." From Soelle's account, one is given to understand that I introduce this distinction in presenting my "understanding of language in theology" and that it is a distinction between "modes of language," specifically, between "the language of prayer and sermons on the one hand, and the language of theological reflection on the other." But, in point of fact, the distinction as I make it is not introduced in connection with a discussion of theological language, nor is my reason for making it that the terms and categories of first-order religious discourse are different from those of the second-order discourse of theology. On the contrary, on my own account, the difference between witness and theology is the difference between existential positions, or the rationalization of such positions, on the one hand, and critical reflection on the meaning and truth of such positions, on the other. "In other words, what distinguishes theology proper from the thought and speech about God that make up Christian witness generally is that theology is either the process or the product of critically reflecting on that witness with a view to satisfying the twin criteria of appropriateness and understandability."[1] This means, among other things, that I neither say nor imply, as Soelle represents me as doing, that "confessional talk . . . lacks the quality of critical reflection that would render it adequate relative to both criteria," or that "existential talk cannot satisfy these criteria." On the contrary, simply assuming that one's witness and theology both can and should satisfy the same two criteria, I insist only that "to determine whether one's witness is adequate, in the sense of being both appropriate and understandable, requires that one engage in theological reflection."[2]

As for Soelle's remark that "the distinction between witnessing and doing theology. . . seems to be related to the more basic distinction which bourgeois liberalism has made between private and public," suffice it to say that, if such a relation is apparent between the two distinctions as she herself makes use of them, she gives no reason whatever for supposing that my use of the first distinction entails any such relation. Nor, I venture to think, would she ever be likely to give any such reason. For I am confident that it would be at once apparent to any reasonably sympathetic reader of my work that what I mean by bearing witness to one's faith is every bit as public a matter as reflecting on one's witness theologically could possibly be.

The second point requiring comment is the further distinction I make and insist on in the same book between "redemption" and "emancipation" (not, as Soelle sometimes has it, "liberation and emancipation"). According to Soelle, my thesis that theology can and must make this distinction is nothing less than "a frontal attack from the right on any form of liberation theology." Why? Well, because "it is essential for us to decide whether we understand emancipation/liberation as one historical process that allows us to talk about God the liberator who operates in, with, and among us in a liberating way, or whether we must distinguish God's activities into two sets of actions which can be separated within a nonclassical, yet dualistic scheme." Against my distinction, then, Soelle argues that "to distinguish or separate our need to be emancipated from our oppressors, from our need to be reconciled with nature is dangerous because it decries the spiritual identity of the struggle." At least three things need to be said about Soelle's criticisms at this point if the real issues between us are to be sorted out.

First of all, it is clear from her repeated confusion of the two concepts that Soelle recognizes no difference between "distinguishing" things, on the one hand, and "separating" them, on the other. Evidently, in her world, rather as in David Hume's, anything that can be distinguished can be separated, so that one is forced either to avoid distinctions or else to tolerate separations. The difficulty, however, is that, without ever arguing that hers is the *only* world, Soelle acts as though everyone else had to live in it, too—even someone, like myself, who not only professes to live in another world but also thinks and speaks accordingly. Consequently, she invariably reasons as though to distinguish between redemption and emancipation, as I argue an adequate theology must do, is *eo ipso* to separate them, and so to make a frontal attack on the very position that any liberation theology is bound to maintain.

But the second thing to be said is that this reasoning can be made to appear plausible only because Soelle conveniently ignores my own very different way of thinking and speaking. If I insist, as I do, that redemption and emancipation must be distinguished as "two quite different, even if closely related processes," I also make clear in the very same sentence that both processes are comprised in "the one process of liberation whose necessary ground is God."[3] Moreover, just because I myself am as concerned as Soelle or any other liberation theologian could be that redemption and emancipation never be separated, I stress explicitly and repeatedly that their inseparability is "just as fundamental" as their distinguishability: "both processes are so grounded in the one being of God that neither they nor our own participation in them can ever be separated or played off against one another. The one liberating work of God, in which each of us is given and called to play our part, is a redeeming *and* an emancipating work."[4] Simply to ignore all such statements as though I never made them may indeed lead one to conclude that all I would be able to find in "the little catechism picture" that Soelle takes to be a good example of "the oneness of the process of liberation" would be a case of "the confusion of two liberation events which must be distinguished." But my guess is that anyone who takes seriously what I actually say will allow for my finding something very different in that picture: an eloquent symbol of the integral relation between two liberation events which, while they must indeed be distinguished, cannot be separated, either in theory or in practice.

And yet, if what Soelle takes issue with in her criticisms is not what I say but what she makes me mean, I do not suppose for a moment that there are no real issues between us. On the contrary, the third thing I must say is that, as much as I find myself agreeing with her positions, I remain troubled by the negations with which she invariably accompanies them. Thus, while I could readily accept her affirmation of "the multi-dimensionality of the need for liberation" as expressing the same difference-in-unity that I myself want to affirm, I am put off by her flat denial of any "special religious dimension." Or, again, while I, too, would maintain that "concepts of God must be evaluated according to a functional criterion," I could not disavow all interest in "a metaphysical truth claim about God's being in itself," nor could I ever suppose that all truth is so "essentially related to our making it come true" that "truth cannot be said to occur apart from us." Or, still again, while I quite agree with Soelle that "we know of redemption and liberation only through our participation," I stumble at her claim that "there is nothing God could give us without our involvement."

Of course, I, too, would have to say that we ourselves are and must be participants in our salvation no less than in our creation. But the fact that there is some world for us and our fellow creatures to exist and to act in is no more our own doing than is the fact that there is a certain relatively fixed and stable order to the world that allows for the possibility of more good than evil being realized through the exercise of our creaturely freedom. All this is solely God's work as Creator, a sheer gift that is indeed given us "without our involvement." And the same is true of God's work as Redeemer, whereby, notwithstanding our own transience, death, and sin, we are each embraced together with all our fellow creatures in God's own boundless and everlasting life. This, too, is God's work alone, *extra nos, sine nobis, et contra nos,* although God's redemption can become our salvation only insofar as it meets with our own response of faith working through love.

In sum: what I take to be the real issues between Soelle and myself all have to do with how any theology, including any liberation theology worthy of the name, properly construes the reference of the concept-symbol "God." Does it refer merely to what we can just as well call "nature," or to a "historical process" that Soelle further specifies only as "the liberating force in history as well as in nature"? Or does it refer, as I maintain, to the one universal individual who, as the sole ultimate ground of all being and meaning, unsurpassably transcends all nature and history even while being unsurpassably involved in them? I do not question that even here there may be merely verbal issues and misunderstandings that only further discussion can remove. But, as much as I welcome such discussion, I strongly suspect that it will only make all the clearer this strictly theological difference between us.

Notes

1. Schubert M. Ogden, *Faith and Freedom: Toward a Theology of Liberation* (Nashville: Abingdon, 1979), p. 26.
2. Ibid., p. 27.
3. Ibid., p. 36; see p. 99.
4. Ibid., p. 100; see, e.g., p. 95.

2

Liberation and Salvation: A First World View

Lee Cormie

In starkly different ways, the naive optimism of the 1950s which linked economic and technological advances with normative conceptions of cultural evolution, the social ferment of the 1960s, and the quiet desperation of the 1970s, all give witness to the inability of the ascendant classes within American society to comprehend the moral significance of their complicity—at times their conscious advocacy—of the economic, social, and spiritual oppression of millions. In this essay, Lee Cormie describes the impact of international capitalism upon "less advanced" societies as well as upon women, blacks, and the working poor within American society itself. Pointing to the fact that feminist, black, and Third World liberation theologians are in agreement that the capitalist world system and the worldview or "rationality" associated with it are in large part responsible for sexism, racism, and the economic exploitation of the poor, Cormie says that theologians of the First World must acknowledge the privileged perspective of the oppressed. More specifically, they must unite themselves with the liberation theologians already engaged in the task of "demonstrating the irrationality of the dominant rationality" in order to prepare the way for the emergence of a more humane cultural vision.

Lee Cormie is a member of the Faculty of Theology, St. Michael's College of the University of Toronto. He is also coordinator of the Theologians Project of Theology in the Americas, a five-year ecumenical project bringing together social activists, church leaders, theologians, and social scientists with the aim of contributing to the revitalization of theology and theological education through commitment to justice. Brian Mahan is a Ph. D. candidate at the Divinity School of the University of Chicago.

21

"If we are not able to speak about the real deaths of our people today, we will not be able to speak about the life and resurrection of Jesus Christ."

—Gustavo Gutiérrez[1]

Postwar Optimism

The years after World War II saw a growing optimism in the United States about the future. The war itself had finally rescued the economy from the Depression, and the great task of rebuilding the wartorn economies of allies and foes alike only contributed to further development of the domestic economy. The uncertainty over the international balance of power in the immediate postwar years soon gave way to a new sense of national purpose as the U.S. government took up the mantle of defender of freedom throughout the world. Internally, it was widely asserted, the expanding economy would soon make room for everyone, promoting the highest standard of living in the world and eliminating the still-evident effects of past injustices such as slavery.

Throughout the 1950s optimism grew and by the early 1960s influential commentators felt justified in proclaiming that "there is today a rough consensus among intellectuals on political issues: the acceptance of a welfare state; a system of mixed economy and political pluralism."[2] Such a consensus, unprecedented in history, had emerged because, in this view, "the fundamental political problems of the Industrial Revolution have been solved" in the U.S. and other developed countries.[3] And for the remaining problems there is a widespread consensus among the experts about the technical fixes in the economy and government policy necessary to remedy the problems, or at least a rough consensus about the frame of reference within which to consider such problems. There were no longer any disputes at this level; the democratic-capitalist form of society, evident in the U.S., Western Europe, and Japan, had won the day. Indeed, the other nations in the world were seen as evolving toward this type of society; and the exceptions, a communist society like Russia, for example, were interpreted as merely pathological deviations of this development, a "disease" of the transition from traditional to modern society.[4] Of course, many underdeveloped countries still had a long way to go to catch up. But social scientists and government policy-makers were optimistic about the possibilities for development in these countries, and foreign aid would help them along this path; the 1960s was the Decade of Development.

The age was, then, one of the end of ideology. Indeed, it was clear to these influential thinkers that the U.S. was "the good society itself in operation,"[5] and that people in other societies were naturally aspiring to achieve success in similar terms. There could be little debate about that. Indeed, these theorists claimed, the increasing adaptability of societies to their environment in the course of social evolution requires just the sorts of developments reflected in U.S. society.[6]

But no sooner had the end of ideology been declared than it abruptly ended. For the 1960s also witnessed the eruption of a number of challenges to this happy view of the U.S. and its place in the world. There were the civil rights and black power movements which revealed once again the pervasiveness of racism within the U.S. The antiwar movement challenged the prevailing view of the U.S. as defender of freedom and democracy throughout the world. Moreover, rooted as so much of it was in colleges and universities, it also generated widespread challenges to the whole educational system, both its internal dynamics and its links to the military-industrial complex. In the midst of these movements, feminists challenged the sexism enshrined in dominant values and institutions, even within the family itself. And workers, like those at the General Motors factory in Lordstown, Ohio, once again exposed the dangerous and dehumanizing working conditions that even relatively well-paid workers must suffer.

These movements articulated a wide range of criticisms of our society, its internal order, and its role in the world system. Though taken singly many of these criticisms simply reflect different moral judgments about prevailing patterns in economy, society, and personal life; taken collectively they call into question the very roots of the structures which undergird these patterns. And they also call into question the prevailing frameworks for interpreting ourselves and the world, frameworks which have guided our actions as individuals, and the policies of political movements, social institutions, and government agencies. Ultimately these movements have challenged us to unfold fundamentally different ways of understanding and acting in the world.

As bearers of belief and values, as well as social institutions with their priorities reflected in their actual policies, the churches were inevitably caught up in this questioning. Christians involved in the various movements referred to above, and in opposition to these movements in support of so-called "traditional" values, struggled to articulate the meaning of their faith in the light of contemporary events, and to align church policies accordingly. Inevitably there has been a profusion of new theologies, and of new sects and movements, including the quasi-religious pop psychology movements, as large numbers of people search for meaning in their lives. These developments are often referred to, from the perspective of the major denominations, as the "crises" in theology and in the church, and they are reflected in reduced attendance at Sunday services and budgetary crises in many churches. There are few signs that the crises are over.

In the midst of these developments three theological currents focusing on the theme of "liberation" have emerged which are having a significant impact in the U.S. and throughout the world: Latin American liberation theology, black theology, and feminist theology. These three theological currents emerged and have developed within different concrete contexts. Though all converge around the notion of liberation as a central theological and political theme of our time, it is not at all clear how much they converge, if at all, in their understanding of what is at stake politically and theologically in "liberation." In this paper, I would like to offer some tentative reflections on the meanings of these three theologies in their concrete historical contexts in terms of the question, "Liberation from what?"[7]

In particular, I would like to offer these reflections from the point of view of the U.S., and their relevance to the majority of Americans, including many in the so-called middle class. For it is usually assumed, especially in the U.S., that these theologies are relevant only for Third World people, and perhaps Third World people here at home, like blacks, Hispanics, native Americans, and other minority groups. There is even a tendency to see feminist theology as a minority group or Third World theology, in spite of the fact that women account for 51 percent of the population.

But is seems to me that these liberation theologies, and the politics which inspire them and are inspired by them, have a far greater relevance. For they share a common starting point, all the more significant to the extent that they have emerged from different concrete contexts: the rejection of the dominant worldview shaping influential interpretations of the world and of human nature, of pain and suffering, and of the possibilities for transcending them. To the extent that this worldview shapes the policies of politicians and governments, it affects the life and death of millions, and the quality of life for us all. To the extent that these theologies are accurate in exposing the irrationality of the dominant worldview, they call us all to involvement in the struggles to unfold a new order inspired by new values and new belief in the possibilities for transcending current evils.[8]

Developmental Theories

Latin American liberation theology emerged in the midst of profound economic, political, cultural, and religious upheavals in Latin America. It began in the 1960s among ordinary Christians who felt called by their faith to work for and with the poor,[9] but who became increasingly dissatisfied with the prevailing strategies, both political and theological, for responding to their problems. Concerning economic and political development, the prevailing paradigm in the post-World War II period was the developmental perspective.

Developmentalists interpreted the different types of political, economic, social, and cultural development evident in the world as different stages on a continuum from traditional (or primitive) to modern societies. The First World nations, the "advanced" nations, were seen as merely the last stages so far of a developmental process through which all nations were expected to proceed. This process of development itself was conceptualized as essentially a matter internal to nations, although foreign nations could help or hinder this process in various ways. Some theorists emphasized the conversion to modern values as the key to development; here Weber's *Protestant Ethic and the Spirit of Capitalism*[10] stood as a model of analysis. Without denying the importance of values, other theorists pointed to the social and political changes needed to promote self-sustaining economic growth. At this point the optimism of all these theories is crucial. For these theorists assumed that capitalist economic development in the First World along with democratic politics had improved life for all who lived in these countries. And that Third World countries too could enjoy the benefits of compound interest forever if only their leaders would follow appropriate policies.[11]

There were clear policy implications in these theories. Third World governments should do all they can to promote industrialization. After World War II many Latin American governments deliberately attempted to do so. For example, they set up tariffs to promote internal production, hoping to promote internal economic development and to alleviate the balance of payments problems caused by imports. The problem with this and other strategies is that they did not work, at least from the point of view of the majority of Latin Americans.[12]

By the end of the 1950s, the limitations of the strategy of import substitution were apparent and industrial expansion slowed down as the demands of the limited portion of the population with money were met; the majority simply could not afford to consume much. Foreign exchange deficits remained a problem, no longer caused so much by importing consumer goods as by importing technology and capital goods to promote internal development; indeed, local producers found themselves increasingly dependent on sophisticated technologies which could be bought only from the advanced countries. In addition, the tariff walls set up to promote local industry permitted outsiders to move in, and with their advantages in technical, managerial, and financial resources they were able to drive many local firms out of business, at the same time sending royalties and a high percentage of profits out of these countries—this was the period of the rise of the multinational corporations, all based in the First World. Governments, feeling the pinch, expanded local money supplies, thus fueling inflation. They had to borrow more externally, consequently spending ever larger amounts of their foreign exchange reserves on debt servicing to foreign banks and international agencies.[13]

Inevitably these efforts at development promoted widespread social changes. Indeed, there was development for a few. The national bourgeoisie often prospered, although increasingly they were subservient to the policies and interests of the multinational corporations. A small middle class of professional and technical workers also flourished, along with some workers. But growing unemployment, fueled by labor-saving technologies, the flood of unemployed peasants moving to the cities in search of jobs, and a growing population, meant poverty for the great majority. Inevitably, this turn of events, so contrary to the optimism of the developmentalist theories, increased social tensions and prompted the search for new theories and new policies. Chile, during the years when Allende was president, was the most obvious example in Latin America of this revitalized search for alternatives.

At a theoretical level the critique of developmentalism generated a radically new theory of domination and dependence among nations at the core and on the periphery of the capitalist world system. The key claim of this theory is that development and underdevelopment, rather than being two different stages on a ladder of evolutionary development, are but the two sides of the one coin of the development of the capitalist world system. This means that underdevelopment is in some significant ways caused by the development of the advanced capitalist countries.

The point is not that production and even real income did not increase in Third World countries in the post-World War II period, or even that they won't continue increasing. It is, rather, that the development which occurs is very uneven. This characteristic of the development process can be vividly seen in many Latin American cities in the juxtaposition of expensive high-rise apartments reflecting luxurious standards of living for a few with slums where thousands of people live without adequate food and water.[14] The explanation for this uneven development is to be found, according to these theorists, in the nature of the relations between the core and the periphery in the world economy. For development in the periphery has always proceeded according to the requirements of the core, specifically the requirements of corporate elites in their efforts to promote greater profit margins for their companies. So at a purely economic level decisions are not made in terms of local interests. Beyond this, however, international capitalism has tended to reinforce class structures in poor countries which serve its interests, further inhibiting internal development. Yet even when local leaders have the best interests of their people in mind they confront the structures of the world system which dictate lower prices for their products (produced at the same levels of productivity) than for the products of the First World. Moreover, the terms of trade themselves appear to be deteriorating, so that they can expect to get even less, relatively speaking, in the future.

Development in the periphery, then, proceeding rationally, i.e., in terms of profitability, intensifies unevenness; it promotes for the minority an increasing income which enables them to become more closely integrated socially, culturally, ideologically, and politically among themselves and into the world system, so conspicuously evident in their adoption of First World patterns of consumption. At the same time, it promotes the impoverishment of the masses who are marginal to the system, a source of cost in a system that does not depend on their labor or their purchasing power (based on wages) since demand originates elsewhere.[15] Since the traditional ways of life of these people have already been undermined by capitalist development, they can look forward to starvation. Some estimates place half the world's population in this category.[16]

A New Rationality

Developmentalist theories were wrong. But the problem with these theories does not lie simply with their mistaken optimism, though these theories, especially in their optimistic version, helped to obscure the real operation of interests in the world economy; i.e., they were influential ideologies. Rather, the problem lies in the basic categories, such as the discrete nation, and the frame of reference itself which tends to assume continuous, smooth growth. In many respects these theories literally distract attention from the key factors and issues in development. Clearly, new policies informed by new theories are necessary if the majority of people are even to eat. These new theories, however, are not simply modifications of old theories; for, as we have seen, they constitute nothing less than a new paradigm. And as this thinking informs and is informed by the struggles for a new socialist order, within nations, and ultimately a new world order, it amounts to nothing less than a new rationality, a fundamentally different way of thinking about ourselves and the world.

Inevitably this search for a new rationality transformed theology and the churches.[17] In essence, the horizon of meaning changed fundamentally, and so did Christian sensibilities about the Bible and the Christian tradition.[18] No longer could political action for social justice be considered secondary to the spiritual dimensions of the faith as it had been in the dominant theology inherited from Maritain with its distinction of planes and thus the insistence on the connection between liberation and salvation as historical tasks and gifts. No longer could theory, even in theology, be divorced from action, and thus the emphasis on praxis. No longer could development efforts depend on the technical expertise of a few and the good will of the majority, and thus the emphasis on the role of critical social scientific analysis both in politics and in theology; concretely, this means that the issue of capitalism versus socialism becomes a central theological issue. No longer could the growing gap between the social interests of the wealthy minority and the marginalized majority be ignored, and thus the emphasis on commitment to the poor and oppressed as the first act in doing theology. No longer could the actual practice of Christians and of the Church be ignored, and thus the emphasis on the critical social scientific analysis of the Church's role in society. No longer could the Bible be interpreted through the eyes of the discrete, autonomous "rational" individual of liberal thought, and thus the emphasis on the collective dimension of salvation and on biblical faith as doing justice.

These and other aspects of liberation theology clearly add up to a new paradigm for theology, and, these theologians insist, a new way of doing theology, a new method.[19] This is a method which in its commitment to analysis, action, and theological reflection embodies a revitalized spirituality, a concrete way of living out faith in the God of Moses and Jesus which understands the gift of salvation as intimately bound up with the struggles of the oppressed for liberation in history.[20]

Were Optimistic Theories Based on Facts?

Upon hearing about First World involvement in the underdevelopment of the Third World, many Christians propose a theology of relinquishment as a response to the call for liberation.[21] The logic is simple. If the rich nations have benefited from the development of underdevelopment in the poor nations, then these nations ought to be willing to relinquish the advantages and wealth they have acquired.

The important thing to note about this emphasis on a theology of relinquishment is that it can leave unchallenged the impression that, while the optimistic theories of national development which have dominated public discussions and policy making in the post-world War II period were wrong as far as the Third World is concerned, they have been correct as far as the U.S. has been concerned. But have they?

The most influential views of development in the U.S. in the postwar era predicted ever increasing affluence and upward mobility in a post-industrial society.[22] Not only were people generally going to be more affluent, but their work would itself promote the exercise of initiative, a sense of autonomy, and interpersonal skills;[23] for unskilled, manual work was quickly giving way to white-collar work requiring education, initiative, and independence in the era of high technology. And these transformations in the structures of everyday life would promote fuller self-development and a more truly democratic, less prejudiced political process in which each interest group in society could pursue its interests.

A look at the pattern of income distribution in the U.S., however, quickly undermines this perspective on American life. For there has been no significant alteration of income or wealth distribution in the U.S. since World War II.[24]

It is often argued that even if there has been no fundamental redistribution of income, there has been an expansion of everyone's income, so that all, or nearly all, have enough. And that if work for the majority of people is not itself fulfilling, nevertheless people have abundant leisure time and disposable income to develop themselves and their interests in whatever unique ways they wish. It is true that there has been some growth in real income for individuals and families since World War II. But the reports concerning these trends usually do not take account of two facts. First, there are the increased costs of living due to the breakup of traditional living patterns and of various forms of community support and self-sufficiency built into them; and to the penetration of the market into every sphere of life, even into those which traditionally have been the most personal and private.[25] And second, there is the fact that increasingly family income in the U.S. depends on the work of both spouses; the appearance of affluence, even the ability to go further into debt, rely for most on the crucial factor of the second income. The truth is, then, that despite the high degree of visibility of the affluent lifestyle in the media, the bottom 70 percent or so of the population has *at best* barely been keeping up with inflation and the increasing costs of living. Indeed, the bottom 30 percent or so of families in the U.S. are living in outright poverty, even by government standards; they are simply unable to keep up. Furthermore, another 20 to 30 percent of American families fail to earn enough to be able to live by what the government labels a "moderate" standard of living.

The budget for this "moderate but adequate standard of living," as calculated by the Bureau of Labor Statistics, projects the following kinds of spending patterns for an urban family of four: It assumes that the family will own a toaster that lasts thirty-three years, a refrigerator and a stove that will each last seventeen years, a vacuum cleaner that will last fourteen years, and a TV set that will last ten years. It assumes that the father will buy one year-round suit every four years, and one topcoat every eight and one-half years; the mother will buy three street dresses every two years. Once every three months the parents can go to the movies; and one of them can go alone once a year. This budget includes no allowance for savings to meet periods of illness or unemployment, nor does it allow for savings for the children's higher education. A used car may be purchased every four years; and there is an allowance for a tune-up once a year, a brake-relining every three years, and a front-end alignment every four years. In 1975 the moderate budget was set at $15,500 for an urban family of four, and out of this income Social Security, income, and other taxes must be paid. Over 50 percent of the families in the U.S. failed to earn this much income in 1975. And subsequent increases in the cost of living and inflation have further swelled the ranks of those who cannot attain even this moderate standard of living.[26]

The most important point about these data is that they do not even begin to portray the suffering which the majority of American's experience in a society where the dominant institutions define the good life in terms of affluence. Moreover, they do not tell of the poor health, substandard living conditions, concern about jobs, and constant worry about money which confront most people every day.[27] The epidemic rates of alcoholism and other forms of drug abuse, of rape, wife-beating, child abuse, and other forms of violence, of psychosomatic diseases like certain kinds of ulcers and heart disease, suggest the depths of anguish and alienation which many experience in our society. Of course, the poor are more likely to get sick, too. After age forty-five they are about twice as likely as moderately well-off people to have arthritis, asthma, diabetes, heart conditions, hypertension, back problems, hearing and vision impairments.

It is only the top 30 percent or so of the U.S. population which could be said to be affluent in any sense, and an even smaller percentage which can be said to be securely affluent. For example, in 1974 only 20 percent of U.S.

families made $20,000 or more. And less than 5 percent have incomes that make possible the truly affluent lifestyles which so dominate the media[28] and have come to be the norm.

Yet, these lifestyles have been promoted so well that many people, who like the majority of Americans have virtually no chance of achieving such affluence, feel guilty for their failures.[29] And others, usually those who have made it, persist in believing that anyone can make it if only they try hard enough. Nevertheless, the data reveal that, like the gap between rich and poor nations, there is a growing gap in absolute terms in income (and wealth) between rich and poor within the U.S.[30] Similar data and analyses undermine the rosy pictures of the transformation of work; the majority of American workers, about 60 percent, are solidly working-class in terms of the kind of work they do, work which is frequently unhealthy, dangerous, and boring along with not paying very well.[31] Moreover, there is growing evidence that much highly touted middle-class work brings with it its own cost, in terms of constant anxiety, profound sense of disconnection, sense of meaninglessness—tendencies which in their pathological forms are identified with narcissism, a syndrome appearing with increasing frequency in therapists' offices.[32]

Clearly, there have been some genuine success stories of ascent up the ladder of success. We all undoubtedly know people who have made it, and these successful few (relatively speaking) are constantly paraded before us by the media and all too often by social scientists. Nevertheless, the story is false for a majority of Americans; the optimistic theories about the affluent post-industrial society have distorted our understanding of ourselves and our world, and inhibited our ability to do anything about it. The story is especially false for certain groups of Americans, blacks and women in particular.

A brief look at some data will help to make the point. First, although the median weekly income of black workers more than doubled between 1967 and 1976, the absolute dollar gap between black and white workers has increased, from $34 in 1967 to $44 in 1973 to $52 by 1976. In terms of family income, between 1970 and 1975 the absolute dollar gap between black and white median income increased from $3,957 to $4,717. And as a percentage of white income, median black family income has fallen from 64 percent in 1970 to 61 percent in 1975. Similarly, labor-force participation rates have been lower for blacks; between 1960 and 1975 black workers were twice as likely to be unemployed due to loss of job and twice as likely not to enter the labor force or find re-employment.[33] In a society where meeting human needs depends almost entirely on income these differences have life-and-death significance for many blacks. Statistics indicate a fate for persons of Spanish-speaking origin which places them as a group better off than blacks and worse off than whites, though "better" and "worse" are meaningless concepts in terms of the actual lives of the millions of people, whether black, Hispanic, or white, who actually live in poverty.

The data concerning women's wages and unemployment rates also reveal patterns of discrimination. According to the prevalent view women were entering the paid labor force in the postwar era to earn some extra money to be used by the family in pursuit of luxuries. As well, of course, there were women who were, like many men, seeking professional careers with all the rewards that they bring. However, women have been crowded into low-skilled work, work as nurses' aides, health service workers, telephone operators, and the like, in which at least 85 percent of the jobs are held by women.[34] Not surprisingly, these jobs tend to be low paying. In 1974 women earned 57 percent of the median income of men, $6,772 versus $11,835. These figures actually represent a decline, for women earned 63.9 percent of men's median income in 1955. Clearly, the gap in absolute terms between women's and men's income was also increasing, from $1,533 in 1955 to $5,062 in 1974. And as for the claim that women work just to have extra money, 71 percent of all women in the wage-labor force in 1974 were single, widowed, divorced, or separated, or married to husbands who earned less than $9,999 per year in 1973. And of course, women are more likely to be unemployed than men.[35] And female-headed families were five times as likely as male-headed families to be in poverty. As you might expect by now, minority women suffer the most; at least 50 percent of all families headed by black or Spanish-speaking women are poor by official government standards.[36]

These data suggest that there are patterns of discrimination against women, blacks, Hispanics, and other minorities, which along with the class divisions are built into the very functioning and historical evolution of our society. In spite of the optimism of theories and policies in the postwar era, things are not getting any better for these groups, or for the majority of Americans. Indeed they may well be getting worse.

The failures of these theories and policies have led to a search for new ways of understanding and organizing for change. In particular, among women and blacks, the critique of old theories has generated new perspectives on racism and sexism in relation to the development of the capitalist system. The key involves a rejection of the point of view which sees both racism and sexism as only psychological and/or cultural factors in favor of looking at the ways in which different groups of people get caught up at different times, in different ways, in different places in the uneven development of the capitalist world economy.

The Capitalist System

We have already seen that from the beginning of the capitalist era development in the nations of the periphery has proceeded largely in terms of an agenda set in the core nations. This means that as the capitalist system has expanded to cover the world the ways in which different groups of people go about producing all the necessities and luxuries which make life in a society possible and even "good" have been undermined and transformed, not according to the ideals, values, and the interests of the majority of local people, but in response to needs defined in terms of capital accumulation by elites at the center, in collusion with local elites.

One of the major needs of this system is for cheap labor. Inevitably peoples of color have been incorporated into the system as the cheapest kind of labor. So the capitalist world order which emerged in the sixteenth century was both a class order, insofar as the crucial division is between those who own and control the means of production and those who have only their labor to sell, and a racial order. Workers in the core countries may have had only their labor to sell, but in theory at least they were free to sell it where they would and to do with the rest of their time and energy what they would. Africans, however, became members of the slave class, exported to the plantation economies of the New World, i.e., the economies on the periphery of the world system.[37] In the world economy at that time, then, the core nations were dependent on the trading of slaves and slave production for the accumulation of wealth which fueled capitalist development, just as the plantations were dependent on merchant capitalism both for slaves and for markets for their products. In this context an elaborate social, ideological, and moral order, drawing on a pre-existing derogatory imagery of darkness, barbarism, and heathenism, was erected whose function was to legitimate this particular division of labor and status.[38] Bringing civilization, and all too often Christianity, to the primitives justified the worldwide destruction of other peoples, their cultures, economies, and institutions. And internally, racism served the interests of capital accumulation all too frequently at the level of politics by convincing low-status whites that being white was more significant than being poor.

The Place of Blacks in the System

In this perspective race is simultaneously an economic, political, cultural, and psychological reality, one which has survived even as it has changed with changes in each of these spheres. Clearly, slavery did not disappear with the demise of the plantation economy and the Civil War. For in the period after the Civil War, most blacks were relegated to the work in peonagelike sharecropping and tenancy operations; and racism continued to be a useful political weapon in defending the status quo, dividing workers and poor people in their struggles for better wages and working conditions. Gradually, however, expanding industry, in the North at first and then also in the South, provided alternatives to blacks, especially during labor shortages during the two World Wars; this exodus from rural areas was made irreversible with the mechanization of agriculture in the mid-twentieth century. Thus, changes in the processes of capital accumulation generated new opportunities in new situations for blacks. In 1900, for example, about 77 percent of all blacks lived in rural areas; by 1970 only 19 percent lived in rural areas. Clearly, these new opportunities required fundamental changes in the structures of everyday life for a majority of blacks. These changes, however, have not been so beneficial as the dominant theories of national development suggest.

For in the cities only a few blacks gained the privileges and status promised in the American dream. The problem is that in this century two distinct segments have emerged in the labor market corresponding to the division in the economy between the monopoly sector in which industries are dominated by a few corporate giants and the competitive sector involving larger numbers of smaller firms which compete with one another in the traditional sense of the word. Primary-sector jobs tend to involve high wages, good working conditions, employment stability, job security, due process in the administration of work rules, and chances for advancement. In contrast, the secondary-sector jobs tend to involve low wages, poor working conditions, considerable variability in employment, harsh and often arbitrary discipline, and little opportunity for advancement.[39] Largely because of deeply committed and well-organized political action, which in the middle years of this century won substantial concessions from the government and the courts, and because racism becomes less significant as a political weapon for controlling workers in large bureaucracies in government and large corporations where formal "rational" methods of labor management dominate, some blacks have been able to gain access to primary-sector jobs, and to display in their own lives the "success" promised to all in the optimistic theories of the postwar era.[40]

But there have never been enough of these kinds of jobs to go around. And the majority of blacks have been channeled into the least desirable jobs, not simply because of racism as a form of active discrimination but by the structuring of the political economy in this country. Forced off the land by the mechanization of agriculture, they moved to the central cities at a time when industry was already decentralizing and moving to the suburbs.[41] At a time when good jobs in the rapidly expanding corporate and government sectors increasingly demanded education, black children were attending deteriorating inner-city schools.[42] At a time when blacks increasingly need other social services, the flight of industry from northeastern and midwestern cities to the southern rim of the U.S., and abroad, undermines the ability of local governments to supply them. Of course, many who are white, as well as members of other racial minorities, suffer for the same reasons. And this is the point: apart from overt racism (and there remains plenty of that) the structures engendered in the processes of uneven capitalist development in this century channel many Americans into undesirable, poor-paying jobs, or into outright poverty. For clear historical reasons, blacks are highly over-represented in these classes at the bottom of the social ladder in the U.S.

And yet, if recent history has not resulted in an improved quality of life for most blacks, the future holds even less hope. For the weakened position of the U.S. in the world economy portends continuing crisis in the U.S., with the costs being borne especially by working-class and poor people in the form of continuing inflation, higher unemployment, and cutbacks in social services.[43]

That blacks in particular will bear these burdens is already clear, as official government data referred to above reveal. Indeed, these data probably seriously underestimate the extent of the problem. For example, recent estimates place the percentage of unemployed black youth in inner-city areas at 50 to 60 percent.

Clearly, another form of rationality than that promoted by the logic of capitalist accumulation is required if there is to be any hope for the "good life" for a majority of Americans, and if there is to be any hope of eliminating racism. The efforts of blacks to combat racism and to contribute to the creation of a new society in America in the context of changing historical circumstances can be understood in one sense as a deepening quest for this new rationality, for a new way of understanding racism and of organizing to overcome it.[44] Inevitably, these struggles have transformed black theology and the black churches. And not surprisingly, in the late 1960s liberation, as distinct from equality, emerged as a central theme in black theology. With it there was a call to reject structures of oppression as these are manifested in American society, and to reject dominant forms of thinking as these reflected the interests of the oppressors. In particular, there was a call to reject dominant forms of theology, and to articulate a new theology expressive of the experience and faith of oppressed blacks.[45] In the light of the above analyses this kind of liberation theology must be understood ultimately as a challenge to the capitalist system in the U.S., and throughout the world, which inevitably exploits and marginalizes blacks.[46]

The Place of Women in the System

The oppression of women can also be understood in terms of the uneven development fostered by the different strategies of capital accumulation in the U.S. For definitions of women's roles, and indeed the nature of subjectivity itself in both women and men, have been central points of struggle in the shifting relations of production throughout history. It has been suggested, for example, that in early capitalist societies women, because they worked side-by-side with men in the fields and in the home in doing all the jobs necessary to keep the family going, actually had greater equality and more rights than they were to have subsequently.[47] Certainly these societies were patriarchal and oppressive to women, but the undermining of this form of society organized around family production and the emergence of industrial capitalism generated a series of crises in family life. And in ensuing struggles to define "female" and "male" and their respective roles in the family and in the larger society women actually lost ground.

The key to these struggles lies in the transformation of the mode of production. Increasingly women and men and even children were being drawn into industry, undermining the traditional division of labor and emotion in the family.[48] In the face of these pressures members of the new working class fought to preserve traditional values and forms of family life. And by the

1830s or so various types of reformers, including especially ministers and doctors, began to point with alarm to the "crisis in the family." The resolution of these struggles involved on the one hand the increasing privitization of the family as government at various levels—the public realm—took up responsibilities traditionally exercised by the family, such as care for the old, the poor, the sick, and delinquents; and on the other hand, it involved the definition of the role of women in terms of full-time motherhood within the home, her tasks focusing especially around care for children who were coming to be seen for the first time in history as innocent, helpless beings in need of constant attention and careful nurturance.[49]

These developments were somewhat ambiguous. On the one hand, the late nineteenth-century Victorian emphasis on the sanctity of the family and the autonomy of women within it marked an advance for women of all classes. Similarly, the success of movements to eliminate child labor and to limit the kinds of jobs women could do represented real progress in protecting people from the ravages of the capitalist organization of work. On the other hand, this definition of womanhood and the protective legislation embodying it served to limit women's access to higher-paying jobs.[50] Thus these images and policies worked to the advantage of men who were competing for the same jobs; indeed unions were supportive of such legislation while hesitant to unionize women, who were seen as a threat to men's jobs. Thus, like racism, sexism served to divide people, who as workers faced the same problems about wages and working conditions. Moreover, these images and policies also reflected the reality of upper- and middle-class women whose income was not necessary for family survival. Nevertheless, this image of womanhood, and a corresponding image of the family as the focus of women's work, was widely preached by the hosts of experts in the new professions which arose to deal with the crisis in the family: pediatrics, education, social work, public health, household science, recreation.[51] Not surprisingly, working-class women and men reflected similar values, even though women's work in the paid labor force was essential to the survival of many working-class families. And women who worked in the wage-labor force carried the double burden of that work plus the largest share of housework.[52]

Especially important, however, is the fact that the new division of labor and the changing normative images of femininity and masculinity corresponded to fundamental changes in family life. The home came to be seen as the haven in a heartless world of work, the domain of men; children came to be seen as weak, helpless creatures requiring constant attention.[53] And women came to be seen as ideally suited by nature and disposition to be keepers of the home, nurturers of husbands and children. The point is that while there is nothing eternal and inevitable about these arrangements, women and men came to be socialized into these roles. Furthermore, the family came to be the primary locus for the reproduction of mothers and fathers in the particular forms in which we have come to know them.[54] The ill-effects of this division of labor and emotion on women and in them at the deepest levels of their selves, and in those of men, are well-known: the symptoms range from the epidemic rates of wife-beating and child abuse to discrimination in the labor market. Clearly, if this form of oppression is to be overcome, ways of understanding the relationships between psychology and the economy far superior to that provided by older theories are necessary.

The emergence of the women's movement and of feminist theology can be explained in terms of women's entry into the wage-labor force in unprecedented numbers during the middle years of this century.[55] In 1900 only eighteen percent of women between the ages of eighteen and sixty-four worked; and these were mostly young and unmarried women who planned to work a few years, then leave the wage-labor force to marry and have children, never to return again. By 1977 46 percent of all women worked for wages. The greatest portion of this increase has occurred since 1940, and involves married women. In 1940 only 17 percent of all married women worked for wages, but by 1974 the figure was up to 43 percent.[56] There are several reasons for this rapid increase. Many women were drawn into the paid labor force during the two World Wars and, even though the demand for women workers fell sharply right after World War II, they were still looking for the opportunities for additional income, social contacts, and sense of independence and competence which they had experienced in the workplace. A major underlying reason was the rapidly increasing costs of living; as indicated above, most women work out of sheer economic necessity.

But, whatever their personal reasons, women found that they were channeled into the workforce in very discriminating ways, according to values and interests not their own. The major areas of expansion in the labor market in this century have been in service jobs such as beauticians, waitresses, hospital workers, etc. and in clerical work; and employers turned to women as a cheap source of nonunionized labor.[57] It is in this context that women discovered just how unequal they are in the dominant definitions of the division of labor and emotion at home and work.

Clearly another form of rationality is required if women and men are ever to escape the effects of the distorted development of human capacities and sensitivities reflected in dominant stereotypes and incarnated in oppressive structures in both private and public life. In many different ways in the late 1960s and early 1970s women began to organize to change both values and structures.

Inevitably this search for a new rationality has challenged the churches and theology. Feminist theologians have rejected the very categories in which theology has been articulated, perceiving in them a reflection of men's experience and interests which can only distort women's experience. They insist that theology must begin from the experience of the oppressed, that it cannot be done apart from the actual struggles to unfold a new society.[58] And, like the other liberation theologians, they insist that it must involve a new method[59] and a new spirituality.[60] In the light of the above analyses, this kind of liberation theology must be understood ultimately as a challenge to the capitalist system in the U.S. and throughout the world, which inevitably exploits and marginalizes women.[61]

Efforts to Transcend the System

The above analyses of underdevelopment in the Third World, racism, sexism, and class exploitation within the U.S. and throughout the world, all reflect an understanding of capitalism as a world economy which sweeps up and channels different groups of people into the market at different times, in different places, in different ways. Historically, the most significant feature of this dynamic system is the combined and uneven nature of its development. It has fostered the development of slavery alongside "free" wage-labor and unpaid housework alongside "real" work in factories and offices. It promotes staggering concentrations of wealth and power, unprecedented in history, for a minority, alongside a modest if tenuous living for a larger but still small group, the so-called middle classes throughout the world, and alongside outright marginalization and poverty, even starvation, for the largest portion of humanity.[62] In particular, as we have seen, it channels non-white races and women in unequal ways into the system.[63]

This system, however, should not be seen as a juggernaut out of control crushing all in its path. For it is a dynamic system ever generating conflict and change as new groups are incorporated into the system, often in spite of their own militant opposition; in addition, upon entering the marketplace these newer groups come into competition with established groups for goods, services, and opportunities, groups which are themselves continually changing as they confront the tasks of reproducing themselves. One of the central arenas of these conflicts is government programs at local and national levels, as different groups struggle to secure welfare and regulatory policies and judicial decisions which promote their interests. The results of these struggles inevitably influence the process of capital accumulation itself, i.e., the investment and marketing decisions by corporate executives which shape the national and international division of labor. As we have seen above, these decisions made in the interest of corporate profits and growth, often with government support, have profound effects on local communities, regions, and even whole nations. In recent years with the emergence of multinational corporations (MNCs) there has been an enormous expansion in the power of these large corporations; in their decisions to open a factory here and to close one there corporate executives literally have life-and-death power over millions of people. It is no wonder that governments are so responsive to the wishes of these corporate leaders.[64]

But even this power is not without contradiction. There is, for example, a conflict between the need for corporations to maximize profits by minimizing wages on the one hand, and the ability of consumers, most of whom are workers, to consume the products of the corporations on the other. There is also a conflict between the desires of multinational corporate leaders to be able to move freely wherever and whenevei the market dictates in order to maximize profits and corporate strength, and the continued stability of national governments which on the part of core nations to promote an international climate favorable to their own MNCs, and on the part of periphery nations to promote stable national climates for investment.[65]

It is the existence of these and other conflicts which makes politics so important. For the only inevitability in the ongoing development of underdevelopment between nations and within nations, and in the ongoing reproduction of class, racial, and sexual divisions is the inability and/or unwillingness of ordinary people to act to change the system itself. It is for this reason that the symbols and concepts with which people interpret themselves, others, and the world are inevitably caught up in these struggles to perpetuate and to transform the system. In other words, what people *think* makes a world of difference.[66] The three liberation theologies referred to here and the movements which inspired them all testify to the importance of learning to think and even to feel in fundamentally different ways, both because the dominant ways of seeing themselves actually distort their own experience and personal development, and because these dominant perspectives actually contribute to their oppression by inhibiting their ability to change social structures.[67]

There are many examples of such ideological distortion. I would like to choose one which very dramatically reveals how much is at stake in how we interpret the structures of our daily lives. It is not unusual for people to be unemployed in our society, especially, as we have seen, women and blacks and other minorities. Given various forms of welfare, unemployment does not always mean starvation. Nevertheless, it seems to mean a great deal to the unemployed, to be literally a matter of life and death. For a number of studies show that unemployment is closely correlated with separation and divorce, child abuse, suicide, homicide, admission to state mental hospitals and prisons, death from cirrhosis of the liver, heart and kidney disease. But none of these conditions is automatic or inevitable. All are mediated by the prevailing interpretations of employment and unemployment, by the prevailing level of social and political consciousness. If unemployed persons hold themselves responsible, and it is hard not to when prevailing views see "opportunities" everywhere, then these outcomes do seem inevitable. But if family and friends rally to the support of someone who has been victimized by an unjust system, these outcomes may be avoided. Indeed, when active political movements exist, the anger and frustration arising out of unemployment might be channeled creatively in the direction of radical social change.[68]

The analyses being unfolded by these movements, then, suggest that change in the capitalist world economy with its class, racial, and sexual divisions is inevitable. The key questions concern the nature of these changes and the nature of the decision-making process. The distinctive thing about the movements referred to here is that they converge in calling for the transcendence of the present system, not just for reform, in calling for liberation, not just for equality. Moreover, they are organizing so that oppressed peoples themselves can become active participants in this process of unfolding a new history.

Origins of a New Theology

In conclusion, I would like to focus briefly on the theological implications of these claims. Developmentalist theories have much in common with traditional theological claims about meaning in life,[69] and they can only be understood in this context. In particular, these theories, as they picture development both in the First World and the Third World, parallel traditional Christian expectations of the Second Coming of Christ. Yet there is one significant difference, for the striking thing about these theories is that the *eschaton* is collapsed into the present; there is no future-perfect society against which to judge the present. In these theories salvation has been achieved. More concretely, this means that for these theorists there are no longer any problems of great seriousness;[70] after all, in this view "democracy. . . is the good society itself in operation."[71] Accordingly, alternative visions and values retreat into the background in the face of "experts" who have merely to "fine-tune" the economy and polity, to promote the well-being of all in the U.S., and to iron out the remaining obstacles to development in the "underdeveloped" nations. Thus the problem of leisure emerges in the advanced societies. And, perhaps for the first time in history, "boredom" becomes a major worry![72]

These theories are nothing less than secular salvation histories. The tenets of this creed, "more a cluster of attitudes than a well worked-out theology," became "a truly popular religion in the postwar era."[73] And the "secular priesthood" preaching this salvation history has been those responsible for interpreting and implementing national development in the U.S. and maintaining its place in the world system.[74] These secular priests have been the "missionaries of the American way."[75]

Certainly we know that many in the mainline churches simply echo these versions of salvation history, that many churches became houses of worship of the "American way."[76] But the issues go much deeper than simply the moral stance that we take toward U.S. policies at home and abroad. For these theories have shaped the very horizon of meaning in terms of which we have asked, and attempted to answer, questions about ourselves, our world, and our God.

Two elements of this ethos or horizon of meaning are important here. The first is its optimism; remaining problems were reduced to those of individuals who by disposition or bad luck had not yet succeeded. Problems like racism or poverty, then, when they were noticed at all were seen as residual, outside of the major thrust of the system toward equality and affluence for all; in other words, there were no *social* problems, problems requiring structural change by political movements.

The second element is related to this optimism. It is the focusing of questions of meaning and action on the discrete, autonomous, rational individual.[77] Indeed, such an individual, guided in his actions by science, was seen as the very epitome of evolution. Generally, women, blacks, and other racial groups were not thought capable of achieving such heights; in these theories this discrete autonomous individual is a white, First-World, upper-class man. This image of the autonomous individual dominated virtually all the academic disciplines during this period,[78] and theology was no exception.

This ethos of autonomous rationality can be understood in terms of the rapid expansion of the professional, technical, and managerial middle class following World War II (doubling between 1947 and 1964, and again by 1975). Often in their personal life histories individuals in this class, usually white men experienced upward mobility precisely as individuals. Moreover, the very structure of work as scientists, accountants, and managers promotes a sense of linear rationality, a confidence in calculation, and belief in the ability to plan long range. One commentator refers to these as virtues of the head, not the heart.[79] These sensibilities have been enormously influential because it is precisely these people who have high visibility in our society, and who in their roles as interpreters of our society in the media and the schools and as policy makers in government and business influence the thinking of all of us, and indeed the structures of our daily lives.[80]

These sensibilities have been influential in the churches in part because some church members were moving into this class, but more importantly because many church leaders, theological educators, and theologians have adapted "professional" models, taking as their standards of accountability the canons of other professionals.[81] Inevitably, faith in God, sin, and salvation have been interpreted in terms of crises and transitions in the individual life-cycle: illness and death, birth and marriage. Not surprisingly, psychology has become an influential partner in dialogue with theology, especially at the level of pastoral ministry where there has been a strong tendency to equate ministry with counseling.

Of course, both the optimism and the rationality of autonomous individuality came under attack around very concrete social issues, civil rights for blacks, and peace in Southeast Asia, in the middle 1960s, and somewhat later, around women's rights. And many in the churches were in the forefront of these struggles. The optimism of the developmental theories was rejected by many, and there were numerous attempts to break out of the horizon of meaning shaped by the ethos of autonomous rationality; for example, in theological celebrations of play, festivity, and communalism. Certainly these movements were significant, recovering important elements in older theories and in the psyches of their supporters which had been eclipsed. Nevertheless, the new sense of self tended to be expressed at the theoretical level in terms of a rearrangement of elements of autonomous rationality, within the skin of autonomous individuals so to speak.

But, as we have seen, it has been the experience of blacks, women, and

Third World activists, that the chief determinants in their lives, and death, are collective factors, matters of social structures which channel particular groups of people in particular ways within the system. Moreover, they have said that the focus on the individual and the ethos of autonomous rationality in general not only distort their experience, but serve to perpetuate their situations by masking the mechanisms of oppression. Their experience has called forth new paradigms in the social sciences, and a search for a revitalized language to give expression to fears and hopes. Inevitably, as Christians they have sought new ways to talk about their experience of God, new ways to talk about the Church, new ways to do theology.

Gustavo Gutiérrez makes this point very concretely; we cannot speak about the resurrection of Jesus Christ, he says, unless we are able to speak about the real deaths of the people.[82] Clearly the developmentalist perspectives have not enabled us to speak adequately about or to respond to the real deaths of the great majority of Third-World people. Moreover, we have seen above that optimistic theories of development concerning the U.S. do not enable us to speak adequately about the real deaths of blacks and women, or of a majority of American men.

The search for new ways of thinking about and indeed experiencing ourselves, others, and God, goes on. I have suggested in this paper that feminist theology, black theology, and Latin American theology are converging in their interpretations of the sources of oppression in the capitalist world system. Indeed, it is clear from the perspective of the analysis of this world system why these liberation movements are now arising, and why there are others in Asia, Africa, Europe, and Canada coming to similar conclusions regarding the sources of exploitation and oppression and the necessity of overcoming them. It is also clear that in the tasks of further specifying the nature of this system, of unfolding the vision of an alternative, and of working together to bring this about there is an important role for faith in the God who liberates the poor and oppressed. Moreover, the liberation theologians tell us, it is only in the midst of such struggles for liberation in identification with the oppressed that we can hope to rediscover the God of Jesus and the prophets and to work out our own salvation.[83]

Notes

1. Gustavo Gutiérrez, "The Voice of the Poor in the Church," *Proceedings of the Catholic Theological Society of America* 33 (1978), p. 33.

2. Daniel Bell, *The End of Ideology* (New York: Macmillan, 1960; Free Press, 1965), pp. 402-403.

3. Seymour Martin Lipset, *Political Man* (Garden City, N.Y.: Doubleday, Anchor, 1963), p. 442.

4. Walt Whitman Rostow, *The Stages of Economic Growth: A Non-Communist Manifesto* (Cambridge: Cambridge University Press, 1960; 2nd ed. 1971), p. 164.

5. Lipset, *Political Man,* p. 439.

6. Talcott Parsons, *Societies: Evolutionary and Comparative Perspectives* (Englewood Cliffs, N.J.: Prentice-Hall, 1966).

7. The question "Liberation to what?" is also important. It concerns the utopian vision which motivates the members of these movements, the image of a new society which is affirmed to be both desirable and realistic; as such, it is intimately related to theological notions of the New Creation or the Kingdom of God. Though these issues are important, I will not address them here. In general it is clear that no such vision has grasped the imaginations of large numbers of North Americans.

8. Elsewhere, drawing on developments in anthropology, sociology, and hermeneutics, I offer some theoretical and methodological reflections on the terms "worldview" and "cultural nationality" which make more explicit the way they are used here; see Lee Cormie, "Society, History, Meaning: Perspectives from the Social Sciences," *Proceedings of the Catholic Theological Society of America* 34 (1979), pp. 31-47. In other terms, if theology can be understood as the response, drawing on the Bible and on the Christian tradition, to the limit questions which emerge in the horizons of meaning of a people (David Tracy, *Blessed Rage for Order* [New York: Seabury, 1975]), then these liberation theologies can be understood as rejections of the very horizon of meaning in terms of which both questions and answers have typically been articulated.

9. Gustavo Gutiérrez, *A Theology of Liberation: History, Politics, and Salvation,* trans. Sr. Caridad Inda and John Eagleson (Maryknoll, N.Y.: Orbis Books, 1973), pp. 63-66.

10. Max Weber, *The Protestant Ethic and the Spirit of Capitalism* (1904-1905), trans. Talcott Parsons (New York: Scribner's, 1958).

11. For influential statements of these views, see Alex Inkeles, "The Modernization of Man," in *Modernization: The Dynamics of Growth,* ed. Myron Weiner (New York: Basic Books, 1966), pp. 138-150; Daniel Lerner, *The Passing of Traditional Society: Modernizing the Middle East* (New York: Free Press, 1958); David C. McClelland, "The Impulse to Modernization," in *Modernization: The Dynamics of Growth,* pp. 28-39; Talcott Parsons, "Evolutionary Universals in Society," *American Sociological Review* 29 (1964): 339-357; Parsons, *Societies: Evolutionary and Comparative Perspectives*; Rostow, *Stages of Economic Growth.* For critiques of these views, see Samir Amin, *Accumulation on a World Scale: A Critique of the Theory of Underdevelopment,* 2 vols., trans. Brian Pearce (New York: Monthly Review Press, 1974); Susanne J. Bodenheimer, "The Ideology of Developmentalism: American Political Science's Paradigm-Surrogate for Latin American Studies," *Berkeley Journal of Sociology* 17 (1972-73): 517-534; Theotonio Dos Santos, "The Crisis of Development Theory and the Problem of Dependence in Latin America," in *Underdevelopment and Development,* ed. H. Bernstein (Harmondsworth, England: Penguin, 1973), pp. 57-80; Andre Gunder Frank, "Sociology of Development and Underdevelopment of Sociology," in *Dependence and Underdevelopment* by James D. Cockroft, Andre Gunder Frank, and Dale L. Johnson (New York: Doubleday, Anchor, 1972), pp. 321-398; Alejandro Portes, "On the Sociology of Natural Development: Theories and Issues," *American Journal of Sociology* 82 (July 1976): 55-85; Immanuel Wallerstein, *The Modern World System: Capitalist Agriculture and the Origins of the European World Economy in the Sixteenth Century* (New York: Academic Press, 1974); Immanuel Wallerstein, "The Present

State of the Debate on World Inequality," in *World Inequality: Origins and Perspectives on the World System*, ed. Immanuel Wallerstein (Montreal: Black Rose Books, 1975), pp. 12–28. I have reviewed some of the issues at stake in these conflicts of analysis: see Lee Cormie, "The Sociology of National Development and Salvation History," in *Sociology and Human Destiny*, ed. Gregory Baum (New York: Seabury, 1980), pp. 56–85.

12. Joseph A. Kahl, *Modernization, Exploitation and Dependency: Germani, Gonzalez, Casanova, and Cardoso* (New Brunswick, N.J.: Transaction Books, 1976), pp. 1–22.

13. Howard M. Wachtel, *The New Gnomes: Multinational Banks in the Third World* (Washington, D.C.: Transnational Institute, 1977).

14. São Paulo Justice and Peace Commission, *São Paulo: Growth and Poverty* (London: Bowerdean Press, 1978).

15. Samir Amin, *Unequal Development*, trans. Brian Pearce (New York: Monthly Review Press, 1976), p. 194.

16. Richard J. Barnet, *Roots of War* (New York: Penguin, 1973), p. 237.

17. Pablo Richard, "The Theology of Liberation in the Current Situation of Latin America," *New Wine Exchange* 2 (May/June and August 1977): Pablo Richard, "The Latin American Church, 1959-1978," *Cross Currents* 28 (Spring 1978): 34–46

18. Gutiérrez's *A Theology of Liberation* has become for many a classic statement of Latin American liberation theology; see also José Míguez Bonino, *Doing Theology in a Revolutionary Situation* (Philadelphia: Fortress, 1975). For a good introduction to a broad range of currents and interests among these theologians, see Rosino Gibellini, ed. *Frontiers of Theology in Latin America* (Maryknoll, N.Y.: Orbis Books, 1979). For helpful overviews of Latin American liberation theology, see Philip E. Berryman, "Latin American Liberation Theology," *Theological Studies* 34 (September 1973): 14–44; Robert McAfee Brown, *Theology in a New Key: Responding to Liberation Themes* (Philadelphia: Westminster, 1978); Francis Fiorenza, "Latin American Liberation Theology," *Interpretation* 28 (October 1974): 441–457; Alfred T. Hennelly, *Theologies in Conflict: The Challenge of Juan Luis Segundo* (Maryknoll, N.Y.: Orbis Books, 1979). For documentation concerning the Christians for Socialism movement which has inspired much of the Latin American liberation theology, see John Eagleson, ed., *Christians and Socialism: Documentation of the Christians for Socialism Movement in Latin America*, trans. John Drury (Maryknoll, N.Y.: Orbis Books, 1975); Christians for Socialism, *Option for Struggle: Three Documents of Christians for Socialism* (Santiago, 1972; Avila, 1973; Bogotá, 1973) (New York: Church Research and Information Project, 1974); Christians for Socialism, *Option for Struggle II: More Documents of Christians for Socialism* (International Declaration, Quebec, 1975; Portugal, 1974; Spanish migrant workers, 1974) (New York: Church Research and Information Projects, 1975).

19. All these theologians insist that liberation theology is a new way of doing theology; Segundo (*The Liberation of Theology*, trans. John Drury [Maryknoll, N.Y.: Orbis Books, 1976]) has developed some of the implications of this claim in detail.

20. Gutiérrez ("The Voice of the Poor in the Church," p. 32) insists that "out method is our spirituality"; yet relatively little has been written so far on the spirituality of liberation; see Segundo Galilea, "Liberation as an Encounter with Politics and Contemplation," trans. J. P. Donnelly, in *The Mystical and Political Dimensions of the Christian Faith*, ed. Claude Geffre and Gustavo Gutiérrez, Concilium 96 (New York: Herder and Herder, 1974), pp. 163–183; Segundo Galilea, "Liberation Theology and New Tasks Facing Christians," in *Frontiers of Theology in Latin America*; Gustavo Gutiérrez, "Liberation, Theology and Proclamation," trans. J. P. Donnelly, in *The Mystical and Political Dimensions of the Christian Faith*, pp. 57–77.

21. Probably the best-known statement of this position is Marie Augusta Neal, *A Socio-Theology of Letting Go* (New York: Paulist Press, 1977); see also Glenn R. Bucher, "Toward a Liberation Theology for the 'Oppressor,' " *Journal of the American Academy of Religion* 44 (1976): 517–534.

22. Bell, *The End of Ideology*; Daniel Bell, *The Coming of Post-Industrial Society* (New York: Basic Books, 1973); John Kenneth Galbraith, *The Affluent Society* (New York: New American Library, 1958).

23. Melvin L. Kohn, *Class and Conformity: A Study in Values* (1969), 2nd ed. (Chicago: University of Chicago Press, 1977).

24. Richard Parker, *The Myth of the Middle Class* (New York: Liveright, 1972); John Curtis Raines, *Illusions of Success: Middle Class Dreams and Middle Class Realities* (Valley Forge, Pa.: Judson, 1975); Michael Harrington, *The Other America* (Baltimore: Penguin, 1963); Frederick

J. Perella, Jr., *Poverty in American Democracy: A Study of Social Power* (Washington, D.C.: USCC Campaign for Human Development, 1974).

25. Harry Braverman, *Labor and Monopoly Capital* (New York: Monthly Review Press, 1974), pp. 271–283; Michael H. Best and William E. Connolly, *The Politicized Economy* (Lexington, Mass.: Heath, 1976), pp. 75-102.

26. Andrew Levinson, *The Working Class Majority* (New York: Penguin, 1975).

27. Lillian Breslow Rubin, *Words of Pain* (New York: Basic Books, 1976).

28. Herbert Gans, *Deciding What's News* (New York: Pantheon, 1979).

29. Richard Sennett and Johnathan Cobb, *The Hidden Injuries of Class* (New York: Random House, Vintage, 1973).

30. Edward S. Herman, "The Income 'Counter-Revolution,' " *Commonweal* 101 (January 3, 1975): 290–96.

31. Levinson, *The Working Class Majority.*

32. Richard Sennett, *The Fall of Public Man: On the Social Psychology of Capitalism* (New York: Random House, Vintage, 1978); Michael Maccoby, *The Gamesman: The New Corporate Leaders* (New York: Simon and Schuster, 1977, Bantam, 1978); Christopher Lasch, *Haven in a Heartless World* (New York: Basic Books, 1977).

33. Herman Thomas, "Impact of the Economic Crisis on Minorities," in *U.S. Capitalism in Crisis*, ed. Union for Radical Political Economics (New York: Union for Radical Political Economics, 1978; hereafter URPE), pp. 77–87.

34. Lousie Kapp Howe, *Pink Collar Workers* (New York: Avon, 1978).

35. Women's Work Project, "Women in Today's Economic Crisis," in *U.S. Capitalism in Crisis*, pp. 69–77.

36. Thomas, "Impact of the Economic Crisis on Minorities," p. 81.

37. Wallerstein, *The Modern World System*, pp. 86–87; Ira Katznelson, *Black Man, White Cities: Race, Politics, and Migration in the United States, 1900–1930, and in Britain, 1948–1968* (London and New York: Oxford University Press, 1973; Chicago: University of Chicago Press, 1976), pp. xv–xvi.

38. Harold H. Baron, "Racial Domination in Advanced Capitalism: A Theory of Nationalism and Divisions in the Labor Market," in *Labor Market Segmentation*, ed. Richard C. Edwards, Michael Reich, and David M. Gordon (Lexington, Mass.: Heath, 1975), pp. 173–216.

39. Michael Piore, "Notes for a Theory of Labor Market Stratification," in *Labor Market Segmentation*, pp. 125–150.

40. William Julius Wilson, *The Declining Significance of Race* (Chicago: University of Chicago Press, 1978).

41. Brad Heil, "Sunbelt Migration," in *U.S. Capitalism in Crisis,* pp. 87–102.

42. Richard H. de Lone, *Small Futures* (New York: Harcourt, Brace, Jovanovich, 1979).

43. David Mermelstein, ed., *The Economic Crisis Reader* (New York: Random House, Vintage, 1975); William K. Tabb and Larry Sawers, eds., *Marxism and the Metropolis* (New York: Oxford University Press, 1978); URPE, *U.S. Capitalism in Crisis.*

44. Howard Dodson, "Strategies for Liberation: Review to Renew," mimeographed paper of an address given at the conference on "The Black Church and Black Community: Unity and Education for Action," sponsored by the Black Theology Project, Theology in the Americas, Atlanta, Georgia, August 2-7, 1977. Excerpts of this paper were published in *The Witness* 61 (1978), pp. 8–9, 12–13.

45. James H. Cone, *A Black Theology of Liberation* (Philadelphia: Lippincott, 1970); James H. Cone, *God of the Oppressed* (New York: Seabury, 1975); J. Deotis Roberts, *A Black Political Theology* (Philadelphia: Westminster, 1974). For a useful overview of these developments in black theology, along with a selection of the key texts in this period, see Gayraud S. Wilmore and James H. Cone, eds., *Black Theology: A Documentary History, 1966-1979* (Maryknoll, N.Y.: Orbis Books, 1979).

46. Cornel West, "Black Theology and Marxist Thought," in *Black Theology: A Documentary History*, pp. 552–567; "Message to the Black Church and Community," adopted August 6, 1977, by the National Conference of the Black theology Project in Atlanta, Georgia; published in *Cross Currents* 27 (Summer 1977): 140–44.

47. Ann Oakley, *Woman's Work* (New York: Random House, Vintage, 1976); Roberta Hamilton, *The Liberation of Women: A Study of Patriarchy and Capitalism* (London: Allen and Unwin, 1978); Barbara Leslie Easton, "Industrialization and Femininity: A Case Study of Nineteenth-Century New England," *Social Problems* 23 (1976): 389–401.

48. For a series of studies examining the changing status of women in the course of development in a variety of Third-World situations, see The Wellesley Editorial Committee, (*Women and National Development: The Complexities of Change* (Chicago: University of Chicago Press, 1977). For analyses which relate class exploitation and sexism in the historical development of capitalism, see Heleieth I.B. Saffioti, *Women in Class Society,* trans. Michael Vale (New York: Monthly Review Press, 1978); Hamilton, *The Liberation of Women*; Eli Zaretsky, *Capitalism, the Family, and Personal Life* (New York: Harper & Row, 1976).

49. Philippe Aries, *Centuries of Childhood*, trans. Robert Baldick (New York: Random House, Vintage, 1962).

50. Joan Huber, "Toward a Socio-Technological Theory of the Women's Movement," *Social Problems* 23 (1976): 371-388.

51. Barbara Ehrenreich and Deirdre English, *For Her Own Good: 150 Years of the Experts' Advice to Women* (New York: Doubleday, Anchor, 1978); Sheila M. Rothman, *Woman's Proper Place: A History of Changing Ideas and Practices, 1870 to the Present* (New York: Basic Books, 1976).

52. Elise Boulding, "Familial Constraints on Women's Work Roles," in *Women and the Workplace*, ed. Martha Blaxall and Barbara Reagan (Chicago: University of Chicago Press, 1976), pp. 95-117.

53. Lasch, *Haven in a Heartless World*.

54. Nancy Chodorow, *The Reproduction of Mothering: Family Structure and Feminine Personality* (Berkeley: University of California Press, 1978).

55. The expansion of educational opportunities for women, the trend toward reduction in family size, and the example of the civil rights/Black Power movements were also important facts which gave impetus to the women's movement during these years; see Sara Evans, *Personal Politics* (New York: Knopf, 1979); Jo Freeman, *The Politics of Women's Liberation* (New York: Longmans, 1975); Huber, "Toward a Socio-Technological Theory of the Women's Movement," pp. 371-388.

56. Women's Work Project, "Women in Today's Economic Crisis," in *U.S. Capitalism in Crisis*.

57. Howe, *Pink Collar Workers*.

58. In various ways all feminist theologians make these claims; for perhaps the earliest statement of these themes in the recent phase of feminism, see Valerie Saiving, "The Human Condition: A Feminine View," in *Womanspirit Rising: A Feminist Reader in Religion*, ed. Carol P. Christ and Judith Plaskow (1960) (New York: Harper & Row, 1979), pp. 25-42. See also Rosemary Radford Ruether, *Religion and Sexism* (New York: Simon and Schuster, 1974); Walter Burkhardt, ed., *Woman: New Dimensions* (New York: Paulist Press, 1977). For an analysis of these currents in feminist theology, see Carol P. Christ, "The New Feminist Theology: A Review of the Literature," *Religious Studies Review* 3 (October 1977): 203-212. For a discussion of the related issues of moral development, see Beverly Wildung Harrison, "The New Consciousness of Women: A Socio-Political Resource," *Cross Currents* 24 (Winter 1975): 445-461; Carol Gilligan, "In a Different Voice: Women's Conceptions of Self and of Morality," *Harvard Educational Review* 47 (1977): 481-517.

59. Elizabeth Schüssler Fiorenza, "Feminist Theology as a Critical Theology of Liberation," in *Woman: New Dimensions*, pp. 29-50.

60. Elizabeth Schüssler Fiorenza, "Feminist Spirituality, Christian Identity, and Catholic Vision," in *Womanspirit Rising*, pp. 136-148; Judith Plaskow, "The Coming of Lilith: Toward a Feminist Theology," in *Womanspirit Rising*, pp. 198-211; Letty M. Russell, *The Future of Partnership* (Philadelphia: Westminster, 1979).

61. Sheila D. Collins, "Socialism and Femininity: A Necessary Ground for Liberation," *Cross Currents* 26 (1976): 33-47; "The Familial Economy of God," mimeographed paper (1979), available from Theology in the Americas, 475 Riverside Drive, Room 1268, New York, N.Y. 10027; Rosemary Radford Ruether, *New Woman/New Earth: Sexist Ideologies and Human Liberation* (New York: Seabury, 1975); Rosemary Radford Ruether "Sex, Class and Race: The Experience of Women in the American Women's Movement," in *Is Liberation Theology for North America?: The Response of First-World Churches*, ed. Theology for the Americas (New York: Theology in the Americas, 1978), pp. 45-55; Beverly Harrison, "Feminist Theology: Class and Labor Perspectives," in *Is Liberation Theology for North America?*, pp. 21-27.

62. Susan George, *How the Other Half Dies: The Real Reasons for World Hunger* (Montclair, N.J.: Allenheld, Osmun, 1977); Frances M. Lappé and Joseph Collins, *Food First: Beyond the Myth of Scarcity* (Boston: Houghton Mifflin, 1977).

63. The following statement sums up these issues in terms of the U.S.: "Two-thirds of all poor persons in 1974 were either black, of Hispanic origin, elderly, or in families headed by women; some persons, of course, shared some or all of these characteristics. Whites compromise about 66 percent of all poor people, but the proportion of each population in poverty is much higher among blacks (31 percent) and Hispanics (23 percent) than among whites (9 percent)," Richard Edwards, *Contested Terrain* (New York: Basic Books, 1979), pp. 185-186. It should be noted that Edwards is here relying on the government's definition of poverty, a definition that seriously understates the extent of poverty in our society. These data, then, refer to those in the most extreme poverty.

64. Richard J. Barnet and Ronald E. Muller, *Global Reach: The Power of the Multinational Corporations* (New York: Simon and Schuster, 1974).

65. For fuller discussions of the contradictions in the historical development of capitalism, see Erik Olin Wright, *Class, Crisis and the State* (London: NLB Verso, 1979), pp. 111-180; and James O'Connor, *The Fiscal Crisis of the State* (New York: St. Martin's, 1973). For critical overviews of these and related issues concerning the U.S. and its role in the world system, see Richard C. Edwards, Michael Reich, and Thomas Weiskopf, eds., *The Capitalist System* (Englewood Cliffs, N.J.: Prentice-Hall, 1978); and Douglas Dowd, *The Twisted Dream: Capitalist Development in the United States since 1776* (Cambridge, Mass.: Winthrop, 1974).

66. As Gutiérrez insists: "An oppressed and believing people have a right to think. And doing theology is participating in this right to think—a right to think one's faith in the Lord, a right to think one's liberating experiences," "The Voice of the Poor in the Church," p. 30.

67. Recent studies of ideology reveal very clearly that in advanced capitalist societies ideology functions most powerfully in promoting selective perception and articulation of problems and conflicts, i.e., in defining the world and those aspects of it which are changeable or not; see Steven Lukes, *Power: A Radical View* (London: Macmillan, 1974), and "Political Ritual and Social Integration," *Sociology* 9 (1975): 289-308; Michael Mann, "The Social Cohesion of Liberal Democracy," *American Journal of Sociology* 35 (1970): 423-439; David L. Sallach, "Class Domination and Ideological Hegemony," *Sociological Quarterly* 15 (1974): 38-50. For insight into the ways in which the dominant ideology is promoted in the U.S., see Gans, *Deciding What's News*: Frances FitzGerald, *America Revised* (Boston: Little, Brown, 1979).

68. See Eli Zaretsky, "The Effects of the Economic Crisis on the Family," in *U.S. Capitalism in Crisis*, pp. 209-218. As Mills points out, one of the most important tasks of social analysts, and movement leaders, is to interpret "private troubles" as public matters. People "do not usually define the troubles they endure in terms of historical change and institutional contradiction. The sociological imagination enables us to grasp history and biography and the relations between the two within society. That is its task and its promise" C. Wright Mills, *The Sociological Imagination* (New York: Oxford University Press, 1967).

69. Robert A. Nisbet, *Social Change and History* (New York: Oxford University Press, 1970).

70. C. Wright Mills, "Letter to the Left," in *The End of Ideology Debate*, ed. Chaim J. Waxman (New York: Funk & Wagnalls, 1968), pp. 126-140.

71. Lipset, *Political Man*, p. 439.

72. Rostow, *The Stages of Economic Growth*, p. 91.

73. Barnet, *Roots of War*, p. 142.

74. Noam Chomsky, "The Secular Priesthood: Intellectuals and American Power," *Working Papers for a New Society* (May/June 1978: 24-33; David Halberstam, *The Best and the Brightest* (New York: Random House, 1972; Fawcett World, 1973).

75. Barnet, *Roots of War*, p. 142.

76. Will Herberg, *Protestant, Catholic, Jew* (New York: Doubleday, Anchor, 1960); Martin Marty, *Religious Empire* (New York: Harper, Torchbooks, 1977); Dean R. Hoge, *Division in the Protestant House* (Philadelphia: Westminster, 1976); Gibson Winter, *The Suburban Captivity of the Churches* (Chicago: University of Chicago Press, 1962); Langdon Gilkey, "Social and Intellectual Sources of Contemporary Theology in America," *Daedalus* 96 (1967): 69-98.

77. As MacIntyre points out, "The Lipset-Bell vision of the world is informed by a view of rationality which makes liberal, pragmatic man the paradigm of rationality"; in *Against the Self-Images of the Age: Essays on Ideology and Philosophy* (Notre Dame, Ind.: University of Notre Dame Press, 1978), p. 9. I have suggested that this Lipset-Bell vision is simply the scholarly version of a vision which was widely shared among professional middle-class intellectuals in the postwar era. For an analysis of the way in which these assumptions have long shaped public policies in the U.S., see Robert Castel, "La 'guerre à la pauvreté' aux Etats-Unis: le statut de l'indigence dans une sociéte d'abondance," *Acts de la Recherche en sciences sociales* 19 (January

1978): 47–60. For an analysis of how these assumptions have influenced political theories in the U.S., and of the empirical inadequacies of these theories, see C. B. Macpherson, *The Life and Times of Liberal Democracy* (New York: Oxford University Press, 1979).

78. Robert A. LeVine, *Culture, Behavior and Personality* (Chicago: Aldine, 1973), pp. 43–44; Robert T. Hogan and Nicholas P. Emler, "The Biases in Contemporary Social Psychology," *Social Research* 45 (1978): 478–534.

79. Maccoby, *The Gamesman*, pp. 181–224.

80. Gans, *Deciding What's News*; FitzGerald, *America Revised*.

81. Van A. Harvey, review of Anders Nygren, *Meaning and Method: Religious Studies Review* 1 (September 1975): 13–19; and "The Proper Task of Theology: Seven Theses," paper delivered at the American Theological Association meeting in New York City, April 1976 (mimeographed).

82. Gutiérrez, "The Voice of the Poor in the Church," p. 33.

83. It is not an exaggeration to say that in the struggles between these different paradigms there is nothing less than a battle for the human soul. It is precisely because of his awareness of what is at stake in these struggles that Cone, in *God of the Oppressed* (pp. 36, 37), returns to the notion of heresy; in his view, any interpretation of the gospel which fails to see Jesus Christ as the Liberator of the oppressed is heretical. For an exciting and extensive effort to explicate the biblical basis of such a claim and the whole range of related methodological issues, see Norman K. Gottwald, *The Tribes of Yahweh: A Sociology of the Religion of Liberated Israel, 1250–1050 BCE* (Maryknoll, N.Y.: Orbis Books, 1979). Also, for some brief reflections on these issues, see Lee Cormie, "The Hermeneutical Privilege of the Oppressed: Liberation Theologies, Biblical Faith, and Marxist Sociology of Knowledge," *Proceedings of the Catholic Theological Society of America* 33 (1978): 155–181.

Response to Lee Cormie

Brian Mahan

Professor Cormie believes that we are in need of a "new rationality." He has told us that if anything can be said to unite the proponents of various liberation theologies, it is that they share a vehement opposition to the vision of reality which defines the horizon of meaning for contemporary society. The challenge which liberation theology poses to academic theology in America and Europe emerges from reflection upon this fundamental dissatisfaction. This challenge, in turn, takes the form of an invitation: we are invited to participate in the strategy of "demonstrating the irrationality of the dominant rationality." A responsible answer to this invitation presumes some knowledge both of the complex of culturally sponsored predispositions and beliefs associated with the dominant rationality, and of our own necessarily ambivalent feelings regarding them. Here I wish to express a tentative opinion concerning the feasibility of participating in a project which would demonstrate the irrationality of the dominant rationality.

Before proceeding, however, I would like to thank Professor Cormie for his efforts. He has documented his observations with painstaking research and in doing so has provided common ground for discussion with those whose perspectives differ from his own.

The old rationality must be replaced, according to Cormie, not simply because it reflects the worldview of the oppressor, but more importantly because "it shapes influential interpretations of the world and of human nature, of pain, suffering, and the possibilities of transcending them" and because it "shapes the policies of politicians and governments," which in turn affect the lives of millions. Although he maintains a third-person tone while documenting the marginal status of blacks, women, and other members of oppressed groups within contemporary society, it is clear that Professor Cormie's own impatience with the dominant rationality reflects the strength of his identification with those who suffer most intensely within our society. While affirming with him the necessity of adopting, to whatever degree possible, the perspective of those whose suffering has been intensified, prolonged, or worst of all justified by purveyors of the dominant rationality, I am less enthusiastic about his project to discredit that ethos because I cannot share what seems to be an implicit assumption that the dominant rationality can be easily identified, isolated, and dismissed. A rationality by its very nature can exercise power only insofar as it is internalized. It is not so much seen as it is a requisite to seeing; it orders perception and gives it direction, texture, structure, and even style. As Cormie himself intimates, however, a rationality cannot be pictured as something standing over and against us, as fully or even primarily external to our personal patterns of perception and interpretation, either as these apply to everyday living or to the more abstract activities of reflection and theorizing. This is not to say, of course, that a rationality cannot be experienced as an alienating structure, as something that enslaves and coerces; it is only to say that it can become such only to the degree that it has become part of us. It may be the enemy, but unlike the oppressor we find in the flesh, it cannot be imprisoned, executed, or banished, and any attempt to root it out and replace it is undertaken at great risk.

It is knowledge of this intimate character of a rationality which alerts us as to the fact that we are also speaking of ourselves when we speak of the dominant rationality. The very strategies we employ to dismantle it are in part determined by it. Our perception of the dominant rationality as something external to us may account for our inability to understand how closely our ambitions and class interests may color even altruistic visions of liberation. We must unmask ourselves, even as we seek to unmask the evil effects of our social ethic. This unmasking begins with the realization that those of us who have been treated less violently than others whom we can afford to call oppressed stand in an ambivalent, though emotionally charged relation to the dominant rationality. However much we may complain about the inordinate psychic price demanded by the reigning worldview inasmuch as it is an outgrowth of the Protestant ethic, or decry the apotheosis of the technocrat and the scientist, or denounce the enthronement of objectifying and dissecting modes of thinking, we are also familiar with the power of our ethic and fascinated by it. We maintain its formal customs even as we condemn them: we have, for instance, been invited to continue this discussion over sherry—an incongruity that symbolizes our plight.

Briefly then, our confidence in our ability to demonstrate the irrationality of the dominant rationality presumes our ability and willingness to come to terms with our own investment in it. Failure to acknowledge our ambivalence will give birth to subtle forms of resentment: resentments born of conflicts between our conscious intentions and hidden interests; resentments which will cloud our perception of states of affairs and render impotent our strategies to change them. The academic community in general, and the theologian in particular, cannot adopt Mannheim's sanguine view of the role played by the intelligentsia in the emergence of a new worldview. The intelligentsia, Mannheim thought, represents an "unanchored, relatively classless stratum" whose investment in a given worldview is more a matter of choice than of necessity.[1] We know better.

It is particularly important for those of us who give witness to the need for radical cultural change to objectify and reflect upon our own residual attachments to the dominant rationality. It is interesting to note in this regard that certain nineteenth-century South American cultural savants, among them poets and political theorists, anticipated some of the criticisms of North American society associated with contemporary liberation theology. They criticized their neighbors to the north for their inordinate stress upon the virtues of the isolated individual, for their moral and aesthetic insensitivity, for their greed, and for numerous social improprieties associated with "pragmatism" and the growth of technology. César Graña, a sociologist who named this school of Latin American social thought "Americanidad," suggests that the failure of the alternative vision, proposed by these social critics, to mount a serious moral or political challenge to the cultural ethic of North American society, stemmed from the nature of the movement itself. Graña argues that it was the inability of these savants to come to terms with their own desire to share in the worldly efficacy of the North American rationality that resulted in a literary and political idealization of Latin American society: "a gesture of solace and reassurance before the march north of American social energy and economic and political power."[2]

There is no reason to believe that there lurks behind the critique of capitalist society made by the liberation theologians a similar form of misplaced resentment; the facts Professor Cormie has shared with us demonstrate that a major cause of dissatisfaction lies elsewhere. Still, even if criticism of the dominant rationality accurately represents the way things are, it does not follow that a theology for the artisans of a new humanity,[3] the title of the English edition of Juan Luis Segundo's five-volume series, can afford to dismiss certain characteristics of the dominant rationality which have yielded enormous economic and political power. A responsible strategy for discrediting the dominant rationality must include an attempt to isolate characteristics which seem to account for the worldly efficacy of that rationality along with efforts to fuse these with a more humane and egalitarian vision derived from the witness of the oppressed. The ambivalent relation to the dominant rationality which defines members of the more privileged strata of society may in fact be of value in formulating such a strategy. Rather than attempting to root out all residues of the dominant rationality, we would do well to attempt to distinguish qualities of our collective attitudes and behaviors which should be exposed and dismissed from those that should be preserved. We must think synthetically rather than antithetically. We may ask ourselves whether a Gandhi who had not experienced firsthand, and to some extent from the inside, the power of a dominant rationality as it was embodied in the institutions and social conventions of British society could have been as successful as he was in actualizing his own vision of liberation.

Still it is no easy task to form either a personal or culture-wide synthesis between images of human fulfillment and destiny which at first glance appear to be in hopeless conflict; it is difficult because the processes which lead to such syntheses in individual and collective behavior patterns are not fully conscious ones. It is for this compelling reason that the prophetic voices of the oppressed in our midst must be heard; their accusations must be presumed to reveal much about our society which otherwise would remain hidden. But the "privileged perspective" of the oppressed cannot be counted on to provide a total vision of things. Nor can the ethic of the dominant culture be singled out as the enemy to be vanquished. Amilcar Cabral, leader of the successful revolution in Guinea—and cunning exploiter of his own investment in the dominant rationality—has spoken eloquently to his comrades of waging the war for liberation on a second, perhaps more hazardous field of battle:

> We note, however, that one form of struggle which we consider to be fundamental has not been explicitly mentioned. . . . [W]e refer here to the struggle against our own weaknesses. Obviously other cases differ from that of Guinea; but our experience has shown us that in the general framework of daily struggles this battle against ourselves—no matter what difficulties the enemy may create—is the most difficult of all whether for the present or the future of our people.[4]

The "battle against ourselves," according to Cabral, rages when we attempt to give expression to "the inherent contradictions of the economic, social, cultural (and therefore historical) reality of each of our countries." Cabral and Gandhi are individuals who marshalled the spiritual strength to fashion their own ambivalent investment in the dominant rationality of their respective time and place into a powerful instrument for liberation. Their examples should not be lost on us. We must take care that in waging the "battle against ourselves" and against the dominant rationality that we do not destroy what might have been transformed and made new.

Notes

1. Karl Mannheim, *Ideology and Utopia* (New York: Harcourt, Brace, 1936), pp. 163–164.

2. César Graña, *Fact and Symbol: Essays in the Sociology of Art and Literature* (New York: Oxford University Press, 1971), ch. 7.

3. Juan Luis Segundo, *A Theology for Artisans of a New Humanity,* 5 vol. (Maryknoll, N.Y.: Orbis Books, 1972–74).

4. Amilcar Cabral, *Revolution in Guinea: Selected Texts by Amilcar Cabral* (New York: Monthly Review Press, 1969), pp. 91–92.

3

Christian Faith and Political Praxis

James H. Cone

Obedience is not a virtue one immediately associates with black liberation theology; it is a "virtue" more easily associated with a more conservative style or faith—one which stresses conformity to ecclesiastical authority, or to the admonitions of biblical positivism. For James Cone, however, obedience is the heart and soul of the process of human liberation. It is a creative response to God's liberating presence within history and it transforms passive belief into dynamic faith. But faith does not possess innate criteria by which it is enabled to analyze the socio-economic determinants of oppression; it must turn to social theory if it is to avoid investing its dynamism in mere sentimentality or in misguided activity. Liberation theology thus must commit itself to the struggle of the oppressed and it must utilize whatever analytic tools are at its disposal to insure that this commitment bears fruit.

James H. Cone is the Charles A. Briggs Professor of Systematic Theology at Union Theological Seminary in New York. He received his Master of Divinity degree from Garrett Theological Seminary and his M.A. and Ph. D. from Northwestern University. He is the author of Black Theology and Black Power *(New York: Seabury, 1969);* A Black Theology of Liberation *(Philadelphia: Lippincott, 1970);* The Spirituals and the Blues *(New York: Seabury, 1972);* God of the Oppressed *(New York: Seabury, 1975) and co-author with Gayraud S. Wilmore,* Black Theology: A Documentary History, 1966–1979 *(Maryknoll, N.Y.: Orbis Books, 1979). Robin W. Lovin teaches ethics at the Divinity School of the University of Chicago.*

In this essay my concern is to examine the relation of the Christian faith to political praxis, with special reference to the concrete realities of the oppressed and oppressors, whites and blacks, and the Church's responsibility to preach and to live the gospel of Jesus Christ in a highly industrialized and capitalistic society.

What is the Christian faith, and what does it have to say about the rich and the poor, and the social, economic, and political conditions that determine their relationship? To answer this question is not easy in North America because we live in a society that claims to separate Church and state, religion and politics. "Christianity," it is often said, "is concerned with spiritual reality but not with the material conditions of people." This view of the Christian faith is commonly held inside and outside organized churches, thereby supporting the conservative role that religion has often played in politics. If the Christian faith is no more than the cultural and political interests of the rulers transformed into theological categories, then Karl Marx is right in his contention that religion is the opiate of the people, and therefore should be eliminated along with other legitimizing agencies in an oppressive society. But if religion, generally, and the Christian faith, in particular, is an imaginative and apocalyptic vision about the creation of a new humanity that is derived from the historical and political struggles of oppressed peoples, then to describe it as a sedative is to misunderstand religion's essential nature and its latent revolutionary and humanizing thrust in society.

When the meaning of Christianity is derived from the bottom and not from the top of the socio-economic ladder, from people who are engaged in the fight for justice and not from those who seek to maintain the status quo, then something radical and revolutionary happens to the function of the "holy" in the context of the "secular." Viewed from the perspective of oppressed peoples' struggle for freedom, the holy becomes a radical challenge to the legitimacy of the secular structures of power by creating eschatological images about a realm of experience that is not confined to the values of this world. This is the strange and revolutionary character of Christianity that is so often misunderstood by church and non-church people alike. When we permit ourselves to experience the root meaning of the biblical message and to hear the claims that it lays upon all who would dare be Christian, then we will see the radical difference between the established churches and the truth of the gospel. For inherent in the Christian gospel is the refusal to accept the things that are as the things that *ought* to be. This "great refusal" is what makes Christianity what it is, and thus infuses in its very nature a radicality that can never accept the world as it is.

This radical perspective of the biblical faith has not always been presented as an essential part of the Christian gospel. Since the time of the Emperor Constantine, when Christianity became the official religion of the Roman State, the chief interpreters of the Christian tradition have advocated a spiritual view of the gospel that separated the confession of faith from the practice of political justice. Whether we speak of Augustine's identification of slavery with the sins of the slaves, Luther's stand against the Peasants' Revolt, the white American church's endorsement of black slavery, or of contemporary

Euro-American theology's indifference toward the political embodiment of the gospel, it is unquestionably clear that the dominant representatives of the Christian tradition, both Protestant and Catholic alike, have contributed to the political oppression of humanity by defending the economic interests of the rich against the poor. When the gospel is spiritualized so as to render invisible the important economic distinctions between the haves and the have-nots, the dialectical relation between faith and the practice of political justice is also obscured.

Recently, the assumed separation between faith and political praxis has been seriously challenged by the appearance of liberation theologies in North and South America, Africa, and Asia. Whether we speak of black theology, feminist theology, or African theology, liberation theology in all forms rejects the dichotomy between spiritual and physical salvation, between faith and political praxis, and insists on their dialectical relationship. Liberation theology has been created by people who consciously seek to speak to and for the victims of the economic and political injustices as represented in racism, classism, and sexism. The advocates of this new theology are intolerant of any perspective on Christianity that fails to relate the gospel of Jesus to the economic and social conditions of people. They contend that the gospel embraces the whole person in human society, in work and play. This means that the gospel is inseparably connected with the bodily liberation of the poor.

Because I am a black North American theologian whose political and religious consciousness has been shaped in and by black people's historical fight for justice, I agree with my theological colleagues in Africa, Asia, and Latin America who contend that the gospel cannot be separated from the concrete struggles for freedom among the oppressed of the land. Indeed, this theological conviction has been an integral part of the black religious tradition from its beginning,[1] and it was reinforced in my own theological consciousness during the civil-rights movement and in the context of the rise of Black Power.

The civil-rights movement of the 1950s and 1960s, which was created and largely centered in the black churches with Martin Luther King, Jr., as its charismatic leader, demonstrated the continuing relevancy of black religion in the struggle for political and social justice. Not only were political sessions held in the context of church worship, but many black ministers withdrew from formal denominational ties in order to devote themselves full-time to "sit-ins," "freedom rides," and other political activities. The increasing violence of the existing structures of North American society, as well as black people's determination to assert their freedom in opposition to it, led many black civil-rights workers to question Martin King's uncompromising devotion to the principle of nonviolence. Thus, in the context of the James Meredith March in Mississippi (Spring 1966), and in light of many years of the carefully organized violence of white societal structures, Willie Ricks sounded the cry of Black Power. Stokely Carmichael and others enthusiastically accepted this intellectual challenge and defined its political and social relevance in American society.[2]

Black theology was born in response to the rise of Black Power and in the context of the National Committee of Negro Churchmen.[3] From the beginning black theology was interpreted as the theological arm of Black Power with the responsibility to define the religious meaning of our prior political commitment to black liberation. The initial move in this direction was the publication of the "Black Power" statement (July 1966)[4] in which an ecumenical group of black churchmen defended the right of black people to empower themselves against the encroachments of white racism. Following the "Black Power" statement, many black church people began to move away from Martin King's rigid commitment to nonviolence and to express their solidarity with James Forman's Marxist and revolutionary "Black Manifesto."[5] Although we respected the integrity of Martin King's commitment to the struggle for justice, we nevertheless felt that his nonviolent method for radical change in societal structures was not radical enough, and his methods were too dependent upon the possibility of change in the hearts of the white oppressors. The problem of King's assumption was that it did not take seriously enough Henry H. Garnet's claim that "if [slaves] would be free, they must themselves strike the blow."[6]

The theological meaning of Garnet's assertion for black Christians had to be worked out in the historical context of white violence. As black people were being systematically exterminated through American military structures (dramatically symbolized in the Watts, Detroit, and Newark abortive insurrections), we black theologians had to ask: What has the gospel to do with life and death, and the struggle of people to be free in an extreme situation of oppression? The existential and political implications of this question forced us to take a new look at the theological enterprise. We concluded that the beginning and the end of the Christian faith is found in the struggle for justice on behalf of the victims of oppressive societal structures. Whatever else Christian theology might be, it must take sides with the victims who are economically and politically oppressed. If theology does not side with the victims of economic injustice, it cannot represent *the Victim,* Jesus of Nazareth, who was crucified because he was a threat to the political and religious structures of his time. That insight impressed itself on our consciousness to such a degree that we began to speak of a black theology of liberation.[7] Our central concern was to show that the Christian faith, as lived by oppressed black people in particular, and oppressed people generally, has been—and more importantly *can be*—an instrument of economic and political freedom.

It is out of the historical context of the black church's identification of the Christian gospel with the political liberation of the poor that I would like to say a word about faith and work, theology and the practice of political justice. In this essay, I will try to state what faith demands of praxis and what praxis demands of faith. The discussion will begin with a description of faith in the context of black theology, and then proceed to an examination of the praxis inherent in that faith.

Faith in Christ the Liberator

Faith is a religious term that expresses a person's commitment to the ultimate. According to Paul Tillich, "faith is a total and centered act of the personal self, the act of unconditional, infinite, and ultimate concern."[8] In its broadest theological sense, faith may refer to one's commitment to things of this world, or more narrowly limited to God in organized religion. The distinctive characteristic of faith is its total commitment to that which functions as the ultimate in one's life, giving it order and meaning. Faith is that total commitment which gives a people their identity, and this determines what they must do in order to actualize in society what they believe is necessary for the attainment of their peoplehood.

When faith is understood as commitment to an ultimate concern, then it is obvious that there can be no separation between faith and obedience because obedience determines faith. I know what your faith is, *not* by what you confess, but *only* by what you do. I will say more about this particular point in our discussion of praxis. At this juncture, I merely want to emphasize that the very nature of faith demands a practical activity commensurate with its confession.

Within the general definition of faith, I am dealing with the Christian faith which may be defined as that total commitment arising from Jesus of Nazareth: his life, death, and resurrection. Faith, as defined in the Christian context, is not belief in propositional truths designated as important by organized churches; rather it is an ultimate commitment to a particular God who revealed the fullness of divinity in the human presence of Jesus Christ.

In order to clarify the sociological content of my theological affirmation, it is necessary to state the source of my faith perspective. My view of the Christian gospel is derived from the biblical message, as interpreted in the liberation struggle of an oppressed black North American community, and as reinforced by similar interpretations among oppressed peoples fighting for freedom throughout the world. From the dialectical relationship of these historical contexts arises the theological conviction that the Bible is the story of God's liberation of victims from economic and political oppression. Historically, the story begins with the liberation of Israelite slaves from Egypt and the establishment of the covenant at Sinai.

> You have seen what I did to the Egyptians, and how I bore you on eagles' wings and brought you to myself. *Now therefore,* if you obey my voice and keep my covenant, you shall be my own possession among all peoples; for all the earth is mine, and you shall be to me a kingdom of priests and a holy nation [Exod. 19:4–6, RSV].

In the Old Testament, faith in God is based on an historical event of rescue wherein Israelite slaves become God's free people with the responsibility of spreading freedom throughout the land. Faith is accepting the gift of freedom and putting one's absolute trust in the promise of God to be with the little ones in times of distress. When Israel lapses from this faith in God's righteousness and forgets its slave heritage by treating the poor unjustly, divine love is transformed into wrath. The God of the Old Testament is the God of justice whose revelation is identical with the liberation of the oppressed. The basic human sin is the attempt to be God, to take his place by ordering the societal structures according to one's own political interests. Sin is not primarily a religious impurity, but rather it is the social, political, and economic oppression of the poor. It is the denial of the humanity of the neighbor through unjust political and economic arrangements. When the prophets lay God's demands before the kings and priests of Israel, the demands are identical with justice for the poor and the weak. A faith that expresses itself in rituals is not enough:

I hate, I despise your feasts,
and I take no delight in your solemn assemblies.
Even though you offer me your burnt offering and cereal offering,
I will not accept them,
and the peace offerings of your fatted beasts I will not look upon.
Take away from me the noise of your songs;
to the melody of your harp I will not listen.
But let justice roll down like waters,
and righteousness like an ever-flowing stream [Amos 5:21-24, RSV].

Amos and other prophets contend that Israel will be sent back to servitude, not because the people failed to attend religious services, but because of the *economic* oppression of the poor.

The same theme of God's solidarity with the victim is found in the New Testament, where it receives a universal expression in the particularity of Jesus' life, death, and resurrection. The appearance of Jesus as the Oppressed One cautions us against any easy identification with his ministry. By North American standards Jesus could be considered neither a successful person, nor could he be considered morally respectable. He identified with the prostitutes and drunkards, the unemployed and the poor, not because he felt sorry for them, but in order to reveal God's judgment against social and religious structures that oppress the weak. Jesus was born like the poor, he lived with them, and on the cross he died like them.

If Jesus is the divine revelation of God's intention for humanity, then faith is nothing but trust in the One who came in Christ for the liberation of the poor. To place one's trust in this God means that one's value-system is no longer derived from the established structures of the world, but from one's struggle against these unjust structures.

It is significant that the biblical theme of God's solidarity with the historical liberation of the oppressed is notably absent in the songs and sermons of white missionaries when they introduced their version of Christianity to African slaves in North America. Like all oppressors who interpret the gospel in the light of their right to dominate others, white preachers contended that God willed Africans to be slaves, and they cited biblical references to Noah's curse upon Ham and to Paul's "slaves, be obedient to your masters" (Col. 3:22) as the theological justification for their claim. But black slaves rejected the white distortions of the gospel and insisted that God willed their freedom and not their slavery. As evidence, they pointed to the Exodus, the prophets, and Jesus' preaching of the gospel to the poor and not to the rich. Through sermons, prayers, and songs, black slaves created a version of Christianity qualitatively different from that of their masters. The distinctiveness of black faith was its focus on God's will to liberate those who are oppressed. That was why the independent black churches were created in the North and the "invisible" (secret) churches were formed in the South. Black people were determined to fashion a faith that was identical with their political fight for justice. In the ecstasy of their church services was born their encounter with the God of Moses and Jesus. They bestowed upon them the power to actualize in their present history the freedom they experienced in their worship and read about in the scriptures.

> Oh Freedom! Oh Freedom!
> Oh Freedom! Oh Freedom!
> And before I'll be a slave,
> I'll be buried in my grave,
> And go home to my Lord and be free.[9]

The historical embodiment of black faith is found not only in the creation of separate institutional black churches with songs, prayers, and sermons about liberation, but it is also found in the presence of black faith outside the confessional and organizational framework of black denominations. Black faith is found in "secular" songs and stories, slave insurrections, and protest assemblies. When I speak of black faith, I am referring only secondarily to organized religion and primarily to black people's collective acknowledgment of the spirit of liberation in their midst, a spirit that empowers them to struggle for freedom even though the odds are against them. This is the historical matrix out of which my hermeneutical perspective has been formed.

Since other oppressed peoples are making similar claims regarding God's solidarity with the poor, the North American black perspective is reinforced and enlarged. Indeed, the universal dimension of the biblical faith, so central in the New Testament, is found in God's will to make liberation not simply the property of one people, but of all humankind. Wherever people are being oppressed, divine righteousness is disclosed in their historical struggle to be other than what is intended by oppressive rulers.

Faith then is a human response to the liberating presence of the divine Spirit in an oppressed community. God's Spirit is liberating, because God gives people the courage and power to resist dehumanization and slavery. Through faith oppressed people receive the gift of a new humanity that can only be realized in the historical process of liberation. But since faith does not include in its confession the social analysis needed to implement its eschatological vision of freedom, it must relate itself to a social theory in order to actualize in society what it confesses in worship. This leads us to an analysis of praxis.

Faith and Praxis

In philosophical and theological circles, praxis is a term closely related to the philosophy of Karl Marx. It is perhaps best summarized in Marx's often quoted eleventh thesis on Feuerbach: "The philosophers have only *interpreted* the world in various ways; the point however is to change it."[10] Praxis is that directed activity toward freedom wherein people recognize that truth is not primarily a question of theory, but it is a practical question. In practice people must prove the truth by destroying the existing relations of untruth. As Gajo Petrovic says: *"The question of the essence of freedom . . . is not only a question. It is at once participation in the production of freedom.* It is an activity through which freedom frees itself."[11]

In a broad sense, praxis is connected with the Christian idea of obedience and is identical with the horizontal implementation of the vertical dimension of faith. According to the New Testament, Jesus says, "Not everyone who says to me, 'Lord, Lord,' shall enter the kingdom of heaven, but he who does the will of my Father who is in heaven" (Matt. 7:21, RSV). A similar point is made in 1 John. "He who does right is righteous . . . If one says, 'I love God,' and hates his brother [or sister], he is a liar; for he who does not love his brother [or sister] whom he has seen, cannot love God whom he has not seen" (1 John 4:20, RSV).

Inherent in the biblical faith is the obedience that defines it. In contemporary theology no one made this point more clearly than Dietrich Bonhoeffer: *"Only he who believes is obedient, and only he who is obedient believes."* Bonhoeffer continues: "It is quite unbiblical to hold the first proposition without the second. . . . Faith is only real when there is obedience, never without it, and faith only becomes faith in the act of obedience." Therefore he says: "Only the obedient believe. . . . Without this preliminary step of obedience, our faith is only a pious humbug, and leads us to grace which is not costly."[12]

In North America, black slaves' perception of this biblical insight enabled them to make the distinction between the confession of faith and the obedience that validated it. They knew that their slavery invalidated white religion. That's why they sang: "Everybody talking about heaven ain't going there." Some slaves even contended that "No white people went to heaven."[13]

On one occasion a white minister's sermon was interrupted by an elderly slave with the question: "Is us slaves gonna be free in Heaven?" The white preacher paused with surprise and anger. But Uncle Silas was persistent: "Is God gonna free us slaves when we get to Heaven?" The remainder of the incident was described by a slave who was present:

> Old white preacher pult out his handkerchief an' wiped de sweat fum his face. "Jesus says come unto Me ye who are free fum sin an' I will give you salvation." "Gonna give us freedom 'long wid salvation?" asked Uncle Silas. "De Lawd gives an' de Lawd takes away, and he dat is widout sin is gonna have life everlastin','" preached the preacher. Den he went ahead preachin' fast-like, widout payin' no 'tention to Uncle Silas.[14]

Uncle Silas was insisting on the practical implications of faith which the white preacher had no intention of granting, especially in view of the economic and political consequences.

Because oppressors do not reorder the structures of society on the basis of an appeal to the practical implications of faith, praxis is more than the biblical understanding of obedience. It is this "more" that gives it its distinctive identity. Praxis is a specific kind of obedience which is organized around a social theory of reality in order to implement in society the freedom inherent in faith. If faith is the belief that God created all for freedom, then praxis is the social theory used to analyze the structures of injustice so that we will know what must be done for the historical realization of freedom. To sing about freedom and to pray for its coming is not enough. Freedom must be actualized in history by oppressed peoples who accept the intellectual challenge to analyze the world for the purposes of changing it.

The focus on praxis for the purpose of societal change is what distinguishes Marx from Hegel and liberation theology from other theologies of freedom. That is why Marx studied the economic forces in society, and why liberation theologians in Latin America find his social theory so basic in the development of their theological enterprise. For the same reason black liberation theologians also relate their theological program to social theories about racism. Feminist theologians do the same in their analysis of sexism. While there are different emphases among liberation theologians regarding the major historical contradictions in society, they all agree that there is a need to relate theology to a social theory of reality because they share the conviction that truth is found in the active transformation of unjust societal structures.

For liberation theologians, faith and praxis belong together because faith can only be expressed in a political commitment to the humanization of society. We believe that inherent in faith is the love of God which can only be manifested in love of the neighbor. Gutiérrez writes: "To know God is to do justice." He continues: "It is not enough to say that the love of God is inseparable from the love of one's neighbor. It must be added that the love for God is unavoidably expressed *through* love of one's neighbor."[15] But in order to protect love from sentimentality, we must analyze it in the fabric of social relationships where people are situated in their economic, cultural, and racial coordinates. What does it mean to love the exploited social classes, the dominated people, or a marginated race?

It is in the attempt to answer this question that we also realize that praxis is inseparably connected with faith that expresses itself in love of the neighbor. If the masses are our neighbors, then we will find it impossible to tolerate economic structures that are destructive of their humanity. Love demands justice, i.e., the creation of a space in the world so that love can realize itself in human relations. To love the neighbor requires more than a pious feeling in my heart. It requires social and political analysis so that piety will not become a substitute for justice.

The truth of the gospel then is a truth that must be done and not simply spoken. To speak the truth without doing the truth is to contradict the truth one claims to affirm. The Church is good at writing resolutions and preaching sermons against this or that idea, but the denunciation of injustice is not only a spoken "word" or a written "text." "It is an action, a stand."[16] The word is only a gesture of commitment. This gesture must be concretized by social analysis so that the oppressed will be empowered to challenge the unjust societal arrangements.

The concretization of faith actualized through love can only be done by connecting faith with the praxis of justice. The theological assumption that necessitates the connection of faith with praxis is found in Jesus Christ. The incarnation connects faith with life and work. By becoming human in Jesus, God connects faith with the social, political, and economic conditions of people, and establishes the theological conclusion that we cannot be faithful to the Creator without receiving the political command to structure creation according to freedom.

The best way to understand the relation of faith and praxis is to reverse the order found in Bonhoeffer's contention that "only the obedient believe." To be sure, ontologically, faith is prior to obedience and thus is its foundation. But practically, obedience comes before faith. We do not first receive faith from God or the Church and then seek to live that faith in the world. It is the other way around. One meets God in the process of historical liberation. In the historical context of the struggle for freedom, one receives the gift of divine freedom wherein the realization occurs that the eternal structures of creation are empowering the oppressed in their fight for justice. This realization is the gift of faith.

Faith then is not a datum, but rather a commitment that arises out of the struggle for freedom and not before. The power that throws us into the struggle for freedom before we are consciously aware of its connection with faith can be called the prevenient grace of God. This grace is ontologically prior to justification and sanctification because it is grounded in the creative will of God. Therefore, when we are justified and sanctified by the grace of God, the recognition of both experiences occurs in the struggle of freedom, and it is a gift of God.

By putting obedience prior to faith on the sociological plane, we protect ourselves from the heresy of substituting faith for action. We must never allow a prayer for justice to become a replacement for an act against injustice. But if our act against oppression is to have meaning, and not be purposeless, then obedience must connect itself with a social theory of change. *Why* are people poor, and *who* benefits from their poverty? In an attempt to answer this question, theology must actualize its Christian identity through social analysis and political participation on behalf of the victims of economic injustice.

When theology defines the meaning of Christian obedience in terms structured in sociology and politics, it becomes global in its outlook by analyzing international capitalism and multinational corporations. What oppressors do to the poor in North America, they also do to poor countries. The world becomes their domain for economic exploitation. Thus, Holiday Inn, Gulf Oil, and other multinational corporations are present in South Africa and other Third World countries exploiting the victims. Anyone who would be Christian by taking a stand with the victims should connect their obedience with praxis, i.e., a social theory of change that will disclose both the causes of injustice and what must be done to eliminate injustice.

However, persons who would cast their lot with the victims must not forget that the existing structures are powerful and complex. Its creators intend it that way, so that any action which challenges their existence will appear both immoral and useless. Oppressors want people to think that change is impossible. That is the function of the military and the atomic bomb. They want to scare the victims so that any social and political analysis will lead to despair. This is what Martin King called the "paralysis of analysis." But the truth is otherwise. If analysis does not elicit hope for change, then it is incorrect. The constituent definition of humanity is that people are agents of history, capable of changing the world.

Because hope is the foundation of praxis, praxis can never be separated from faith. The Christian's faith is grounded in the promise of God and is actualized in the process of liberation in history. Praxis without faith leads to despair. Despair is the logical consequence of a praxis that does not know the eschatological hope derived from historical struggle. Without hope there is no struggle. It was this eschatological knowledge derived from Jesus' cross and resurrection that enabled black North American slaves to struggle in history, and not be defeated by their historical limitations. To be sure, they sang about the fear of "sinking down" and the dread of being a "motherless child." They experienced trouble and the agony of being alone where "I couldn't hear nobody pray." They encountered death and expressed it in song:

> Soon one mornin', death comes a creepin' in my room
> O my Lawd, O my Lawd, what shall I do?
> Death done been here, took my mother an' gone,
> O my Lawd, what shall I do?

In these songs are expressed the harsh realities of history and the deep sense of dread at the very thought of death. But because the slaves believed that death had been conquered in Jesus' resurrection, they could also transcend death by interpreting salvation as a heavenly, eschatological reality. That was why they also sang:

> You needn't mind my dying,
> Jesus' goin' to make up my dying bed.
> In my room I know,
> Somebody is going to cry,
> All I ask you to do for me,
> Just close my dying eyes.

This is not passive resignation, but rather an eschatological expression of an historical commitment that refuses to adjust itself to the power of oppressors. This is what the praxis of faith in a Christian context is all about.

Notes

1. The best historical account of the black religious tradition is Gayraud S. Wilmore, *Black Religion and Black Radicalism* (New York: Doubleday, 1972) and James H. Cone, *Black Theology and Black Power* (New York: Seabury, 1969), ch. 4. For other historical accounts of black religion in North America, see Cecil Cone, *The Identity Crisis in Black Theology* (Nashville: AMEC, 1975), ch. 11, and Joseph Washington, *Black Religion* (Boston: Beacon, 1964).

2. For an account of the rise of black power, see Stokeley Carmichael and Charles Hamilton,*Black Power: The Politics of Liberation in America* (New York: Random House, 1967). For Martin Luther King's response to black power, see his *Where Do We Go From Here: Chaos or Community?* (Boston: Beacon, 1967).

3. The National Committee of Negro Churchmen was an *ad hoc* ecumenical group of black ministers that was later formalized into a permanent body under the name: National Conference of Black Churchmen, with headquarters in Atlanta, Georgia. This was the black church organization that struggled to respond to the creative politics of black power.

4. Originally this statement appeared as an ad in *The New York Times*. This statement was the first of a series of policy statements that were to come from NCBC in order to help define the political direction of the black church in the 1960s and 1970s. Most of these documents are reprinted in Gayraud S. Wilmore and James H. Cone, *Black Theology: A Documentary History 1966-1979* (Maryknoll, N.Y.: Orbis Books, 1979).

5. Perhaps no document or person disturbed the religious complacency of the white and black church more than Forman and his "Black Manifesto." For an interpretation of this document and the events surrounding it, see Gayraud S. Wilmore and James H. Cone, *Black Theology: A Documentary History 1966-1979* (Maryknoll, N.Y.: Orbis Books, 1979).

6. See Henry H. Garnet, "Address to the Slaves of the United States of America" in David Walker and Henry H. Garnet, *Appeal and an Address to the Slaves of the United States of America* (New York: Arno, 1969), originally 1929 (Appeal) and 1943 (Address).

7. The first book on "black theology" was my *Black Theology and Black Power* (New York: Seabury, 1969). Although the theme of liberation is present in that volume, the theological focus of the liberation theme appeared more directly in my second volume, *A Black Theology of Liberation* (Philadelphia: Lippincott, 1970). Other books on black theology include J. Deotis Roberts, *Liberation and Reconciliation: A Black Theology* (Philadelphia: Westminster, 1971): Cecil Cone, *Identity Crisis in Black Theology* (Nashville: AMEC, 1975): and my *God of the Oppressed* (New York: Seabury, 1975).

8. Paul Tillich, *Dynamics of Faith* (New York: Harper, Torchbook, 1958), p. 8.

9. For a theological interpretation of the black spirituals in particular and black religion generally, see my *The Spirituals and the Blues* (New York: Seabury, 1972).

10. Karl Marx and Friedrich Engels, *Marx and Engels: Basic Writings on Politics and Philosophy* (Garden City, N.Y.: Doubleday, 1959), p. 120.

11. Gajo Petrovic, *Marx in the Mid-Twentieth Century* (New York: Doubleday, 1967), p. 120.

12. Dietrich Bonhoeffer, *The Cost of Discipleship* (New York: Macmillan, 1969), pp. 54, 55.

13. Cited in Lawrence Levine, *Black Culture and Black Consciousness: Afro-American Folk Thought from Slavery to Freedom* (New York: Oxford University Press, 1977), p. 34.

14. Ibid., p. 46.

15. Gustavo Gutiérrez, *A Theology of Liberation* (Maryknoll, N.Y.: Orbis Books, 1973), pp.199, 200.

16. Ibid., p. 268.

Response to James H. Cone

Robin W. Lovin

Professor Cone confronts us squarely with the difficulty of being serious about the Christian faith. That faith, in contrast to some of the other, more agreeable faiths that are available to us, involves an ultimate commitment to Jesus Christ, and as Professor Cone puts it, "the appearance of Jesus as the Oppressed One prevents any easy identification with his ministry."

I want to dwell on that for just a moment, because I think that the impact not only of this paper, but of Cone's theology as a whole rests on his refusal to let us evade that requirement of discipleship. Given the contrast between oppressor and the oppressed, the victims and the victors, and given the fact that most of us live our lives somewhere in between those two poles, our most common choice is to think positively, act confidently, and hope that folks generally will take us for victors, and not victims. We are, moreover, vigorously urged on in that direction by our parents, our psychoanalysts, our spouses, or the advertising industry—to say nothing of our preachers.

So the unpopular task that falls to Professor Cone and other theologians of liberation in North America is to remind a nominally Christian success-oriented culture that Jesus took the opposite course, that real Christianity is possible only when we can identify ourselves as victims—and then wager everything on the notion that to be a victim is not to be the loser, but to inherit God's promise of liberation and resurrection.

"To place one's trust in this God," Professor Cone tells us, "means that one's value-system is no longer derived from the established structures of the world, but from one's struggle against these unjust structures."

At the same time, that statement makes it abundantly clear that the faith of which Cone speaks expresses itself in action. Faith requires a *praxis,* or it simply no longer exists—as an earlier theologian who identified himself as James also told us.

Professor Cone is especially concerned to identify two features of that praxis. First, praxis in theological terms is obedience; it is action undertaken in response to that One who let himself be victimized by oppressive structures precisely so that he could break their power over us. Second, praxis in social terms is effective action; it is action guided by a social theory that accurately depicts what is going on at our present moment in history, and identifies the real sources of oppression against which we should direct our efforts for change.

Praxis as obedience partakes in the immediacy of faith; it shares in the certainty of God's solidarity with the oppressed and the hope for liberation that Professor Cone has illustrated in the spirituals. But praxis as effective action never proceeds without some middle term between the faith and the deed. Before we can act on our identification with Jesus the Oppressed One, we require a method of analysis or a mode of reasoning that will fit our resistance to the realities of the situation. We turn to social theory, not because faith is weak, but precisely because it is too compelling to waste its power in useless action.

If that is Professor Cone's main point—the point that a serious faith always requires something more than just faith as a guide to action—then I am in entire agreement.

However, it ill becomes a critic to indicate agreement and let it go at that. So, assuming now that I have correctly set out the foundations of the paper we have just read, I do want to go on to raise three further questions that seem to arise for a praxis based on social theory.

First, I think I would like some clarification of my relationship as a theologian and a Christian to others who may be using the same social theory, but who are neither theologians nor Christians. There are a great many social theories available, and I think Professor Cone is quite right to suggest that the choice between them should be directed in some way by one's theology. A social theory that leads to despair or a sense of impotence is to be rejected, however correct it may be technically. Precisely because there is a variety of schools of social thought, engaged in self-conscious rivalry eliciting an almost sectarian loyalty from their partisans, I am in the odd position as a Christian that once I select the social theory that will guide my praxis, I have in effect also joined somebody else's "church." I have acquired not only a theory, but a loyalty and an identity. I am no longer merely Christian or merely theologian, but I am a Marxist or a Weberian, or a structural-functionalist, or whatever.

How do I deal with that identity? Since I am to use social theory as a guide to action, does my theological agenda depend in some important ways on the problems and issues this group of theorists chooses to address? Do I owe to the theorists who shape their position a certain amount of loyalty and mutual support, not unlike my loyalty to my fellow Christians, or do they remain simply a neutral group whose work I use, but who do not themselves impose any claims on me? This would seem to be a particularly crucial issue where the social theory in question is Marxism—for while I know of no country East or West where Weberians are subject to persecution as political deviants, it happens not infrequently that Marxists are the targets of such repression.

My first question, then, is whether social theory can ever be merely a tool in the hands of theology, or whether it does not, under present conditions, become a system of political loyalties unto itself? And if that is so, how do we understand that set of loyalties theologically?

My second question has to do with the relationship between social theory and social action. It is perhaps not so much a question as a cautionary note: I am afraid that the "paralysis of analysis" to which Professor Cone refers may not be simply the result of bad social theory. It may be a characteristic of *all* social theory. The danger in making social theory your guide to action is that you may be stuck with the results when social theory leads to inaction. For example, during the years from, say, 1964 to 1974, people concerned about racial integration in public education got into the bad habit of letting social scientists make their case for them. Where we had formerly relied on legal or moral or theological cases for desegregation, we now had the *Coleman Report,* scientific proof, you see, that desegregated education produced results. Instead of arguing that desegregation was faithful or just, we could now argue that it was sociologically sound. And that worked well for a decade, until Coleman said he wasn't sure whether his results depended on race or class, and other researchers weighed in with evidence that the results of desegregation are much more ambiguous than Coleman thought, and the end result is that from a sociological point of view, these probably are not compelling reasons one way or the other for pursuing social desegregation.

Now, it does not much matter for my present purposes what you think about desegregation: the point is that when you give the technical methods of social investigation and social theory power to guide your choice of action, you tend to let certain other kinds of arguments wither, and you are apt to find over the long run that the social theoretical imperatives are rather less clear than you first thought. My second question, or caution, then, is this: when you have chosen what seems to be an appropriate social theory, can you be sure *over the long run* that it will continue to energize and direct your action instead of leaving you in a state of confusion?

My third, and final, question follows from that second concern: Is social theory enough? Granted that there must be some middle term between the immediacy of faith and an effective Christian praxis, can we rely exclusively on social theory to fill that mediating role? My own hunch, or proposal, would be that alongside of social theory, we need a public social ethic to mediate adequately between Christian faith and Christian praxis. Along with a theory of how things work, we need a theory of how things *ought to be,* an ethical theory that is tied not to the particular, revelatory experiences of faith, but to a public language of justice that articulates specific claims. Generally speaking, liberation theology has been suspicious of this business of ethics. Too often, it seems that ethics requires us to take the immediate experience of oppression and liberation and translate it into cool, rational terms that lose the sense of divine power and divine wrath behind the claims of the dispossessed. That does sometimes happen in ethics, and when it happens, that's unfortunate. But if we once admit, with Professor Cone, that the praxis of liberation needs to be guided by something more than immediate experience, might we not set ethical theory alongside social theory as a guiding element in that practical effort? There has been some discussion in theological circles about the possibility of an ethics of liberation. I am more concerned about a liberating use of the ethics currently available, and I wonder whether Professor Cone today sees some possibilities for that alongside the problems he has noted with it in the past.

4

Black Theologies of Liberation: A Structural-Developmental Analysis

James W. Fowler

If theology is to interpret faith to the modern world, it must be guided not only by the norms of Scripture and tradition, but also by informed descriptions and analyses of faith as it is actually experienced—both collectively and individually. It is for this reason that James W. Fowler's theory of the structural-developmental stages of faith, which has already proven its value to practical theology (particularly to religious educators and pastoral counselors), promises to enrich the perspective of systematic theology as well.

Although it is Fowler's operative assumption that more highly differentiated stages of faith generally suggest more adequate strategies for constructing "a world of meaning in faith," in the essay that follows he does not presume to recommend the work of some black liberation theologians over that of others on the basis of the stage theory. Instead, Fowler employs his theory in a manner which highlights the strengths and weaknesses of two distinct "styles" adopted by various black liberation theologians. It is his hope that this exercise will aid theologians who wish to fuse aspects of both of these post-"mass consciousness" styles of theologizing into a higher synthesis.

James W. Fowler is Professor of Theology and Human Development and Director of the Center for Faith Development at Candler School of Theology of Emory University in Atlanta, Georgia. He is the author of several recent books including To See the Kingdom: The Theological Vision of H. Richard Niebuhr *(Nashville: Abingdon, 1974);* Life Maps: Conversations on the Journey of Faith, *with Sam Keen (Minneapolis: Winston, 1978);* Trajectories in Faith: Five Life Stories, *with Robin W. Lovin and others (Nashville: Abingdon, 1980); and* Stages of Faith *(San Francisco: Harper and Row, 1981). He was co-editor with Antoine Vergote of* Toward Moral and Religious Maturity *(Morristown, N.J.: Silver Burdett, 1980). He is also an Asso-*

*ciate in Education at the Harvard Graduate School of Education. The fol-
lowing article was originally the third lecture of the Thirkield Jones Lecture
at Gammon Theological Seminary in Atlanta, Georgia, in 1974. It has been
revised and expanded for this volume.*

Structural-Developmental Stages of Faith

In other writings I have offered provisional statements of a structural
developmental theory of faith.[1] Faith, I maintain, is a universal feature of
human beings. By faith we relate to others and to groups in trust and loyalty.
By faith we shape our lives in relation to centers of value and power which
give us value and which promise to sustain our lives. By faith we—as individuals and in groups—respond to transcendence and shape our lives with reference to it. Faith may be—and is meant to be—religious. But many persons
today shape their life meanings and purposes in communities other than religious communities and with symbols and values other than those of organized religion.[2] Our reflection on faith needs to include both the religious
and nonreligious centers of our commitment and trust.[3]

Using the structural-developmental approaches pioneered by Jean Piaget
in cognitive development[4] and by Lawrence Kohlberg in moral development,[5]
I and my associates, through the analysis of some four hundred interviews,
have identified seven stage-like "styles" or ways of constructing one's world
of meaning in faith. Since the analysis of black theologies of liberation which
follows employs these stages as analytic categories, I include a brief recent
overview of them here. We believe that these stage-like positions are develop-
mentally related to each other. They emerge sequentially, and persons cannot
skip over a stage. Previous stages, however, continue to be part of one's overall way of being in faith, and "regressions" or return to previous stages are
possible. Movement from one stage to the next requires physical and emotional maturation, as well as cognitive development. While all of these are
necessary for stage transition, no one of them—or all of them in combina-
tion—is sufficient to bring about a change of stage. The challenges of our
lives, the communities with which we share our symbolization of meanings,
the contents of our "theologies," and the initiative of the Holy Spirit, all play
vital roles in determining whether, and at what rate, we are supported and
challenged to stage transition.

Here are the stages:

Undifferentiated Faith

The preconceptual, largely prelinguistic stage in which the infant unconsciously forms a disposition toward its world.

Trust, courage, hope, and love are fused in an undifferentiated way and
contend with sensed threats of abandonment, inconsistencies, and dep-

rivations in its environment. Though really a pre-stage, and largely inaccessible to empirical inquiry of the kind we pursue, the quality of mutuality and the strength of trust, autonomy, hope, and courage (or their opposites) developed in this phase, underlie or undermine all that comes later in faith development.

Transition to Stage 1 begins with the convergence of thought and language, opening up the use of symbols in speech and ritual play.

Stage 1. Intuitive-Projective Faith

The fantasy-filled, imitative phase in which the child can be powerfully and permanently influenced by the examples, moods, actions, and language of the visible faith of primal adults.

The stage most typical of the child of three to seven, it is marked by a relative fluidity of thought patterns. The child is continually encountering novelties for which no stable operations of knowing have been formed. The imaginative processes underlying fantasy are unrestricted and uninhibited by logical thought. In league with forms of knowing dominated by perception, imagination in this stage is extremely productive of long-lasting images and feelings (positive and negative) which later, more stable and self-reflective valuing and thinking will have to order and sort out. This is the stage of first self-awareness. The "self-aware" child is egocentric as regards the perspectives of others. Here we find first awareness of death and sex, and of the strong taboos by which cultures and families insulate those powerful areas.

The emergence of concrete operational thinking underlies the transition to Stage 2. Affectively, the resolution of Oedipal issues or their submersion in latency are important accompanying factors. At the heart of the transition is the child's growing concern to *know* how things are and to clarify for him/herself the bases of distinctions between what is real and what only seems to be.

Stage 2. Mythic-Literal Faith

The stage in which persons begin to take on for themselves the stories, beliefs, and observances that symbolize belonging to their communities. Beliefs are appropriated with literal interpretations, as are moral rules and attitudes. Symbols are taken as one-dimensional and literal in meaning.

In this stage the rise of concrete operations leads to the curbing and ordering of the previous stage's imaginative composing of the world. The episodic quality of intuitive-projective faith gives way to a more linear, narrative construction of coherence and meaning. Story becomes the major way of giving unity and value to experience. This is the faith stage of the school child (though we sometimes find its structures dominant in adolescents and in adults). Marked by increased accuracy in taking the perspective of other persons, Stage 2 composes a world based on reciprocal fairness and an immanent justice based on reciprocity. The actors in its cosmic stories are anthropomorphic, though lacking full personality. It can be affected deeply and powerfully by symbolic and dramatic materials, and can describe in endlessly detailed narrative what has occurred. Stage 2 does not, however, step back from the flow of its stories to formulate reflective, conceptual meanings. For this stage the meaning is both carried and "trapped" in the narrative.

The implicit clash or contradictions of stories leads to reflection on meanings. The transition to formal operational thought makes such reflection possible and necessary. Previous literalism breaks down; new "cognitive conceit" (Elkind) leads to disillusionment with previous teachers and teachings. Conflicts between authoritative stories (i.e., Genesis on creation vs. evolutionary theory) must be faced. The emergence of mutual interpersonal perspective-taking ("I see you seeing me; I see me as you see me; I see you seeing me seeing you") creates the need for a more personal relationship with the unifying power of the ultimate environment.

Stage 3. Synthetic-Conventional Faith

The person's experience of the world now extends beyond the family. A number of spheres demand attention: family, school or work, peers, street society and media, and perhaps religion. Faith must provide a coherent orientation in the midst of that more complex and diverse range of involvements. Faith must synthesize values and information; it must provide a basis for identity and outlook.

Stage 3 typically has its rise and ascendency in adolescence, but for many adults it becomes a permanent equilibration. It structures the ultimate environment in interpersonal terms. Its images of unifying value and power derive from the extension of qualities experienced in personal relationships. It is a "conformist" stage in the sense that it is acutely tuned to the expectations and judgments of significant others, and as yet does not have a sure enough grasp on its own identity and autonomous judgment to construct and maintain an independent perspective. While beliefs and values are deeply felt, they typically are tacitly held—the person "dwells" in them and the meaning world they mediate. But there has not been occasion to step reflectively outside them to examine them explicitly or systematically. At Stage 3 a person has an "ideology," a more or less consistent clustering of values and beliefs, but has not objectified it for examination, and in a sense is unaware of having it. Differences of outlook with others are experienced as differences in "kind" of person. Authority is located in the incumbents of traditional authority-roles (if perceived as personally worthy) or in the consensus of a valued, face-to-face group.

Factors contributing to the breakdown of Stage 3 and to readiness for transition may include any one or more of the following: serious clashes or contradictions between valued authority sources; marked changes, by officially sanctioned leaders, of policies or practices previously deemed sacred and unbreakable (e.g., in the Catholic Church changing the Mass from Latin to the vernacular, or no longer requiring abstinence from meat on Friday); the encounter with experiences or perspectives that lead to critical reflection on how one's beliefs and values have formed and changed, and on how "relative" they are to one's particular group or background.

Stage 4. Individuative-Reflective Faith

The movement from Stage 3 to Stage 4 is particularly critical, for it is in this transition that the late adolescent or adult must begin to take seriously the burden of responsibility for his or her own commitments, lifestyle, beliefs, and attitudes. Where genuine movement toward Stage 4 is underway the person must face certain unavoidable tensions: individuality vs. being defined by a group or group membership; subjectivity and the power of one's strongly felt but unexamined feelings vs. objectivity and the requirement of critical reflection; self-fulfillment or self-actualization as a primary concern vs. service to and being for others; the question of being committed to the relative vs. struggle with the possibility of an absolute.

This stage most appropriately takes form in young adulthood (but let us remember that many adults do *not* construct it and that for a significant group it emerges only in the mid-thirties or forties). It is marked by a double development. The self, previously sustained in its identity and faith compositions by an interpersonal circle of significant others, now claims an identity no longer defined by the composite of one's roles or meanings to others. To sustain that new identity it composes a meaning frame conscious of its own boundaries and inner-connections, and aware of its self as a "worldview." Self (identity) and outlook (worldview) are differentiated from those of others, and become acknowledged factors in the reactions, interpretations, and judgments one makes on the actions of the self and others. It expresses its intuitions of coherence in an ultimate environment in terms of an explicit system of meanings. Stage 4 typically translates symbols into conceptual meanings. This is a "demythologizing" stage. It is likely to attend minimally to unconscious factors influencing its judgments and behavior.

Restless with the self-images and outlook maintained by Stage 4, persons ready for transition find themselves attending to what may feel like anarchic and disturbing inner voices. Elements from a childish past, images and energies from a deeper self, a gnawing sense of the sterility and flatness of the meanings one serves—any or all of those may signal readiness for something new. Stories, symbols, myths, paradoxes from one's own or other traditions may insist on breaking in upon the neatness of one's previous faith. Disillusionment with one's compromises, and recognition that life is more complex than Stage 4's logic of clear distinctions and abstract concepts can comprehend, press one toward a more dialectical and multileveled approach to life-truth.

Stage 5. Conjunctive Faith

This stage involves the integration into self and outlook of much that was suppressed or evaded in the interest of Stage 4's self-certainty and conscious cognitive and affective adaptation to reality. This stage develops a "second naiveté" (Ricoeur) in which symbolic power is reunited with conceptual meanings. Here there must also be a new reclaiming and re-working of one's past. There must be an opening to the voices of one's "deeper self." Importantly, this involves a critical recognition of one's *social* unconscious—the myths, ideal images, and prejudices built deeply into the self-system by virtue of one's nurture within a particular social class, religious tradition, ethnic group, or the like.

> Unusual before mid-life, Stage 5 knows the sacrament of defeat and the reality of irrevocable commitments and acts. What the previous stage struggled to clarify, in terms of the boundaries of self and outlook, this stage now makes porous and permeable. Alive to paradox and the truth in apparent contradictions, this stage strives to unify opposites in mind and experience. It generates and maintains vulnerability to the strange truths of those who are "other." Ready for closeness to that which is different and threatening to self and outlook (including new depths of experience in spirituality and religious revelation), this stage's commitment to justice is freed from the confines of tribe, class, religious community, or nation. And with the seriousness that can arise when life is more than half over, this stage is ready to spend and be spent for the cause of conserving and cultivating the possibility of others' generating identity and meaning.

Stage 5 can appreciate symbols, myths, and rituals (its own and others') because it has been grasped, in some measure, by the depth of reality to which they refer. It also sees the divisions of the human family vividly because it has been apprehended by the possibility (and imperative) of an inclusive community of being. But this stage remains divided. It lives and acts between an untransformed world and a transforming vision and loyalties. In some few cases this division yields to the call of the radical actualization that we call Stage 6.

Stage 6. Universalizing Faith

This stage is exceedingly rare. The persons best described by this stage have generated faith compositions in which their felt sense of an ultimate environment is inclusive of all being. They become incarnators and actualizers of the spirit of a fulfilled human community.

They are "contagious" in the sense that they create zones of liberation from the social, political, economic, and ideological shackles we place and endure on human futurity. Living with felt participation in a Power that unifies and transforms the world, universalizers are often experienced as subversive of the structures (including religious structures) by which we sustain our individual and corporate survival, security, and significance. Many persons in this stage die at the hands of those whom they hope to change. Universalizers are often more honored and revered after death than during their lives. The rare persons who may be described by this stage have a special grace that makes them seem more lucid, more simple, and yet somehow more fully human than the rest of us. Their community is universal in extent. Particularities are cherished because they are vessels of the universal, and are thereby valuable apart from any utilitarian considerations. Life is both loved and held to loosely. Such persons are ready for fellowship with persons at any of the other stages and from any other faith tradition.

Theology and Faith

Now we turn to the real business of this writing. I ask you to join me in an examination of theology—and especially recent writings in the black theologies of liberation—with the categories of the structural developmental stages of faith. Accordingly, I shift my focus somewhat away from faith as a phenomenon in individual and group life. Here we shall be looking instead at theology and the interaction between theology and faith. I shall, however, maintain the developmental perspective and employ it in our discussion.

Theology is indissolubly connected with faith. Faith is a *person's or people's apprehension of themselves, their neighbors, and their world, as related to transcendent being, value, and power, and their ways of shaping their lives in accordance with that apprehension.* Faith is the fundamental disposition a person or a people hold toward the ultimate conditions of their existence. Faith can be expressed and symbolized by ritual, prayers, dance, cultic observances of all kinds, ethics, social action, myths, codes of laws, poetry, preaching, music, and statuary art or painting. Faith can be expressed or communicated in many ways. It is a particular bias of Christianity that the most normative expressions of its faith have tended (since the second or third century A.D.), to be verbal, and to take the form of systematic, prose discourse about faith and its contents. Christian theology, in the formal sense, has been and is the effort, through language, to express, explain, and criticize the faith of Christian persons and communities.

Theology must perform a double duty. It must try to bring present faith to clear expression and give it systematic explanation and application. But simultaneously it must also keep present faith in normative dialogue with the sources and norms of faith—the Scriptures, the tradition, and the contemporary experience of the being and action of God. Theology, if we oversimplify, may be seen as providing models *of* faith and models *for* faith. To perform its task it must be in touch with and resonant with the experiences and faith which it tries to express. Theology cannot be simply an intellectual exercise pursued for its own sake, though it does have a legitimate intellectual component. Nor can it be merely an aesthetic creation—a mere medium of self-expression—though it needs all the artistry and aesthetic power we can give it. Theology must be the reflective expression, strung tense between the sources of revelation and the outlook, attitudes, and actions of a people, pursued for the sake of informing, guiding, and shaping that people's individual and corporate action.

Parenthetically, I want to observe that one of the cardinal contributions of black, feminist, and Third World theologies of liberation to the larger theological enterprise is their seriousness about keeping theological reflection integrally involved with the struggling community of faith. I am not being anti-intellectual when I say that much of academic theology is caught today in a serious case of university captivity. In itself such theology may be harmless. But it is positively subversive of the gospel when it seduces or comforts young (or older) would-be servants of God into thinking that by doing privatistic thinking about God, in abstraction from concrete involvement in God's worldly works, we somehow are investing ourselves in God's service.

The Re-emergence of Political Criteria for Theological Adequacy

Now I want to address with you the question of criteria for the adequacy of theology. I have already referred in a general way to some of these criteria of adequacy: (1) There is the requirement that a theology be grounded in the Christian memory and promise. The Scriptures and tradition of the Church, which mediate the incarnational knowledge of God's disposition toward humanity, are normative for Christian theology. (2) There is the requirement that theology carry on its reflection from, in the midst of, and as a participant in, the concrete life and faith of a people. Theology must attend to the needs, hopes, illusions, and particular circumstances of those for whom it works. It must be informed in its work by their *current* experiences of the power, reality, and working of God (or, we might also say, by their experience of the seeming impotence, absence, or inactivity of God).

But just here we come up against a serious set of problems. How inclusive can or must this phrase "a people" be? Is it to be universal—inclusive of all persons? Is it to be nationally, ethnically, racially, denominationally, sexually, or ideologically determined? In Thomas Aquinas' day Christian theologians could presume that they were writing theology for all Christendom. And that meant, practically speaking, the whole world, for all people were considered to be at least *potentially* Christian. So long as the sacramental and political power structure of the Church remained intact, theology could do its work from a presumptively universal standpoint. We know that in practice there have always been dissenters to this presumption, both before and after the Reformation. There have been the Hussites, the Anabaptists, the Levellers, the Quakers, not to mention those massive dissenters, Luther, Calvin, Zwingli, and Knox. (These latter figures, we might point out, did not so much dispute the possibility of a universal theological standpoint, and the use of authority and coercion to enforce it, as they objected to those services being provided by Rome.) Nonetheless, with all those dissenters, the magisterial reformers included, individual conscience, and the collective conscience of groups of like-minded folk, came to be seen in a new way as constituting a criterion alongside Scripture and tradition for the adequacy of theology.

With the Renaissance and Enlightenment and their separation of science, philosophy, and the arts from religious control, new kinds of *secular* criteria for the adequacy of theology were generated and applied. Out of the history of religious warfare and persecution came a growing consciousness, in the seventeenth and eighteenth centuries, of the need for *toleration* as a criterion for theological adequacy.

With the Philosophes and the French Revolution there came a powerful impulse toward clarifying *political* criteria for the adequacy of theology. Karl Marx was the heir of this thinking and he, more than any figure before him in the modern period, pointed to the entanglement of religion and theology in the political, social, and economic patterns of society. Since Marx's time sociology, economics, political science—and theology itself—have developed and sharpened the conceptual tools he forged for evaluating the role of religion and theology in economic and political struggles. More to the point, Marx's ideas, insights, and theories have spurred to action countless revolutionary leaders and movements, most of them anti-Christian and antireligious.

There is growing evidence that many black slaves in America, in the process of becoming Christian, exercised a very well-developed set of social and political criteria in their appropriation of the slave-masters' religion.[6] My friend Herbert Edwards has a formula which expresses this in wry understatement. He says of the slaves' appropriation of the biblical message: "They *took more* than they were *given:* and they *accepted less* than they were *offered.*" And as Major Jones said to me in a conversation: "The masters did not mean for them to learn about Exodus, but they did." He went on, "The more they got of the gospel the more unwilling they were to accept their position in life."

The theologies of liberation today represent the internalization into theology of the socio-political critique of class-bound, economically-conditioned, racistic, and status-quo-sanctioning religion. A prime criterion of theological adequacy and validity has re-emerged with these theologies. *Liberation,* the account of God's identification with and action on behalf of the oppressed, has become for many *the* cardinal index of the validity and faithfulness of any Christian theology. With the theologies of liberation there has emerged a new frankness about the limits to inclusiveness in the community of faith. There is suspicion of any claim that one is doing theology from a universalizing standpoint. Communities of faith are coming to be seen as coterminous with those communities that result from racial, social-class, and ideological barriers. God, it is claimed, cannot be the benefactor of both the oppressed and the oppressors.

Developmental Criteria for Theological Adequacy

To this point I have been trying to trace the re-emergence of one of the most important kinds of criteria currently being applied in testing the adequacy or criterion of theology—a political and economic criterion. I am in essential agreement with Warner Traynham in his excellent book, *Christian Faith in Black and White,* when he claims that the theme of liberation and the restoration of just relations between people outweighs its twin theme of sanctification in the biblical tradition. He says: "We have to reassert the liberation theme of the gospel because for so long our concerns for sanctification overshadowed it and, while the two themes complement each other, that of liberation is fundamental."[7] Now to set up the tension I want to face and work with in this chapter, I must ask you to focus with me on structural developmental stages of faith as another source of criteria for theological adequacy.

Let's look first at the value biases which I—partly consciously and partly unconsciously—built into this developmental schema. First of all, following Piaget, Kohlberg, and other structural-developmentalists, I have assumed that more complex and more highly differentiated forms of thought and interpretation are more adequate than the less complex and less differentiated. A simpler way to say this is that I have presumed that each higher stage of faith incorporates into itself the qualities and abilities of each of the preceding stages, combining them in transformed ways. Corollary to this assumption is the belief that the higher stages are more adequate because they allow for a more comprehensive, inclusive, and accurate knowing of a complex world. So far this point may seem to have significance merely for the structural characteristics of theological thinking. It is important to see, however, that there are assumptions about the *content* of theology tied into it as well. Let's take, for example, the question of the extensiveness of inclusion in community—precisely the same issue we were looking at before with the theologies of liberation.

In Stage 0, the stage of *"undifferentiated faith,"* the infant's "community" is necessarily limited to those providing care and nurture, and to possible siblings. In Stage 1, "Intuitive-Projective" faith, although there may be a wider circle of acquaintances, it is still primarily the family or extended family which provides those relationships by which the child forms a view of self, of the world, and of what is important, sacred, or sublime in it. Stage 2, "Mythic-Literal" faith, involves a widening of community to include usually a schooling and a peer, and sometimes a church world. Most often it is still the case that the values of primal or familial others continue to be determinative. At Stage 3, "Synthetic-Conventional" faith, the person has found class, racial, regional, and religious identifications with significant others. Because this now includes relations in multiple spheres of life, there may be conflicts between some loyalties and identifications (such as between peers' values and those of parents). But the contradictions are maintained in some kind of synthesis of given elements, and without any real fundamental examination of and decision about the values and attitudes thus embraced.

Stage 4, "Individuative-Reflective" faith, involves necessarily a cracking open of previously unexamined attachments, loyalties, and underlying values. For it is of the essence of Stage Four that fundamental alternatives to one's deepest affiliations and affections must be acknowledged and reckoned with. One's "embeddedness" in the values, beliefs, and practices of the persons or groups who have been most important to one is no longer a matter that can be taken for granted. Serious alternatives are challengingly present; life-defining choices and commitments must be made. At this point persons can—and often do—reaffirm the faith or community which has nurtured them. But when this happens there usually must be available an ideologically potent reformulation of that faith or worldview. It must exact from the person a new, deepened, and intentional commitment, and provide boundaries and a communal identity that have new firmness. Stage 4 wants to keep communal boundaries sharp and clear. Ideological purity is an important matter. Inclusion and exclusion are taken seriously; and justification for one's choice must ever be at the ready.

Stage 5, our "Conjunctive" stage, marks the development of a readiness to be close to and to learn from groups and worldviews quite different from one's own. Stage 5 sees that the faith and commitments of others, while not one's own, can have integrity and truth. It sees that "truth" is multidimensional and multiperspectival. While unready to discard its own belief and identification boundaries, Stage 5 experiences the paradoxical recognition that beyond our highly diverse, pluralistic experiences and beliefs, we human beings are more like each other than we are different from each other. Stage 5 recognition of a oneness which comprehends and transcends our manyness, however, is experienced as paradoxical. It is an affirmation made and acted on in spite of needs and defenses which militate against it. At Stage 6, "universalizing" faith, it seems that this paradoxical quality is overcome; participation is possible in a genuinely universal commonwealth of being.

The point I wanted to make in this rather long illustration is that the developmental schema has some normative value assumptions relative to the *content* of theology built into it. Using the same illustration, let me point to a few other value commitments implied in the developmental perspective which constitute criteria for the adequacy of theology.

Here I would call attention to the fact that the developmental perspective implies the desirability of a theology which calls for reflective awareness over against the embeddedness of Synthetic-conventional faith. Paulo Freire's great book, *The Pedagogy of the Oppressed*,[8] describes a method and offers an educational theology, as it were, which are designed to assist persons to break out of a mass-consciousness into critical awareness of who they are and of who they are called to be. This is something like what must happen in any real transition from Stage 3 to Stage 4. This Stage 4, "Individuative-Reflective" faith, is not necessarily individual*istic* faith. Rather it is faith for which the person of faith takes a measure of personal responsibility. He or she no longer swims in an ethos of unexamined values and attitudes and expectations, like a fish who has no control over the water which supports and engulfs it. *This value bias of the developmental perspective suggests that an important criterion for any theology's adequacy is whether it helps clarify and sharpen a person's awareness of values being served, and whether it encourages the assumption of responsibility for affirming or rejecting them.*

There is at least one other important value commitment implied in the developmental perspective which can be applied as a criterion for theological adequacy. This may initially seem to fly in the face of my previous point concerning the increasing adequacy of stages as one moves through the schema. But the contradiction is only an apparent one. Optimally, each person deserves theological and communal support for fully developing and realizing each of the stages. The Stage 2 "Mythic-Literal" faith of a child can be much richer and more vibrant if the child has not been forced too quickly to supplant the fantasy and imagination of Stage 1 with a premature, coercive accommodation to orthodox beliefs and norms. Similarly, Stage 5, "Conjunctive" faith can be extraordinarily rich when a person has been enabled to carry forward the capacity to be thrilled and informed by the myths, legends, poetry, and music of his or her tradition—many of which are first appropriated in Stage 2.

In summary, we may say that the developmental perspective implies three principal value biases which can be translated into criteria for theological adequacy:

1. A theology is to be preferred which will support the most developed stage of the person's or community's faith, and provide models *of* and *for* further development.

2. Theologies are to be preferred which stimulate development in the self-awareness of a person's or group's operative values, and which sponsor responsible self-determination in relation to them.

3. A person or community at a given stage of faith is best nurtured by theological communication appropriate to that stage. (There is evidence that

we have difficulty comprehending theological communication pitched more than one stage beyond our own.)

Theologies of Liberation in Developmental Perspective

I propose now that we try to bring certain of the black theologies of liberation and this developmental perspective into dialogue. It is my hope that I will be able to convey to you some of the insights which developing this dialogue has generated for me.

Permit me, parenthetically, to insert a personal word here. I have been working on the interplay between theology and developmental psychology for some time now. For the greater part of that time I have devoted myself primarily to the effort to master the principles and methods of developmental psychology—a new field to me. We have pursued the effort to conduct empirical research on the basis of which to construct and refine a stage theory of faith development. My theological anchorage for this work has been rooted most deeply in the theology of H. Richard Niebuhr, the subject of my first book.[9] Other theologians from his generation—or shaped by his generation—were also my teachers. During this period the theology of the sovereignty of God, developed as Niebuhr had worked it out in his books *The Meaning of Revelation, Radical Monotheism and Western Culture,* and *The Responsible Self,* pretty well expressed my own faith. Under that influence the so-called "death of God" flap in theology did not shake me or grab my imagination. Nor did the various "theologies of play" seem very helpful or useful to me. As for the "Theology of Hope" I had already found most of it, I thought, in Niebuhr's often unrecognized theological appropriation of a Marxist view of history[10]—not unlike that of Ernst Bloch—who had been so important for Moltmann, Pannenberg, Metz, and the others in that wing.

But when the invitation came to undertake the present writing, and when, simultaneous with these preparations, I began to read Niebuhr again with Rudolph Featherstone, then finishing his doctorate in black theology and West African traditional religions, something began to stir in me. As I re-read Cone,[11] as I dealt with Gayraud Wilmore's splendid *Black Religion and Black Radicalism,*[12] as I read Major Jones' contribution to the theology of hope, and especially, as I ran head on into William R. Jones' *Is God a White Racist?*[13] I began to be aware that certain theological commitments I had held, and certain canons of adequacy for theology formerly central to me, were undergoing radical changes.

I do not mean to bore you with this account of my own growing awareness. Nor do I mean to engage in name-dropping. What I am trying to indicate is that the dialogue I am going to offer here is not one artifically contrived and designed for pedagogical purposes. Rather it is an attempt to lay honestly before you the issues which a serious encounter with black theologies of liberation has raised for me and my previous thinking.

Permit me to say just one more word of personal explanation. In drawing on the structural-developmentalists in psychology there inevitably crept into my theory-building and research efforts a tendency to focus too singularly on development as a *personal* and *internal* matter. I tended in this first phase of my work not to take seriously enough the way economic, social-class, ethnic, racial, and political factors in a person's or group's environment inter-play with the process of development in faith. The tendency in structural-developmental theory to separate the *form* of thought from the *content* of thought or faith is a kind of corollary to this too individualistic, too inward-looking focus on faith. On each of these counts the theologies of liberation have provided a powerful corrective stimulus and challenge. I have recognized and embraced the challenge represented by liberation theologies—black, feminist, and Latin American—but I recognize only too clearly that I have not yet fully assimilated the transformation in my thinking which is now in process.

But from where I now stand it seems to me that an examination of the major black theologies of liberation, through the lenses of a developmental perspective, brings into view two main camps. As with any typology the designation of these two camps will involve some force-fitting and blurring of fine distinctions, but limitations of space leave us little choice in this regard. Nonetheless, it does seem to me that the principal differences between these two camps can fruitfully be discussed in terms of developmental stages. Let me inject here that I am *not* suggesting that one of these groups of theologians is necessarily more mature or more Christian than the other. What I will be suggesting, rather, is that the principal differences in their theological work seem to derive from their holding different perceptions of those for whom they are writing and their needs. One group seems to address itself primarily to persons who are in transition from a Stage 3 to a Stage 4 type of faith. The other group seems to assume that their audience is primarily in Stage 5 in faith orientation and outlook. Our analysis will show that while there are these *implicit* developmental criteria for theology at work here, there are also *explicit* political criteria for theological adequacy firmly in the picture, and that sometimes the two types of criteria are in conflict and tension with each other.

The "Ideological" Theologians

Stage 4, "Individuative-Reflective" faith is that which develops when one "breaks out" of the structure of values, myths, and images supplied by the nurturing environments(s). Stage 4 involves beginning to win a critical awareness of one's operative values, and attitudes, and their bases in societal, economic, racial, political, and religious patterns. Characteristic of Stage 4 faith is a tendency to see things in terms of dichotomies. In theologies focused at Stage 4 there tend to be sharp distinctions, necessitating either/or choices, between concepts like the following:

reason	vs.	revelation
particularity	vs.	universality
subjectivity	vs.	objectivity
oppressors	vs.	oppressed
black	vs.	white
humanism	vs.	theism
the present	vs.	the past and future

and so on.

Theologies focused at Stage 4 put a premium on the establishment and maintenance of firm, clear boundaries. Language is intentionally *passionate,* and there is an appeal to new commitment, and to action on the basis of new commitment. A principal goal of theologies focused at Stage 4 is to bring about change. Whether intentional or not, the theologies focused at Stage 4 tend to have the characteristics of *ideologies.* That is to say, they want to offer a specific worldview, addressed to a particular group, in the service of a particular set of needs or goals of that group. Because of these characteristics I propose to refer to these theologians whose work focused at Stage 4 as the "Ideological Theologians." (I am aware that "ideological" is often taken as a pejorative label; I do not intend it so; rather I mean it here to be descriptive.) We will return in a moment to the ideological group, which includes James Cone,[14] Albert Cleage,[15] and their critic, William R. Jones.[16]

The "Theologians of Balance"

Stage 5, "Conjunctive" faith represents a position in which the dichotomies separated by Stage 4 are rejoined and viewed as complementary, polar tensions. We saw that Stage 4 finds it necessary to make either/or, exclusive commitments. But Stage 5's integrity depends upon a somewhat paradoxical affirmation of both sides of a polarity. Theologies conceived so as to focus in Stage 5 tend to take polar opposites into themselves, affirming a kind of "both/and" approach. They want to affirm both *particularity and universality* as necessary affirmations for theology. They want to speak from the standpoints of both *subjectivity and objectivity.*

The line between the *oppressor and the oppressed* is seen as passing through people and groups rather than *between* them.

Black and white are seen as complementary experiences, and both are needed for "truth."

They will offer both *humanism and theism.*

They will focus on the present but refuse to separate it from *past* and *future.*

I propose that we call these Stage 5-focused theologians the "Theologians of Balance." Critics of this group are quick to point out that in their efforts to be theologically comprehensive they often operate unknowingly in ideological ways too. That is to say, they also may be seen as expressing worldviews which are drawn specifically from the experiences and needs of particular groups and which serve the special interests of these groups. The "Theologians of Balance" would deny any ideological intent. They regard ideology as a pitfall for theology. Their goal is to provide a kind of passionately disinterested perspective on God's work in and God's will for history. They aim to be passionate in attending to God's work in and will for history. They aim to be passionate in attending to God's way with humankind, but to be disinterested or objective in the interpretation and application of what they discern. Among the "Theologians of Balance" I would include Joseph Washington (at least the Joseph Washington of the *Politics of God*),[17] J. Deotis Roberts,[18] Major J. Jones,[19] and Warner Traynham.[20]

Some Comparisons and Differences

We have identified the two major groups, at least in abstract terms. I propose now to try to flesh out in a more concrete way some of the differences between these two groups. In this comparison I hope I will succeed in communicating my profound appreciation for the truths or strengths on both sides. In what follows I try to be suggestive rather than exhaustive. We will look at differences regarding (1) *The tasks of theology,* (2) *the understanding of God's relation to history,* (3) *perspectives on time,* and (4) *views of sin and evil.*

The Tasks of Theology

The *Ideological Theologians* tend to take a frankly utilitarian attitude toward theology. Theology is directly connected to the intention to bring about change. Any theology which does not directly relate to and contribute to the liberation of the oppressed—despite its other possible virtues—is not Christian (or useful) theology. Theology takes its hermeneutical focus and its criteria of relevance from its primary commitment to the liberation of the oppressed. The Scriptures, tradition, and present experiences are selectively normative for theology, depending upon their relevance to this central commitment. The intellectual canons traditional in theology are of decidedly secondary importance. And this theology knows it can speak only on behalf of the oppressed. It must avoid the double consciousness of also trying to take the part of the oppressor.

The *Theologians of Balance,* on the other hand, are suspicious of utilitarian uses of theology. Theology, for them must be subordinated to no other causes or loyalties than loyalty to God's kingdom. To be sure, liberation of the oppressed is a central loyalty and a high imperative, but it must be held in second place to the larger and more comprehensive task of discerning the will and working of God. Scripture, tradition, present experience, and the imperative of liberation must all be affirmed as norms and sources of theology. The intellectual canons of theology must also be taken seriously. The theologian, while identifying primarily with one group or standpoint, must make the effort to discern theological truth for the *human* community, including the oppressed *and* the oppressors.

The Understanding of God's Relation to History

For the *Ideological Theologians* God is either identified with the oppressed or with the oppressor. It cannot be both ways. Those who want to continue to speak of God as sovereign in history (Cone and Cleage) see him as having committed himself faithfully to the dispossessed. In Cone's words: "Black theology cannot accept a view of God which does not represent him as being for blacks and thus against whites. Living in a world of white oppressors, black people have no time for a neutral God."[21] William R. Jones takes a behaviorist view of God. For him God must be regarded as the "sum of his acts." For Jones the massive fact of maldistributed ethnic suffering makes it problematic simultaneously to claim that God is sovereign in history and that God has decisively sided with the oppressed. For him God is either sovereign and pernicious, or beneficent and less than omnipotent. Whether you go with Cone and Cleage, or with William R. Jones, God must be seen as *either/or.* And the critical question determining whether God can be loved and trusted is whether (and how) he is really faithful, with power, to the cause of the liberation of the oppressed.

For the *Theologians of Balance* the first word about God is that God intends and is committed to the fulfillment of his creation. God is a structure-intending-righteousness in the process of history. God is the loving, faithful sovereign whose judgment is the other side of his love, and whose wisdom and righteousness exceed human understanding. This sovereign God causes his rain to fall on the just and the unjust in a cosmic graciousness. He has no favorites, but wills—and is working in visible and invisible ways—to realize his kingdom on earth. Through the incarnation God identifies with and participates in the suffering of the victims of misused human freedom. In the crucifixion and resurrection of Jesus the Christ the principle of a vicarious suffering, through which the whole world is being redeemed, is both demonstrated and established. In sum, God is faithful and loyal to the cause of fulfilling creation. Though human beings, in our freedom, seek to do evil, God employs even the evil action and the consequential suffering, in the redemption and restoration and completion of his kingdom.

The Perspectives on Time

The *Ideological Theologians* decisively reject what Herbert Edwards calls the eschatological justification of suffering: "By and by, when the morning comes . . . we'll understand it better by and by." The Ideological Theologians tend to demand evidence that God is vindicating his commitment to the liberation of the oppressed in the realizable present. For them the biblical testimonies to past "liberation-exaltation events" may be paradigms by which to see God's present liberating work. But, on the whole, the credit-line of divine support for black liberation must show cashable resources in the present, or there is little use in talking about it.

The *Theologians of Balance* generally take a longer-range view. With Augustine they testify that we hang suspended in the present, between a long memory of God's faithfulness and a long future of God's promise. They remind us that Israel spent four hundred years in Egypt and a considerable time in Babylon on the way toward being worthy of their election. And they caution us against the presumption that God should carry out his liberating activity according to *our* prescription and timetable.

Views of Sin and Evil

From the standpoint of the *Ideological Theologians,* sin fundamentally consists in a separation or alienation from a person or group's true identity. It is a failure of self-affirmation, a lack in the courage to be. The sin of un-being (to coin a phrase) is manifest in *quietism* and *resignation*. To quote Cone again, "According to Black Theology, the sin of the oppressed is not that they are responsible for their own enslavement—far from it. Their sin is that of trying to 'understand' the enslaver, to 'love' him on his own terms."[22] Sin is the acceptance of oppressive denials or limitations of personhood, shrouded as such oppression always is, in mystifying religious rationale.

Evil, for the Ideological Theologians, is largely the direct consequence of power discrepancies. Evil is the cumulative result of centuries of enforced inequality. No suffering is good. Ethnic suffering and the conditions that produce it must be expunged. The power discrepancy must be obliterated. No one—and especially not the beneficiary of the present, oppressive order—has the right to claim or speak about a necessary redemptive quality of the suffering of the oppressed.

For the *Theologians of Balance,* on the other hand, sin and evil are the consequence of misused human freedom. Excessive pride, leading to idolatry, is the essential form of sin. The cumulative results of human sin are structures of injustice and oppression. These structures of evil carry the seeds of their own destruction within them. To be sure they must be opposed and fought. But even as Christians are fighting these structures they must remember that the line dividing the just from the unjust passes through the heart of every person, and not between persons and groups. In the struggle against structures of evil and oppressors Christians must struggle as those who hope for the redemption of the oppressor.

Suffering and evil are baffling and perplexing phenomena. But we can trust that the God who is loyal to all being is working redemptively in and through suffering to transform human hearts and minds.

Conclusions

I have not set up this set of comparisons so as now to choose one alternative and negate the other. There was no "straw man" intended in the comparison and contrast of the Ideological Theologians and the Theologians of Balance.

This inability or unwillingness to decide between them, however, is not to suggest that preaching, religious education, and economic or socio-political initiatives informed by one of these positions will not be quite different from those same activities informed by the other. The differences are real and deep-going.

What I want to affirm is the importance of maintaining *both* positions and the tensions between them. I suspect that whenever you have *genuine* theological passion and vitality you will have *both* Stage 4- and Stage 5-focused theologies. It is striking to notice how the principal emphases of yesterday's Stage 4-focused theologies find resonant places in today's Stage 5-focused theologies.

It is my impression that the black churches, to a striking degree, do in fact work at maintaining both these options and the tensions between them. It is the task of the Stage 4 theologies to keep affirming and clarifying the particularities of the black experience, and the specialty of the angle of vision on God's way and work which it offers. These theologies also have the task of recruiting and supporting persons in the transition from conventionally fostered faith and self-images, to those for which they themselves take an aware responsibility. This latter function is one of the clear justifications for speaking of them as liberating theologies. The development from Stage 3 faith to a Stage 4 faith is a genuine liberation which lays the necessary foundation for more concrete socio-political liberating action.

It would seem to be the task of the Stage 5 theologies, on the other hand, to hold up the linkage of the black experience and the black church to the larger community of Christian and human faith. In order to avoid a specious and merely intellectual resolution of the great polar tensions of the life of faith, however, the Stage 5 theologies need on-going involvement with the *un*intellectual, struggling people of faith. They also need the sharp, critical warnings from the Stage 4 theologies that faith resolutions won too easily can be what Bonhoeffer called "cheap grace" and what Sartre called "bad faith." There is always the danger, when the Stage 5 model is held up as solely normative, that its proponents may be justly accused as Jeremiah accused the false prophets in his day: "Peace, peace, they say, though there is no peace" (Jer. 6:14).

Both these positions can be misused. There are misuses that derive from political and socio-economic motives. And there are misuses that derive from failures to have and apply developmental criteria. The best check against misuse of these kinds, it seems to me, is the strong preservation at present of both theological approaches, and of the debate between them, in the course of acting theologically in the struggles for a more human and Godly world. Out of the dialectic of their interaction there likely will emerge a more comprehensive theological synthesis that will include the strengths of both.

As a possible contribution to that dialectic I want to leave you with a series of questions—critical questions—addressed to the members of each of these two camps. First I address the Ideological Theologians:

1. Can a purely utilitarian theology retain religious sufficiency? Does it not sooner or later require an admission that the Deity, as so understood and used, is merely a function of human need and a symbol of a particular group's aspiration and self-righteousness? (This, to me, is the question which William Jones' book raises with most power.)

2. Can the God of the Christian tradition be portrayed accurately either as having favorites (and special targets of abuse) or as totally uninvolved in any effectual way in history?

3. Is it not an excess of self-affirmation—bordering on solipsism—to demand that God vindicate his righteousness and goodness on *our* terms, or our group's terms (i.e., within our time-frame and according to our needs and expectations)?

4. Is it either wise or Christian to affirm, even for ideological purposes, that the line between oppressed and oppressors, sinless and sinners, the elect and the damned, can be drawn *between* persons and groups?

Second, I have some questions for the Theologians of Balance:

1. Is there not something incongruent about addressing accusations of excessive hubris and pride to persons or groups whose ability to affirm self-worth and pride has been so consistently and systematically under attack?

2. In the presence of structural injustice and institutionalized evil, is it not at best an evasion—and at worst a conspiracy with the *status quo*—to speak too easily of universal community, the sister- and brotherhood of humankind, and of God's transcendence of all our particular claims for and needs of him?

3. When persons are blocked by concrete political, economic, and social barriers to the assumption of full personhood, is it not irresponsible to speak to them of waiting expectantly for the liberating work of God and to ask them to participate in that work only by aggressive suffering?

4. Is not there something myopic about charges that the Ideological Theologians are less than Christian when your own theodicies and theologies of liberation have failed to provide any sufficiently radical critique of the way theologies of balance have been used to inculcate quietism and to buttress the *status quo?*

To conclude: Probably the greatest danger for us who make our living talking about faith—teacher and preacher alike—is that we, in practical terms, tend to sever action and theological reflection. In these matters the Gospel dictum is unerringly right when it says, "Seek ye first the Kingdom of Heaven, and all these things"—including theological understanding—"will be added unto you" (Matt. 6:33).

Notes

1. James W. Fowler and Sam Keen, *Life-Maps: Conversations on the Journey of Faith* (Minneapolis: Winston Press, 1978): James W. Fowler, "Faith and the Structuring of Meaning," in *Toward Moral and Religious Maturity,* ed. Fowler and Antoine Vergote (Morristown, N.J.: Silver Burdett, 1980); James W. Fowler and Robin W. Lovin, and others *Trajectories in Faith: Five Life Stories* (Nashville: Abingdon, 1980).

2. Three books by W. C. Smith, *The Meaning and End of Religion* (New York: Harper & Row, 1978); *Belief and History* (Charlottesville: University Press of Virginia, 1977); and *Faith and Belief* (Princeton, N.J.: Princeton University Press, 1979). See also Robert N. Bellah, *Beyond Belief* (New York: Harper & Row, 1970).

3. Paul Tillich, *Dynamics of Faith* (New York: Harper, 1956): H. Richard Niebuhr, *Radical Monotheism and Western Culture* (New York: Harper & Row, 1960); and James W. Fowler, *To See the Kingdom: The Theological Vision of H. Richard Niebuhr* (Nashville: Abingdon, 1974).

4. Jean Piaget and Bärbel Inhelder, *The Psychology of the Child* (New York: Basic Books, 1969). Jean Piaget, "Piaget's Theory," in *Carmichael's Manual of Child Psychology,* 3rd ed., ed Paul H. Mussen (New York: John Wiley & Sons, 1970), pp. 703–732.

5. Lawrence Kohlberg, "Stage and Sequence: the Cognitive Developmental Approach to Socialization," in *Handbook of Socialization Theory and Research,* ed. David A. Goslin (Skokie, Ill.: Rand McNally College Publishing Co., 1969), pp. 347–480. See also Lawrence Kohlberg, *Collected Papers on Moral Development,* (San Francisco: Harper and Row, 1981).

6. Gayraud S. Wilmore, *Black Religion and Black Radicalism* (New York: Doubleday, Anchor, 1973). See esp. Ch. 1–4.

7. Warner R. Traynham, *Christian Faith in Black and White: A Primer from the Black Perspective* (Philadelphia: Lippincott, 1970; Wakefield, Mass.: Parameter Press, 1973), p. 19.

8. Paulo Freire, *The Pedagogy of the Oppressed* (New York: Herder and Herder, 1970).

9. Fowler, *To See the Kingdom.*

10. See ibid., especially ch. 2.

11. James H. Cone, *Black Theology and Black Power* (New York: Seabury, 1969); *A Black Theology of Liberation* (Philadelphia: Lippincott, 1970): *The Spirituals and the Blues* (New York: Seabury, 1972); and *God of the Oppressed* (New York: Seabury, 1975).

12. Gayraud S. Wilmore, *Black Religion and Black Radicalism* (Garden City, N.Y.: Doubleday, Anchor, 1973).

13. William R. Jones, *Is God a White Racist?* (New York: Doubleday, Anchor, 1973).

14. See note 11. Although in Note 11 I have included Cone's *The God of the Oppressed,* that text was not available to me when the main theses of this comparison were being formed. In the latter volume Cone takes some important steps beyond the Ideological position as I will develop it here. Most notably, he shifts the focus of his critique of religion from a dominant concern with its collusion with racism to include a strengthened and very significant analysis of religion's entanglement with social class. Also suggesting that Cone has taken a further step in the direction of what I will be calling a Theology of Balance is his insistence that Christian theology must take seriously in its work the truth claims of non-Chritian religious traditions. For Cone's analysis of class and religion, see *God of the Oppressed,* ch. 3. For his reference to non-Christian religions, see ibid., p. 104.

15. Albert Cleage, *The Black Messiah* (New York: Sheed and Ward, 1968).

16. See Jones, *Is God a White Racist?*

17. Joseph Washington, *The Politics of God* (Boston: Beacon, 1967).

18. J. Deotis Roberts, *Liberation and Reconciliation: A Black Theology* (Philadelphia: Westminster, 1971).

19. Major J. Jones, *Black Awareness: A Theology of Hope* (Nashville: Abingdon, 1971); and *Christian Ethics for Black Theology* (Nashville: Abingdon, 1974).

20. See Traynham, *Christian Faith in Black and White.*

21. Cone, *Liberation: A Black Theology of Liberation,* p. 131. This is another point which Cone has modified somewhat in his *God of the Oppressed.* There he discussed how the love and grace of God, which are for all people, take the form of God's judgment in the experience of the oppressors. As such, God's judgment on oppression and those by whom it is continued, is part of God's redemptive and liberative activity.

22. Cone, *Liberation,* pp. 100–101. The changes alluded to in Cone's later work seem to illustrate and bear out this observation.

5

Toward a Feminist Biblical Hermeneutics: Biblical Interpretation and Liberation Theology

Elisabeth Schüssler Fiorenza

Whitehead once said that the goal toward which philosophical theory should move must be defined in terms of "concreteness and adequacy." Although Elisabeth Schüssler Fiorenza might not describe herself as a Whiteheadian, she clearly demands that these same criteria be adopted by theologians. Schüssler Fiorenza's essay begins with an account of the current academic standing of the "advocacy position" adopted by liberation theologians, which suggests that many academic theologians perceive this methodological stance as unhistorical, superfluous—even faddish. Interpreting these characterizations as transparent functions of self-interest, Schüssler Fiorenza suggests that the hermeneutic method of Juan Luis Segundo represents a qualitative advance over pitatively objective methodologies. Still, Segundo's method has one notable defect: it fails to extend its hermeneutics of suspicion to Scripture itself. A feminist biblical hermeneutics, according to Schüssler Fiorenza, is able to contribute to the "advocacy approach" of liberation theology by uncovering and denouncing biblical traditions which perpetuate violence, alienation, and oppression, and by affirming those biblical traditions which enhance and inform the liberation experiences and visions of the People of God.

Elisabeth Schüssler Fiorenza, Professor of Theology at the University of Notre Dame, has published a study on ministries of women in the church, Der vergessene Partner, *1964, and a book on priesthood in the New Testament, which concentrates on the Book of Revelation,* Priester für Gott, *1972. She has authored* The Apocalypse *(Chicago: Franciscan Herald, 1976),* Invitation to Revelation *(New York: Doubleday Image Books, 1981), and edited* Aspects of Religious Propaganda in Judaism and Early Christianity *(Notre*

91

Dame, Ind.: University of Notre Dame Press, 1976). She was the Harry Emerson Fosdick Visiting Professor at Union Theological Seminary in New York in 1974–1975, has served on the editorial boards of major biblical journals and societies, and is active in the women's liberation movement in the churches. She has published numerous studies on feminist theology and women in early Christianity.

To discuss the relationship between liberation theology and biblical interpretation in general, and to ask for the function of the Bible in the struggle of women for liberation in particular, is to enter an intellectual and emotional minefield. One must detect and lay bare the contradictions between historical exegesis and systematic theology, between value-neutral scientific inquiry and "advocacy" scholarship, between universal-objectivist preconceptions of academic theology and the critical partiality of liberation theologies. To attempt this in a short paper entails, by necessity, a simplification and typologization of a complex set of theological problems.

To raise the issue of the contemporary meaning and authority of the Bible from a feminist theological perspective, and to do this from the marginalized position of a woman in the academy,[1] is to expose oneself to triple jeopardy. Establishment academic theologians and exegetes will reject such an endeavor as unscientific, biased, and overly conditioned by contemporary questions, and therefore unhistorical, or they will refuse to accept it as a serious exegetical or theological question because the issue is raised by a woman. Liberation and political theologians will, at best, consider such a feminist theological endeavor as one problem among others, or at worst, label it as "middle class" and peripheral to the struggle of oppressed people. After all, how can middle-class white women worry about the ERA or the sex of God, when people die of starvation, are tortured in prisons, or vegetate below poverty level in the black and Hispanic ghettos of American cities? However, such an objection against feminist theology and the women's movement overlooks the fact that more than half of the poor and hungry in the world are women and children dependent on women.[2] Not only do women and children represent the majority of the "oppressed," but poor and Third World women suffer the triple oppression of sexism, racism, and classism. If liberation theologians make the "option for the oppressed" the key to their theological endeavors, then they must become conscious of the fact that "the oppressed" are women.

Feminist theology, therefore, not only challenges academic theology to take its own intellectual presuppositions seriously, but it also asks other liberation theologies to concretize their option for the oppressed. Finally, the feminist theologian challenges not only the supposedly neutral and objective stance of the academic theologian, but she also must qualify the definition of the advocacy stance of liberation theology as "option for the oppressed." Her involvement in liberation theology is not "altruistic," but it is based on the acknowledgment and analysis of her own oppression as a woman in sexist, cultural, and theological institutions. Having acknowledged the dimensions of her own oppression, she can no longer advocate the value-neutral, detached stance of the academician. In other words, feminist theologians' experience of oppression is different from those of Latin American theologians, for instance, who often do not belong to the poor, but have made the cause of the oppressed their own.[3] Such an emphasis on the differences in the approaches of different liberation theologies is important. Robert McAfee Brown has pointed out, "What we see depends on where we are standing."[4]

Moreover, the Native American theologian Vine Deloria[5] has cautioned that one way of co-opting liberation theology is to classify all minorities as oppressed and in need of liberation. Christian theologians often add to this that we are all under sin and therefore all equally oppressed: male and female, black, white, and red. In co-opting the terms "oppression," and generalizing it so much that it becomes meaningless, the liberal establishment successfully neutralizes specific analyses of oppression and prohibits oppressed groups from formulating their own goals and strategies for liberation. Therefore, it seems to be methodologically inappropriate to speak in generalized terms about oppression or about liberation theology in the singular.

The "Advocacy" Stance of Liberation Theologies

This insight has far-reaching consequences for the methodological approach of this paper. Instead of asking for the Scriptural *loci* of liberation theology in general, or critically evaluating their approach from a "superior" methodological historical-critical point of view, I have decided to concentrate on one specific issue of contention between so-called academic theology and all forms of liberation theology. The basic insight of liberation theologies and their methodological starting-point is the insight that all theology knowingly or not is by definition always engaged for or against the oppressed. Intellectual neutrality is not possible in a historical world of exploitation and oppression. If this is the case then theology cannot talk about human existence in general, or about biblical theology in particular, without identifying whose human existence is meant and about whose God biblical symbols and texts speak.

This avowed "advocacy" stance of all liberation theologies seems to be the major point of contention between academic historical-critical or liberal-systematic theology on the one side and liberation theology on the other side. For instance, in many exegetical and theological circles a feminist interpretation of the Bible or the reconstruction of early Christianity is not the proper substantive historical and theological subject matter for serious academic theology. Since such a feminist interpretation is sparked by the women's movement and openly confesses its allegiance to it, academic theologians consider it to be a popular "fad," and judge it not to be a serious historical-theological problem for historical-critical scholarship.[6] Since this interpretative approach is already prejudiced by the explicit advocacy position of the inquiring scholar, no value-neutral scientific inquiry is possible. Therefore, no one publicly identified with the "feminist cause" in theology and society can be considered to be a "serious" scholar. Or as one of my colleagues remarked about a professor who wrote a rather moderate article on women in the Old Testament: "It's a shame! In writing this article she may have ruined her whole scholarly career."

The ideal of historical-critical studies that all exegetical inquiry should be a value-neutral and objective historical description of the past overlooks the fact that biblical studies as *"canonical"* studies are already "engaged," insofar as the Bible is not just a document of past history, but functions as Holy Scripture in Christian communities today.[7] The *biblical* exegete and theologian, in distinction from the historian of antiquity, never searches solely for the historical meaning of a passage, but also raises the question of the Bible's meaning and authority for today. The argument that the "hermeneutical privilege of the oppressed"[8] or the feminist interest in the role of women in the New Testament is too engaged or biased pertains, therefore, to all biblical inquiry *qua* biblical inquiry, and not only to the study and use of the Bible by liberation theologians. Insofar as biblical studies are "canonical" studies, they are related to and inspired by their *Sitz im Leben* in the Christian Church of the past and the present. The feminist analysis of the Bible is just one example of such an ecclesial contextuality and of the theological commitment of biblical studies in general.

This fact is recognized by Schubert Ogden, who nevertheless objects to the "advocacy" stance of liberation theology. He argues that all existing liberation theologies are in danger of becoming ideologies in the Marxist sense insofar as they, like other traditional theological enterprises, are "the rationalization of positions already taken."[9] Rather than engaging in a critical reflection on their own positions, liberation theologies rationalize, with the help of the Bible, the positions of the oppressed instead of those of the oppressors. Insofar as they attempt to rationalize the prior claims of Christian faith and their own option for the oppressed, they are not theologizing but witnessing. Theology as a "second act" exists according to Latin American liberation theologians, not "for its own sake," but for the sake of the Church's witness, its liberating praxis.

One must, however, question whether this statement adequately characterizes the "advocacy" stance of liberation theologians. Ogden suggests that the only way theology—be it academic or liberation theology—can become emancipated is by conceiving its task as that of a critical reflection on its own position. He then proceeds to work out a "still more adequate theology of liberation than any of them has as yet achieved."[10] However, he not only fails to reflect critically on the political standpoint and implications of his own process theology, but he also goes on to talk about "women's theology" and to explore the "being of God in himself" as if he had never studied feminist theology.

While Ogden accuses liberation theologians of too "provincial an understanding of bondage," James Cone insists to the contrary that the option for the oppressed should become the starting point of all theology: "If Christian theology is an explication of the meaning of the gospel for our time, must not theology itself have liberation as its starting point or run the risk of being, at best, idle talk, and at worst blasphemy?"[11] Such a provocative formulation should not, however, be classified as mere "rhetoric,"[12] but must be seen as an indicator of serious theological differences in the understanding of the task and function of theology.

This disagreement about the function and goal of theology has serious implications for the way theologians understand the task of biblical interpretation. As a feminist theologian I have taken the "advocacy" position, but do not think that this option excludes "critical reflection" on my own feminist position. Such a critical reflection must not only be applied to the "advocacy" position of liberation theologies, but it must also be extended to the ways exegetes and theologians have construed the relationship between the biblical past and its meanings, and explicated the claim of Christian theology that the Bible has authority and significance for Christians today.

Such a critical reflection indicates *first* that biblical and theological interpretation has always taken an advocacy position without clearly reflecting upon it. Such an advocacy position is not unique to liberation theologies.

Second, in order to reflect critically on the funcion of liberation theologians' explicit advocacy position in the process of biblical theological interpretation, I have chosen to discuss two concrete examples of liberation theological hermeneutics. This is necessary because it is methodologically incorrect to reduce every advocacy stance and every analysis of concrete structures of oppression by liberation theologies to one common level. I will argue that liberation theologies, because of their option for a specific group of oppressed people, e.g., women or Native Americans, must develop, within the overall interpretative approach of a critical theology of liberation, more adequate heuristic interpretative models appropriate to specific forms of oppression. In short, the biblical interpretation of liberation theologians must become more concrete, or more "provincial," before an "interstructuring" of different interpretative models, and a more universal formulation of the task of a critical theology of liberation can be attempted.

T. S. Kuhn's[13] categories of scientific paradigms and heuristic models, which evolved in the methodological discussions of the natural sciences, provide a conceptual theoretical framework that allows for the advocacy stance of liberation theologies, as well as for their distinctive interpretative approaches. According to Kuhn, a paradigm represents a coherent research tradition, and creates a scientific community. Since paradigms determine how scientists see the world and how they conceive of theoretical problems, a shift in paradigm also means a transformation of the scientific imagination, and thus demands an "intellectual conversion" which allows the community of scientists to see old "data" in a completely new perspective. For a period of time different paradigms may be competing for the allegiance of the scientific community until one paradigm replaces the other or gives way to a third.

The usefulness of this theory for biblical and theological studies in general and for our discussion here is obvious. It shows the conditioned nature of all scientific investigation, and maintains that no neutral observation language and value-free standpoint is possible insofar as all scientific investigations demand commitment to a particular research approach, and are carried out by a community of scholars dedicated to such a theoretical perspective. Moreover, this theory helps us to understand that theological approaches, like all other scientific theories, are not falsified, but replaced, not because we find new "data," but because we find new ways of looking at old data and problems. Research paradigms are therefore not necessarily exclusive of each other. They can exist alongside each other until they are finally replaced by a new paradigm.

Paradigms in Biblical Interpretation

The debate around the "advocacy" stance of liberation theology and the "value-neutral" stance of academic theology appears to reflect such a shift in theological paradigms. Since the Bible as Holy Scripture is a historical book, but at the same time claims to have significance and authority for Christians today, theological scholarship has developed different paradigms to resolve this tension between the historical and theological claims of the Bible.[14]

The *first* paradigm, which I will call the "doctrinal paradigm," understands the Bible in terms of divine revelation and canonical authority. This paradigm is concerned with the truth-claims, authority, and meaning of the Bible for Christian faith today. It conceives of biblical authority in ahistorical, dogmatic terms. In its most consistent form it insists on the verbal inspiration and literary inerrancy of biblical writings. In this understanding the Bible does not just communicate the Word of God, but it *is* the Word of God. It is not simply a record of revelation, but revelation itself. As such, it functions as proof-text, "first principle," or *norma normans non normata*. The tension between the historical and contemporary meaning of the Bible can be dissolved by means of allegory, typology, or the distinction between the literal sense and the spiritual sense of Scripture.

The most widely used method is proof-texting, which provides the ultimate theological arguments or rationalizations for a position already taken. The general formula is: "Scripture says, therefore . . ." or "This argument is also borne out by Scripture." The proof-texting method presupposes that the Bible reveals eternal truth and timeless principles which can be separated from their historical expression. Biblical writings are only important for theology insofar as they are a source of "proof-texts" or "principles" which can be taken out of their historical context. Biblical texts function as theological justification for the moral, doctrinal, or institutional interests of the Christian community. Insofar as liberation theology too exclusively and abstractly focuses on certain biblical texts, e.g., the Exodus-texts,[15] certain prophetic indictments against the rich in Luke 4:16–30, or the Last Judgment in Matthew 25:31–45, it could be in danger of submitting to the "proof-texting" or the allegorical method.

The *second* paradigm of historical-critical exegesis was developed in confrontation with the dogmatic use of Scripture and the doctrinal authority of the Church. It linked its attack on the doctrinal paradigm with an understanding of exegesis and history that is objective, value-free, rationalist, and scientific. Modeled after the natural sciences, historical-critical exegesis seeks to achieve a purely objective reading of the texts and a scientific presentation of the historical facts. As objective, scientific exegesis, it identifies theological truth with historical facticity. According to James Barr, in this paradigm:

> A biblical account of some event is approached and evaluated primarily not in terms of significance but in terms of correspondence with external reality. Veracity as correspondence with empirical actuality has precedence over veracity as significance.[16]

Although academic historical-criticism has become suspicious of the objectivist-factual understanding of biblical texts, it still adheres to the dogma of value-neutral, detached interpretation. Academic historical-critical scholarship reconstructs as accurately as possible the historical meaning of the Bible, but on methodological grounds it refuses to discuss the significance of biblical texts for the contemporary community of faith. Therefore, academic biblical exegesis must limit itself to historical and literary inquiry, but strictly speaking, it is not a theological endeavor.

It is obvious that liberation theologians must distance themselves from such an understanding of biblical interpretation since they focus on the significance of the Bible for the liberation struggle. However, it is interesting to note that José Miranda,[17] the prolific biblical exegete among the Latin American liberation theologians, adheres to this paradigm. He insists that the historical-critical method is in itself objective, scientific, and controllable. When Western exegetes frequently miss the true meaning of the text, this is not due to the exegetical method, but it is due to the Greek thought which Western exegesis has adopted, and which it must abandon in favor of a Marxist reading of the Bible. However, it is questionable whether Miranda's distinction between Greek and biblical thought can still be maintained, and whether liberation theology can adopt the value-neutral stance of historical criticism.

The *third* paradigm of biblical interpretation takes seriously the methodological insights of historical-critical scholarship, and at the same time radically questions how it conceives of its interpretive task. This paradigm is justified by two developments in biblical scholarship: the methods of form and redaction criticism have demonstrated how much biblical writings are theological responses to pastoral-practical situations and problems, while the hermeneutic discussions have elaborated how biblical texts can have meaning today.

First: form and redaction critical studies have highlighted the fact that the biblical tradition understands itself not as a doctrinal, exegetical, or historical tradition, but as a living tradition.[18] In order to understand biblical texts it is important not only to translate and interpret a text in its immediate context, but also to know and determine the situation and the community to whom the text is addressed.

The New Testament authors rewrote their traditions in the form of letters, gospels, or apocalypses because they felt theologically compelled to illuminate or to censure the beliefs and praxis of their communities. The biblical books are thus written with the intention of serving the needs of the community of faith, and not of revealing timeless principles, or of transmitting historically accurate records. They, therefore, do not locate revelation only in the past, but also in their own present, thereby revealing a dialectical understanding between present and past. On the one hand the past is significant because revelation happened decisively in Jesus of Nazareth. On the other hand the writers of the New Testament can exercise freedom with respect to the Jesus traditions because they believe that the Jesus who spoke, speaks now to his followers through the Holy Spirit.

However, form and redaction critical studies can be criticized for conceptualizing the situation of early Christian communities too readily in terms of a confessional struggle between different theologies and church groups. Such a reconstruction often reads like the history of the European Reformation in the sixteenth century or a description of a small town in America where five or six churches of different Christian persuasions are built within walking distance of one another.

The studies of the social world of Israel[19] and early Christianity[20] emphasize the fact that it is not sufficient merely to reconstruct the ecclesial setting. Christian faith and revelation are always intertwined within cultural, political, and societal contexts. It does not suffice merely to understand biblical texts as expressions of religious-theological ideas or ecclesial disputes. What is necessary is to analyze their societal-political contexts and functions. For instance, it does not suffice merely to recognize the literary form of the household-code, or its theological imperative in the post-Pauline community tradition, if one does not also ask why these communities appropriated this particular form in their societal-political environment.[21] While the doctrinal paradigm understands miracles as proofs of the divinity of Jesus, the historical-contextual paradigm discusses whether they actually could have happened as they are told, and the form and redaction paradigm debates whether they are a religious expression of the time or a genuine expression of Christian faith, the contextual paradigm points out that miracle-faith was widespread in lower classes who did not have money for medical treatment. Miracle-faith in Jesus is best understood as protest against bodily and political suffering. It gives courage to resist the life-destroying powers of one's society.[22]

Second: The hermeneutical discussion is concerned with the meaning of biblical texts. While one direction of hermeneutics seeks to discover the synchronic ontological, a-temporal, ideal, noematic meaning of written texts by separating it from the diachronic, temporal, communicative, personal, and referential speech-event, another direction does not concentrate so much on the linguisticality of the text as on the involvement of the interpreter with the text. The interpreter always approaches the text with specific ways of raising questions, and thus with a certain understanding of the subject matter with which the text is concerned.[23]

The hermeneutic circle conceives of the relationship between the contemporary interpreter and the historical text as a continuous dialogue that corrects the presuppositions of the interpreter and works out the true meaning of the text. At this point, it becomes clear that in this third paradigm dialogical interpretation is the governing model. While form and redaction criticism show that early Christian communities and "authors" were in constant dialogue with the tradition and the living Lord authorizing this tradition, the hermeneutic circle continues this dialogic endeavor in the act of interpretation. Therefore, this hermeneutic understanding can be combined with the neo-orthodox theological enterprise. Or as Schillebeeckx points out: "The apparent point of departure is the presupposition that what is handed down in tradition and especially the Christian tradition, is always meaningful, and that its meaning must only be deciphered hermeneutically and made actual."[24]

In conclusion: All three paradigms of biblical interpretation espouse a definite stance and allegiance to a research perspective and community. The doctrinal paradigm clearly has its allegiance to the Church and its teachings. The norm by which it evaluates different texts and their truth claims is the *regula fidei.* The scientific paradigm of historical-critical exegesis shares in the objectivist-scientific worldview, and espouses the critical rationality and value-free inquiry of academic scholarship. The hermeneutic-contextual paradigm is interested in the "continuation" of the tradition, and therefore advocates a position in line with neo-orthodox theology, a "hermeneutics of consent."[25] It would be interesting to explore which political interests each of these paradigms serves, but this would go far beyond the task and aim of this paper. The explicit advocacy position, however, of liberation theologies threatens to uncover the hidden political interests of existing biblical interpretative paradigms. This may be one of the main reasons why established theology refuses to reflect critically on its own societal-ecclesial interests and political functions.

Liberation Theology and Biblical Interpretation

The second part of this paper will attempt to explore critically the position of a theology of liberation within the existing paradigms of biblical interpretation. I will do this by discussing two different hermeneutical approaches of liberation theologies. As case studies, I have chosen the hermeneutical model of Juan Luis Segundo as one of the more sophisticated proposals in contemporary theology, and have placed in contrast to it Elizabeth Cady Stanton's approach in proposing the *Woman's Bible*. Both examples indicate that liberation theologies have worked out a distinctive approach to biblical interpretation which leads to a redefinition of the criteria for public theological discourse. Instead of asking whether an approach is appropriate to the Scriptures and adequate to the human condition,[26] one needs to test whether a theological model of biblical interpretation is *adequate* to the historical-literary methods of contemporary interpretation and *appropriate* to the struggle of the oppressed for liberation.

The Interpretative Model of Juan Luis Segundo[27]

While the hermeneutic-contextual approach advocates the elimination of all presuppositions and pre-understandings for the sake of objective-descriptive exegesis, existential hermeneutics defines pre-understanding as the common existential ground between the interpreter and the author of the text. Political theologians have challenged this choice of existential philosophy, while liberation theologians maintain a hermeneutics of engagement instead of a hermeneutics of detachment. Since no complete detachment or value-neutrality is possible, the interpreter must make her/his stance explicit and take an advocacy position in favor of the oppressed. To truly understand the Bible is to read it through the eyes of the oppressed, since the God who speaks in the Bible is the God of the oppressed. For a correct interpretation of the Bible, it is necessary to acknowledge the "hermeneutical privilege of the oppressed" and to develop a hermeneutics "from below."

Since theology is explicitly or implicitly intertwined with the existing social situation, according to Segundo the hermeneutic circle must begin with an experience or analysis of the social reality that leads to suspicion about our real situation. In a second step we apply our ideological suspicion to theology and to all other ideological superstructures. At a third level we experience theological reality in a different way, which in turn leads us to the suspicion that "the prevailing interpretation of the Bible has not taken important pieces of data into account."[28] At a last stage we bring these insights to bear upon the interpretation of Scripture. However, only active commitment to the oppressed and active involvement in their struggle for liberation enable us to see our society and our world differently, and give us a new perspective for looking at the world. This perspective is also taught in the New Testament if the latter is interpreted correctly.

Segundo acknowledges that James Cone has elaborated such a liberation theological interpretation for the black community. He admits his indebtedness to Bultmann, but he reformulates the hermeneutic circle to include action:

> And the circular nature of this interpretation stems from the fact that each new reality obliges us to interpret the word of God afresh, to

change reality accordingly, and then go back and reinterpret the Word
of God again and so on. [emphasis mine][29]

It is apparent that Segundo cannot be accused of rationalizing a previously
taken position. He does not operate within the interpretative tradition of the
doctrinal paradigm. He also clearly distinguishes his own theological interpretation from that of academic historical-critical scholarship by rejecting
the biblical revelation-contemporary application model. According to him
biblical interpretation must reconstruct the second-level learning process of
biblical faith. Faith is identical with the total process of learning in and
through ideologies, whereas the faith responses vis-à-vis certain historical
situations are ideologies. Therefore, faith should not be defined as content or
depositum fidei, but as an educational process throughout biblical and Christian history. Faith expresses the continuity and permanency of divine revelation, whereas ideologies document the historical character of faith and revelation. "Faith then is a liberative process. It is converted into freedom for
history, which means freedom *for ideologies*."[30] It is obvious that Segundo
does not understand ideology as "false" consciousness, but as historical-
societal expression.

According to him, Christian faith is also not to be defined as content,
doctrine, or principle, but as an educational process to which we willingly
entrust ourselves. "In the case of . . . the Bible we learn to learn by entrusting
our life and its meaning to the historical process that is reflected in the expressions embodied in that particular tradition."[31] It is thus clear that Segundo
does not work within the overall approach of either the doctrinal or historical
value-free paradigms, but proposes an interpretative model within the
hermeneutic-contextual paradigm. He shares with neo-orthodoxy the hermeneutical presupposition that Scriptural traditions are meaningful, and that
they can therefore claim our obedience and demand a "hermeneutics of consent." In distinction from neo-orthodox theology, Segundo does not claim
that it is the content of Scripture that is reflected in the Bible as meaningful
and liberative. It is, rather, in the process of learning how to learn that meaning and liberation are seen.

However, this assumption does not take into account the fact that not only
the content of Scripture, but also this second-level learning process can be
distorted. Segundo must, therefore, either demonstrate that this is not the
case, or formalize this learning process to such a degree that the "advocacy"
becomes an abstract principle not applicable to the contents of the Bible. In
other words, Segundo's model does not allow for a critical theological evaluation of biblical ideologies as "false consciousness." One must question
whether historical content and hermeneutic learning can be separated. Such a
proposal also does not allow us to judge whether a text or interpretation is
appropriate and helpful to the struggle of the oppressed for liberation. The
failure to bring a critical evaluation to bear upon the biblical texts and upon
the process of interpretation within Scripture and tradition is one of the reasons why the use of the Bible by liberation theologians often comes close to

"proof texting." To avoid such an impression liberation hermeneutics must reflect on the fact that the process of interpretation of Scripture is not necessarily liberative.

The Hermeneutics of the Woman's Bible

While liberation theologians affirm the Bible as a weapon in the struggle of liberation, and they claim that the God of the Bible is a God of the oppressed, feminist writers since the inauguration of the women's movement in the last century have maintained, to the contrary, that the Bible and Christian theology are inherently sexist, and thereby destructive of women's consciousness. A revisionist interpretation of Scripture and theology, therefore, will either subvert women's struggle for liberation from all sexist oppression and violence, or it will be forced to re-interpret Christian tradition and theology in such a way that nothing "Christian" will remain.

Feminist theology as a critical theology of liberation must defend itself against two sides: While liberation theologians are reluctant to acknowledge that women are exploited and oppressed, radical feminist thinkers claim that feminist consciousness and Christian faith are contradictions in terms. When our daughter Christina was born we announced her baptism with the following statement:

> She is born into a world of oppression
> She is born into a society of discrimination
> She is re-born into a church of inequality. . . .

The reaction of our friends to this announcement illustrates these objections to Christian feminist theology. Some colleagues and students in theology shook their heads and asked whether we had planned a Marxist initiation rite. Or in indignation they pointed to the privileged status of a girl born to middle-class professional parents. However, a very bright college student (who felt suffocated by the patriarchal environment of Notre Dame and was later hospitalized with a nervous breakdown) challenged me on the street saying: How can you do this to her? She will never be able to be a consciousness-raised woman and a committed Christian. Christian faith and the Church are destructive of women-persons who struggle against sexism and for liberation.

The question which feminist theologians must face squarely is thus a foundational theological problem: Is being a woman and being a Christian a primary contradiction which must be resolved in favor of one to the exclusion of the other? Or can both be kept in creative tension so that my being a Christian supports my struggle for liberation as a woman, while my being a feminist enhances and deepens my commitment to live as a Christian.[32] Insofar as feminist theology as a Christian theology is bound to its charter documents in Scripture, it must formulate this problem also with reference to the Bible and biblical revelation. Since the Bible was and is used against women's demand for equality and liberation from societal, cultural, and ecclesial sexism, it must conceive of this task first in critical terms before it can attempt to formulate a hermeneutics of liberation. While the danger of liberation theology is "proof texting," the pitfall to be avoided by feminist theology is apologetics, since such an apologetics does not take the political implications of Scriptural interpretation seriously.

The debate surrounding the *Woman's Bible*,[33] which appeared in 1895 and 1898, may serve here as a case-study for the *political* conditions and implications of feminist biblical interpretation as well as for the radical critical impact of feminist theology for the interpretative task. In her introduction to the *Woman's Bible* Elizabeth Cady Stanton, the initiator of the project, outlined two critical insights for a feminist theological hermeneutics. The Bible is not a "neutral" book, but it is a political weapon against women's struggle for liberation. This is so because the Bible bears the imprint of men who never saw or talked with God.

First: Elizabeth Cady Stanton conceived of biblical interpretation as a political act. The following episode characterizes her own personal conviction of the negative impact of Christian religion on women's situation. She refused to attend a prayer meeting of suffragists that was opened by the singing of the hymn "Guide Us, O Thou Great Jehovah" by Isabella Beecher Hooker. Her reason was that Jehovah had "never taken any active part in the suffrage movement."[34] Because of her experience that Yahweh was not on the side of the oppressed, she realized the great political influence of the Bible. She, therefore, proposed to prepare a revision of the Bible which would collect and interpret (with the help of "higher criticism") all statements referring to women in the Bible. She conceded, however, that she was not very successful in soliciting the help of women scholars because they were

> afraid that their high reputation and scholarly attainments might be compromised by taking part in an enterprise that for a time may prove very unpopular. Hence we may not be able to get help from that class.[35]

And indeed, the project of the *Woman's Bible* proved to be very unpopular because of political implications. Not only did some of the suffragists argue that such a project was either not necessary, or politically unwise, but the National American Woman's Suffrage Association formally rejected it as a political mistake. In the second volume, which appeared in 1898, Cady Stanton sums up this opposition: "Both friend and foe object to the title" and then replies with biting wit to the accusation of a clergyman that the *Woman's Bible* is "the work of women and the devil":

> This is a grave mistake. His Satanic Majesty was not to join the Revising Committee which consists of women alone. Moreover, he has been so busy of late years attending Synods, General Assemblies and Con-

ferences, to prevent the recognition of women delegates, that he has no time to study the languages and "higher criticism."[36]

Although the methods and theological presuppositions of the "higher criticism" of the time are rather outdated today, the political arguments and objectives of a feminist biblical interpretation remain valid. They are outlined by Cady Stanton in her introduction to the first volume. She gives three reasons why such an objective scientific feminist revision and interpretation of the Bible is politically necessary:

1. Throughout history and especially today the Bible is used to keep women in subjection and to hinder their emancipation.

2. Not only men, but especially women are the most faithful believers in the Bible as the Word of God. Not only for men, but also for women the Bible has a numinous authority.

3. No reform is possible in one area of society if it is not advanced also in all other areas. One cannot reform the law and other cultural institutions without also reforming biblical religion which claims the Bible as Holy Scripture. Since "all reforms are interdependent," a critical feminist interpretation is a necessary political endeavor, though perhaps not opportune. If feminists think they can neglect the revision of the Bible because there are more pressing political issues, then they do not recognize the political impact of Scripture upon the churches and society, and also upon the lives of women.

Second: Elizabeth Cady Stanton advocated such a revision of the Bible in terms of "higher criticism." Her insights, therefore, correspond with the results of historical biblical studies of her time. Over and against the doctrinal understanding of the Bible as Word of God, she stresses that the Bible is written by men and reflects patriarchal male interests. "The only point in which I differ from all ecclesiastical teaching is that I do not believe that any man ever saw or talked with God."[37] While the churches teach that such degrading ideas about patriarchal injunctions against women come from God, Cady Stanton maintains that all these degrading texts and ideas emanated from the heads of men. By treating the Bible as a human work and not as a magic fetish, and by denying divine inspiration to the negative biblical statements about women, she claims that her committee has shown more reverence and respect for God than does the clergy or the Church. She concedes that some teachings of the Bible, such as the love-command or the golden rule, are still valid today. Since the teachings and lessons of the Bible differ from each other, the Bible cannot be accepted or rejected as a whole. Therefore, every passage on women must be carefully analyzed and evaluated for its impact on the struggle for the liberation of women.

In conclusion: Although the idea of a *Woman's Bible* consisting only of the biblical texts on women must be rejected today on methodological grounds,[38] biblical scholarship on the whole has proven accurate her contention that the Bible must be studied as a human work, and that biblical interpretation is influenced by the theological mindset and interests of the interpreter. Contemporary feminist interpreters, like some of Cady Stanton's suffragist friends, either reject biblical interpretation as a hopeless feminist endeavor because the Bible is totally sexist, or they attempt to defend the Bible in the face of its radical feminist critics. In doing so they follow Frances Willard, who argued against the radical critique of the *Woman's Bible* that not the biblical message, but only its patriarchal contemporary interpretation preaches the subjugation of women.

> I think that men have read their own selfish theories into the book, that theologians have not in the past sufficiently recognized the progressive quality of its revelation nor adequately discriminated between its records as history and its principles of ethics and religion.[39]

The insight that scholarly biblical interpretations need to be "depatriarchalized" is an important one. However, this critical insight should not be misunderstood as an apologetic defense of the nonpatriarchal character of the Bible's teachings on ethics and religion. It was exactly Elizabeth Cady Stanton's critical insight that the Bible is not just misunderstood, but that its contents and perspectives can be used in the political struggle against women. What Gustavo Gutiérrez says about human historiography in general must also be applied to the writing of the Bible:

> Human history has been written by a white hand, a male hand from the dominating social class. The perspective of the defeated in history is different. Attempts have been made to wipe from their minds the memory of their struggles. This is to deprive them of a source of energy, of an historical will to rebellion.[40]

If we compare Cady Stanton's hermeneutical stance with that of Segundo then we see that she could not accept his understanding of a liberative second-level learning process within Christian history exactly because she shares his "advocacy stance for the oppressed." Cady Stanton cannot begin with the affirmation that the Bible and the God of the Bible are on the side of the oppressed because her experience of the Bible's use as a political weapon against women's struggle for suffrage tells her otherwise.

The subsequent reaction to the *Woman's Bible* also warns liberation theologians that a biblical interpretation that resorts too quickly to the defense of the Bible could misconstrue its advocacy stance for the oppressed. The task of liberation theologians is not to prove that the Bible or the Church can be defended against feminist or socialist attacks. Only when we critically comprehend how the Bible functions in the oppression of women or the poor can we prevent its misuse for further oppression. Otherwise, liberation theology is in danger of succumbing to proof-texting. The advocacy stance of liberation theology can only be construed as a rationalization of preconceived ecclesial or dogmatic positions if it does not fully explore the oppressive aspects of biblical traditions. Because of their advocacy stance for the oppressed, feminist theologians must insist that theological-critical analysis of Christian tradition should not only begin with the time of Constantine, but it also must apply itself to the Christian charter documents themselves.

Because of its allegiance to the "defeated in history," a feminist critical theology maintains that a "hermeneutics of consent" which understands itself as the "actualizing continuation of the Christian history of interpretation" does not suffice. Such a hermeneutics overlooks the fact that Christian Scripture and tradition are not only a source of truth, but also of untruth, repression, and domination. Since the hermeneutic–contextual paradigm seeks only to *understand* biblical texts, it cannot adequately take into account the fact that the Christian past, as well as its interpretations, has victimized women. A critical theology of liberation,[41] therefore, must work out a new interpretative paradigm that can take seriously the claim of liberation theologians that God is on the side of the oppressed. Such a paradigm must also accept the claim of feminist theologians that God has never "taken an active part in the suffrage movement," and that therefore the Bible can function as a male weapon in the political struggle against women's liberation.

Toward a Feminist Interpretive Paradigm
of Emancipatory Praxis[42]

A critical theology of liberation cannot avoid raising the question of the truth-content of the Bible for Christians today. If, for instance, feminist theologians take fully into account the androcentric language, misogynist contents, and patriarchal interests of biblical texts, then we cannot avoid the question of the "canon," or the criterion that allows us to reject oppressive traditions and to detect liberative traditions within biblical texts and history.

First: Such a need for a critical evaluation of the various biblical texts and traditions has always been recognized in the Church. While the doctrinal paradigm insisted that Scripture must be judged by the *regula fidei*, and can only be properly interpreted by the teaching office of the Church, the historical-critical paradigm evaluated the theological truth of biblical texts according to their historicity. The hermeneutic-contextual paradigm has not only established the canon as the pluriform root-model of the Christian community, but it has also underlined the fact that the Bible often includes various contradictory responses to the historical situation of the Israelite or Christian community.

Since not all these responses can equally express Christian revelation, biblical scholarship has attempted to formulate theological criteria to evaluate different biblical traditions. Such a "canon within the canon" can be formulated along philosophical-dogmatic or historical-factual lines. Some theologians distinguish between revelatory essence and historical expression, timeless truth and culturally conditioned language, or constant Christian tradition and changing traditions. When such a canon is formulated along the lines of the hermeneutic–contextual paradigm, scholars juxtapose Jesus and Paul, Pauline theology and early Catholicism, the historical Jesus and the kerygmatic Christ, or Hebrew and Greek thought. Whereas, e.g., Ogden accepts as such a canon the Jesus-traditions of Marxsen,[43] Sobrino emphasizes the Jesus of history as the criterion for liberation theology. Segundo, on the other hand, is methodologically most consistent when he insists that no contentual biblical statement can be singled out as such a criterion because all historical expression of faith is ideological. In line with the hermeneutic-contextual paradigm, he insists that not the content but the process of interpretation within the Bible and Christian history should be normative for liberation theology. Yet such a proposal does not allow for the insight that this process of expressing faith in a historical situation can also be falsified and serve oppressive interests.

Therefore, a critical theology of liberation cannot take the Bible or the biblical faith defined as the total process of learning in and through ideologies as *norma normans non normata*,[44] but must understand them as sources alongside other sources. This point was already made by James Cone, who pointed out that the sources of theology are the Bible as well as our own political situation and experience. However, the norm for black theology is *"Jesus as the Black Christ who provides the necessary soul for black liberation."* ". . . he is the essence of the Christian gospel."[45]

I would be hesitant to postulate that Jesus as the feminist Christ is the canonical norm since we cannot spell out concretely who this feminist Christ is if we do not want to make Christ a formalized *chiffre* or resort to mysticism. This is the argument of Jon Sobrino, who in turn postulates that the historical Jesus is the norm of truth since *"access to the Christ of faith comes through our following of the historical Jesus."*[46] However, such a formulation of the canonical norm for Christian faith presupposes that we can know the historical Jesus and that we can imitate him, since an actual following of Jesus is not possible for us. Moreover, a feminist theologian must question whether the historical man Jesus of Nazareth can be a role model for contemporary women, since feminist psychological liberation means exactly the struggle of women to free themselves from all male internalized norms and models.

Second: I would suggest that the canon and norm for evaluating biblical traditions and their subsequent interpretations cannot be derived from the Bible or the biblical process of learning within and through ideologies, but can only be formulated within and through the struggle for the liberation of women and all oppressed people. It cannot be "universal," but it must be specific and derived from a particular experience of oppression and liberation. The "advocacy stance" of liberation theologies must be sustained at the point of the critical evaluation of biblical texts and traditions. The personally and politically reflected experience of oppression and liberation must become the criterion of "appropriateness" for biblical interpretation.

A hermeneutical understanding which is not only oriented toward an actualizing continuation of biblical history, but also toward a critical evaluation of it, must uncover and denounce biblical traditions and theologies that perpetuate violence, alienation, and oppression. At the same time, such a critical hermeneutics also must delineate those biblical traditions that bring forward the liberating experiences and visions of the people of God. Such a hermeneutics points to the eschatological vision of freedom and salvation, and maintains that such a vision must be historically realized in the community of faith.

A feminist theological interpretation of the Bible that has as its canon the liberation of women from oppressive sexist structures, institutions, and internalized values must, therefore, maintain that only the nonsexist and non-androcentric traditions of the Bible and the nonoppressive traditions of biblical interpretation have the theological authority of revelation if the Bible is not to continue as a tool for the oppression of women. The "advocacy stance" demands that oppressive and destructive biblical traditions cannot be accorded any truth and authority claim today.[47] Nor did they have such a claim at any point in history. Such a critical hermeneutic must be applied to *all* biblical texts and their historical contexts. It should also be applied to their subsequent history of interpretation in order to determine *how* much these traditions and interpretations have contributed to the patriarchal oppression of women. In the same vein, such a critical feminist hermeneutics must rediscover those biblical traditions and interpretations that have transcended their oppressive cultural contexts even though they are embedded in patriarchal culture. These texts and traditions should not be understood as abstract theological ideas or norms, but as faith-responses to concrete historical situations of oppression. For instance, throughout the centuries Christian feminism has claimed Galatians 3:28 as its magna charta, while the patriarchal Church has used 1 Corinthians 14 or 1 Timothy 2 for the cultural and ecclesial oppression of women.[48]

Third: The insight that the Bible is not only a source of truth and revelation, but also a source of violence and domination is basic for liberation theologies. This insight demands a new paradigm of biblical interpretation that does not understand the Bible as archtype, but as prototype.

> A dictionary definition reveals the significant distinction between the words. While both archtype and prototype "denote original models," an archtype is "usually construed as an ideal form that establishes an unchanging pattern. . . ." However, . . . a prototype is not a binding, timeless pattern, but one critically open to the possibility, even the necessity of its own transformation. Thinking in terms of prototypes historicizes myth.[49]

Since the hermeneutic–contextual paradigm has as a goal the appropriation of biblical truth and history, but not its ideological critique, liberation theologians must develop a new critical paradigm of biblical interpretation. T. S.

Kuhn has pointed out that such a new scientific paradigm must also create a new scientific ethos and community.

The hermeneutic-contextual historical paradigm allows for the "advocacy stance" within the hermeneutical circle as a presupposition from which to raise questions, but objects to it as a conviction or definite standpoint. However, a new critical paradigm must reject such a theory as ideological. It must, in turn, insist that all theologians and interpreters of the Bible stand publicly accountable for their own position. It should become methodologically *mandatory* that *all* scholars explicitly discuss their own presuppositions, allegiances, and functions within a theological-political context, and especially those scholars, who in critiques of liberation theology, resort to an artificially construed value-neutrality. Scholars no longer can pretend that what they do is completely "detached" from all political interests. Since we always interpret the Bible and Christian faith from a position within history, scholarly detachment and neutrality must be unmasked as a "fiction" or "false consciousness" that serves definite political interests. Further, theological interpretation must also critically reflect on the political presuppositions and implications of theological "classics" and dogmatic or ethical systems. In other words, not only the content and traditioning process within the Bible, but the whole of Christian tradition should be scrutinized and judged as to whether or not it functions to oppress or liberate people.

Finally, the "advocacy stance" as a criterion or norm for evaluating biblical texts and their political functions should not be mistaken as an abstract, formalized principle. The different forms of a critical theology of liberation must construct specific heuristic models that adequately analyze the mechanisms and structures of contemporary oppression and movements for liberation. On the one hand, too generalized an understanding of oppression and liberation serves the interests of the oppressive systems which cannot tolerate a critical analysis of their dehumanizing mechanisms and structures. At the same time, it prevents the formulation of very specific goals and strategies for the liberation struggle. On the other hand, too particularized an understanding of oppression and liberation prevents an active solidarity among oppressed groups, who can be played out against each other by the established systems. The "advocacy stance" as the criterion or norm for biblical interpretation must, therefore, develop a critical theology of liberation that promotes the solidarity of all oppressed peoples, and at the same time has room enough to develop specific heuristic theological models of oppression and liberation.[50]

In conclusion: Liberation theologians must abandon the hermeneutic-contextual paradigm of biblical interpretation, and construct within the context of a critical theology of liberation, a new interpretative paradigm that has as its aim emancipatory praxis. Such a paradigm of political praxis has, as a research perspective, the critical relationship between theory and practice, between biblical texts and contemporary liberation-movements. This new paradigm of emancipatory praxis must generate new heuristic models of interpretation that can interpret and evaluate biblical traditions and their political function in history in terms of their own canons of liberation.

Notes

1. See Adrienne Rich, "Toward a Woman-Centered University," in *Women and the Power to Change,* ed. Florence Howe (New York: McGraw-Hill), pp. 15–46; and my analysis in "Towards a Liberating and Liberated Theology: Women Theologians and Feminist Theology in the U.S.A.," Concilium 115 (1979) 22–32.

2. See e.g., Lisa Leghorn and M. Roodkowsky, *Who Really Starves? Women and World Hunger* (New York: Friendship Press, 1977); Diane E. Nichole Russel and N. Van de Ven, eds., *Crimes against Women: Processings of the International Tribunal* (Millbrae, Calif.: Les Femmes, 1976); Susan Hill Lindley, "Feminist Theology in a Global Perspective," *The Christian Century,* 96 (April 25, 1979): 465–469.

3. See, for instance, Gustavo Gutiérrez, *A Theology of Liberation* (Maryknoll, N.Y.: Orbis Books, 1973), pp. 204–205: "A spirituality of liberation will center on a *conversion* to the neighbor, the oppressed person, the exploited social class, the despised race, the dominated country. Our conversion to the Lord implies this conversion to the neighbor." Compare the description of feminist conversion by Judith Plaskow, *Sex, Sin, and Grace: Women's Experience and the Theologies of Reinhold Niebuhr and Paul Tillich* (Washington, D.C.: University Press of America, 1980), pp. 171–172: "The woman who, having seen the non-being of social structures, feels herself a whole person, is called upon to become the person she is in that movement. . . . The experience of grace is not the experience of the sole activity of God, but the experience of the emergence of the 'I' as co-creator. . . . Relatedness to God is expressed through the never-ending journey toward self-creation within community, and through the creation of ever wider communities, including both other human beings and the world."

4. Robert McAfee Brown, *Theology in a New Key: Responding to Liberation Themes* (Philadelphia: Westminster, 1978), p. 82.

5. Vine Deloria, "A Native American Perspective on Liberation," in *Mission Trends No. 4: Liberation Theologies,* ed. Gerald H. Anderson and Thomas F. Stransky (New York: Paulist Press, 1979), pp. 261–270.

6. See my article, "Women in Early Christianity: Methodological Considerations," in *Critical History and Biblical Faith in New Testament Perspectives,* ed. T. J. Ryan (Villanova, Pa.: Catholic Theology Society Annual Publications, 1979), pp. 30–58.

7. See my article, "For the Sake of Our Salvation . . . Biblical Interpretation as Theological Task," in *Sin, Salvation, and the Spirit,* ed. Daniel Durken (Collegeville, Minn.: Liturgical Press, 1979), pp. 21–39, for a more extensive discussion of the literature.

8. See Lee Cormie, "The Hermeneutical Privilege of the Oppressed: Liberation Theologies, Biblical Faith, and Marxist Sociology of Knowledge," *Proceedings of the Catholic Theological Society of America* 32 (1977); D. Lockhead, "Hermeneutics and Ideology," *The Ecumenist* 15 (1977): 81–84.

9. Schubert M. Ogden, *Faith and Freedom: Toward a Theology of Liberation* (Nashville: Abingdon, 1979), p. 116.

10. Ibid., p. 32.

11. James H. Cone, *God of the Oppressed* (New York: Seabury, 1975), pp. 51–52.

12. See Charles H. Strain, "Ideology and Alienation: Theses on the Interpretation and Evaluation of Theologies of Liberation," *Journal of the American Academy of Religion* (hereafter *JAAR*) 45 (1977): 474.

13. See Thomas S. Kuhn, *The Structure of Scientific Revolutions* (Chicago: University of Chicago Press, 1962); Ian G. Barbour, *Myth, Models, and Paradigms* (New York: Harper & Row, 1974).

14. See my article, "For the Sake of Our Salvation . . ." for the development of these paradigms. See also for the general paradigm-shift in biblical studies, Walter Wink, *The Bible in*

Human Transformation: Toward a New Paradigm for Biblical Studies (Philadelphia: Fortress, 1973).

15. See, e.g., G. Sauter, " 'Exodus' und 'Befreiung' als theologische Metaphern: Ein Beispiel zur Kritik von Allegorese und missverstandenen Analogien in der Ethik," *EvTh* 38 (1978): 538–559, although one suspects that his criticism leads to a totally depoliticized interpretation.

16. James Barr, *Fundamentalism* (Philadelphia: Westminster, 1978), p. 49.

17. José Miranda, *Marx and the Bible* (Maryknoll, N.Y.: Orbis Books, 1974). See the discussion by J. A. Kirk, "The Bible in Latin American Liberation Theology," in *The Bible and Liberation*, ed. Norman K. Gottwald and Antoinette C. Wire (Berkeley: Radical Religion, 1976), p. 161.

18. See Norman Perrin, *What is Redaction Criticism?* (Philadelphia: Fortress, 1969): Werner G. Kümmel, *Das Neue Testament im 20 Jahrhundert* (Stuttgart: KBW, 1970).

19. See especially Norman K. Gottwald, *The Tribes of Yahweh: A Sociology of the Religion of Liberated Israel, 1250–1050 B.C.E.* (Maryknoll, N.Y.: Orbis Books, 1979).

20. See, e.g., Leander E. Keck, "On the Ethos of Early Christians," *JAAR* 42 (1974): 435–452; John C. Gager, *Kingdom and Community* (Englewood Cliffs, N.J.: Prentice-Hall, 1975); Gerd Theissen, *Sociology of Early Palestinian Christianity* (Philadelphia: Fortress, 1978); Wayne A. Meeks, "The Social World of Early Christianity," *CRS Bulletin* 6 (1975): 1, 4 f.; Willy Schottroff und Wolfgang Stegemann, *Der Gott der kleinen Leute: Sozialgeschichtliche Auslegungen: BD. 2 NT* (Munich: Kaiser, 1979).

21. See my article, "Word, Spirit, and Power: Women in Early Christian Communities," in *Women of Spirit*, ed. Rosemary Radford Ruether and Eleanor McLaughlin (New York: Simon and Schuster, 1979), pp. 29–70; David Balch, *"Let Wives Be Submissive . . ."* (Ann Arbor: University Microfilms International, 1978).

22. See Gerd Theissen, "Synoptische Wundergeschichten im Lichte unseres Sprachverhältnisses," *Wissenschaft und Praxis in Kirche und Gesellschaft* 65 (1976): 289–308; for the interrelation between poverty, violence, and exploitation, cf. Luise Schottroff und Wolfgang Stegemann, *Jesus von Nazareth: Hoffnung der Armen* (Stuttgart: Kohlhammer, 1978).

23. See T. Peters, "The Nature and Role of Presupposition: An Inquiry into Contemporary Hermeneutics," *International Philosophical Quarterly* 14 (1974): 209–222; Frederick Herzog, "Liberation Hermeneutic as Ideology Critique," *Interpretation* 27 (1974): 387–403.

24. Edward Schillebeeckx, *The Understanding of Faith* (New York: Seabury, 1974), p. 130.

25. See especially Peter Stuhlmacher, *Historical Criticism and Theological Interpretation of Scripture: Toward a Hermeneutics of Consent* (Philadelphia: Fortress, 1977), pp. 83 ff.

26. For these criteria, see Ogden, *Faith and Freedom*, p. 26, and especially David Tracy, *Blessed Rage for Order: The New Pluralism in Theology* (New York: Seabury, 1975), pp. 72–79.

27. This whole section is based on an analysis of Juan Luis Segundo, *The Liberation of Theology* (Maryknoll, N.Y.: Orbis Books, 1976).

28. Ibid., p. 9; see also José Míguez Bonino, *Doing Theology in a Revolutionary Situation* (Philadelphia: Fortress, 1975), pp. 86–105, who accepts Professor Casalis' reformulation of the "hermeneutical circle" as "hermeneutical circulation" (p. 102).

29. Segundo, *The Liberation of Theology*, p. 8.

30. Ibid., p. 110.

31. Ibid., p. 179.

32. See my article, "Feminist Spirituality, Christian Identity and the Catholic Vision," in *Womanspirit Rising: A Feminist Reader in Religion*, ed. Carol P. Christ and Judith Plaskow (New York: Harper & Row, 1979), pp. 136–148.

33. Elizabeth Cady Stanton, *The Woman's Bible*, American Women Series: Images and Realities, 2 vol. in 1; reprint of 1895 ed. (New York: Arno).

34. Barbara Welter, "Something Remains to Dare: Introduction to the Woman's Bible," in *The Original Feminist Attack on the Bible (The Woman's Bible)*, by E. Cady Stanton, facsimile ed. (New York: Arno, 1974), p. xxii.

35. Cady Stanton, *The Woman's Bible*, I:9.

36. Ibid., II:7 f.

37. Ibid., I:12.

38. See, however, Marie Fortune and Joann Haugerud, *Study Guide to the Woman's Bible* (Seattle: Coalition Task Force on Women and Religion, 1975) for a contemporary application; and Leonard Swidler, *Biblical Affirmations of Woman* (Philadelphia: Westminster, 1979), who basically follows the same principle.

39. Cited in Cady Stanton, *The Woman's Bible*, II:200.

40. Gustavo Gutiérrez, "Where Hunger Is, God Is Not," *The Witness* 59 (April 1976): 6.

41. For the conceptualization of feminist theology as such a critical theology of liberation, see my article, "Feminist Theology as a Critical Theology of Liberation," in *Woman: New Dimensions*, ed. Walter Burkhardt (New York: Paulist Press, 1977), pp. 19-50.

42. See the pathbreaking article of Francis Schüssler Fiorenza, "Critical Social Theology and Christology: Toward an Understanding of Atonement and Redemption as Emancipatory Solidarity," *Proceedings of the Catholic Theological Society of America* 30 (1975): 63-110.

43. Ogden, *Faith and Freedom*, pp. 44ff., and his article, "The Authority of Scripture for Theology" *Interpretation* 30 (1976): 242-261.

44. For this expression, see David Tracy, "Theological Classics in Contemporary Theology," *Theology Digest* 25 (1977): 347-355.

45. James H. Cone, *Liberation: A Black Theology of Liberation* (Philadelphia: Lippincott, 1970), p. 80.

46. Jon Sobrino, "The Historical Jesus and the Christ of Faith," *Cross Currents* 27 (1977/78): 437-463, 460.

47. Such a proposal should not be misunderstood in the sense of the *Woman's Bible* approach that has singled out for discussion biblical texts on women. The criterion has to be applied to all Biblical texts insofar as they claim authority for today. Such a theological evaluation must also be distinguished from a reconstruction of early Christian history in a feminist perspective. While a feminist reconstruction of early Christian history asks for women's history and heritage, a feminist biblical hermeneutics evaluates the truth-claims of biblical texts for today. Thus both approaches are interdependent but quite distinct.

48. See my analysis in "Word, Spirit, and Power," in *Women of Spirit*.

49. Rachel Blau DuPlessis, "The Critique of Consciousness and Myth in Levertov, Rich, and Rukeyser," *Feminist Studies* 3 (1975): 199-221, 219.

50. Rosemary Radford Ruether, *New Woman/New Earth: Sexist Ideologies and Human Liberation* (New York: Seabury, 1975), pp. 115-132, has called for an "interstructuring" of various models of alienation/liberation.

6

The Political Dimensions of Theology[1]

Langdon Gilkey

Langdon Gilkey agrees with liberation theologians who say that Christianity is called upon to stand with the oppressed in radical opposition to the established order. He also maintains that God's redemptive activity in history is manifest in the sacral character of social structure itself—in the construction and maintenance of the social myths which make social life possible. But our inability or unwillingness to perceive the religious dimension of social organization empowers alienated human consciousness to impose its warped and self-interested interpretations upon the symbols which organize collective life. Since it is for the most part members of the privileged classes who define the contours and character of social interaction, theirs also is the responsibility for limiting the possibilities for self-actualization and social creativity of the disenfranchised. These oppressed experience themselves as fated to a life without hope. Yet, the symbol of the Kingdom calls Christians to affirm the possibility of new life in the face of the void, and to conform themselves to the more ultimate norms which stand in judgment over the oppressive social order.

In the context of the original conference, Gilkey responded to Lee Cormie's paper. The following article which was originally presented as Gilkey's inaugural lecture as the Shailer Mathews Professor in the Divinity School of the University of Chicago represents a fuller exposition of his thoughts. It is reprinted here in a slightly edited form from Langdon Gilkey, "The Political Dimensions of Theology," Journal of Religion *59 (April 1979): 154–68, by permission of The University of Chicago Press. Gilkey is the author of numerous books, including* Message and Existence: An Introduction to Christian Theology *(New York: Seabury, 1979), and* Reaping the Whirlwind: A Christian Interpretation of History *(New York: Seabury, 1977).*

I

If one concentrates on basic motifs rather than on trendy theological language, there seems to be a deep split between an individual and a social interpretation of the Christian religion—between, on the one hand, a committed, personal, existential concentration on inward sin, grace, and reconciliation issuing in a new individual relation to God and, on the other hand, an earnest, courageous concentration on the outer, the social and the political, on liberation within the customs and institutions of outward life and the impersonal relations of society, issuing in a new, objective social order in the historical future.

The deepest substantive question of current theology is, I believe, the mediation of this false opposition, an opposition untrue both to Scripture and to an adequate theological interpretation of history and of human destiny. The overcoming of this split is also crucial for our common social being. It is important that the religious and moral forces, such as they are, of our communities become creatively integrated into our common political life, not only so that Christianity may be an inspiring and shaping factor in social reform and reconstruction, but also so that it may help mitigate those grimmer but real possibilities of our participation in social oppression and social disintegration that lie in our future.

My argument will be that as individual and social cannot be separated in ordinary, secular life, neither can they be separated in religious existence. The central elements of religious existence—our sin, our faith, and our obedience—are as constitutive of a social situation or a social history as they are of a personal, individual situation or history. Consequently the major symbols of Christian faith relevant to life in time—God and his action; human nature and its remaking; sin, grace, and Kingdom—unite rather than separate the individual and the social, the personal and the historical. I think readers, if they should seek to label these remarks theologically, will find this viewpoint a totally confusing mixture of neo-orthodox and liberal emphases. I was asked two weeks ago if I was a "revisionist theologian." I answered that, of course, I was; everytime I read something I have previously written, I say to myself, "God, that needs to be revised!"

I shall begin, if Karl Barth will forgive me, with some anthropological reflections on my theme, though I might as well have begun with my next point, the interpretation of the same themes in the Hebrew Scriptures. If we look at human social existence through the eyes of the most perceptive social scientists, we see two points emphasized that I shall presuppose and illustrate rather than demonstrate in my remarks. The first is the interdependence of the individual with her or his social community. It is out of the community, its ways, language, norms, roles, and viewpoints on the world that each individual arises, becomes a self, and becomes fulfilled. And it is in the community—some community of common interests and aims—that the individual's creative role in life is played out and to which her or his work contributes. Part of our historicity is that we are, and that we are individual selves, however unique that individuality may be, in social community and thus in history. Individual and community dance together down the corridor of time, and so together they exist *coram Deo*, ("in the presence of God"). Taken for granted in ancient cultures (Chinese, Hellenic, Hebrew, Japanese), the truth of this interpretation of individual and community is now a major theme, if not a belated discovery, of any contemporary social science.

The second anthropological-sociological premise of my view is that the social matrix within which we arise and have our human being has a religious dimension; as Tillich liked to say, a "religious substance," or, as I put it a moment ago, subsists, like its individual components, *coram Deo*. Social existence involves and depends on a shared consciousness, a shared system of meanings. This shared system of meanings is structured by symbols that shape or express for that group its understanding of reality; of space and time; of human being and its authenticity; of life and its goods; of appropriate relations, roles, customs, and behavior. These symbols together constitute the unique *gestalt,* the identity or uniqueness, of that social group. To be a member of any community is to be aware of, more, to participate in and to be oneself shaped, energized, and directed by this common symbolic mythos. It is, as Hegel said, to share inwardly the *Geist* of the community, its religious substance.

The "religious" character or quality of this shared mythos constitutive of a community's being can be seen from a multitude of perspectives. An example is the commonly recognized fact that the group (for example, the nation in our day) evokes with ease religious emotions of devotion, commitment, loyalty, self-sacrifice, and that, under pressure, it quickly becomes our "ultimate concern." This religious quality of social bodies is one of the puzzling "facts" about human social existence recognized widely in social science; it requires, I believe, a theological interpretation to be made intelligible.

The security of a community—perhaps the most ultimate of its ultimate concerns—is continually rendered questionable by the passage of time. That is to say, the status of a group is continually shaken by the contingency of its life and the openness, the uncontrollability, of its future. Consequently each group stands in each new moment under the threat of fate, of being unable to control its own course and to secure its own existence. The group, so to speak, must call on the gods or superhuman sacral powers to deal with the problem of its own contingency in time. Now, political existence is the point where the group unites itself in order to steer this course through time, to secure its existence, to defend itself against this threat of fate. Thus is the political life of any people characterized by ultimacy and by sacrality, by sacral rulers given their crucial role by the gods, by a divinely legitimated rule; and this rule will be considered legitimate only because it expresses, is in touch with, and is an agent of, the fundamental grain, pattern, or sovereignity of history. No king but was in the end divinely established; no ruler but sought and received the blessing of communal religion.

The eighteenth century saw clearly this essential relation of religion, privilege, and monarchy, and the nineteenth the relation of religion and society's oppressive superstructure. But both thought that it had been a conspiracy of organized religion, especially of Christianity, that had imported this religious dimension into a potentially secular and so innocent politics. The twentieth century has shown on the contrary that ideology, a religious interpretation of and allegiance to a community's social mythos, springs up inexorably in all politics, that the divine legitimation of rule and the sacral character of a way of life, whether it be a Marxist or a liberal, capitalist ideology, is as much a character of advanced contemporary societies as was the union of religion, myth, and kingship in a traditional society. Ironically, however, each of the twentieth century's religious/political myths claims to be "scientific"!

The same analysis showing the dimension of ultimacy and sacrality in social existence could be made of the *meanings* in a culture's life that generate and permeate activity in the world by its people and of the *norms* by which a people live. The social myths or ethos that make our common life possible have a religious dimension. This is the source of the community's creativity, courage, and confidence; it is also the ground of the demonic in historical life—of blind fanaticism, of infinite arrogance, of imperial ambition, of unlimited cruelty, and of ultimate violence. Even a "secular" analysis of social existence, therefore, uncovers a religious dimension in historical life. This dimension is as yet vague and undefined, the base alike of a community's creativity and of its demonic possibilities. In such an empirical uncovering the real source or referent of this religious dimension, its objective ontological root, is as yet undiscovered and undelineated. And surely any sort of resolution of its stark ambiguity of creativity and of the satanic is as yet unmanifest. All we know through social inquiry is that the religious dimension is very much there; that it is very important if not crucial for the life or being of the community; and that it is clearly the main source of history's capacity for suffering and for nemesis.

II

I will not argue that either Durkheim or Tillich (and surely not Peter Berger!) is to be found full-blown in the Hebrew Scriptures' view of society or of history. However, I do believe that there one does encounter an interpretation of history in terms of Yahweh's actions and purposes with his people that, so to speak, gives helpful clues to the ultimate ground for these empirical social facts I have just rehearsed, or better, that sets these evident facts into an intelligible theological, in this case ontological and anthropological, framework. In these Scriptures the central creative act of Yahweh, the ground and prototype for the later affirmation of his creation of the cosmos itself, was his creation in history of his people Israel. The main "story" of the initial books is the story of Yahweh's calling of his people and his promises to them; of his "mighty acts" (as we fondly used to call them) by which this people's identity and existence were established in and through certain historical events; and of his constitution of the structure of moral and customary behavior, the norms of the community, through the divine law.

Let us note, moreover, that not only is what sociologists would call the "symbolic structure of the community"—its "mythos" concerning the nature of reality, authentic human and social existence, and the norms required to realize that existence—given by Yahweh, but also its particular economic and political structures are regarded as his work. Both the Judges that in the beginning rescue, sustain, and guide the people, and then—though there were variant views and traditions here—the monarchical order of her later life were regarded as the work of Yahweh. In short, while they propound no social theory of community as possessing a religious dimension or substance, the Hebrew Scriptures regarded the community of Israel as divinely established or founded, and its norms of life, its structures of political rule, and its views of reality as aspects of the creative gift of Yahweh to his people in history. The frequently reviled view of Paul that "the powers that be are ordained of God" is not only intelligible sociology, it is also excellent exegesis. In the Hebrew Scriptures, social community, social mores and norms, and economic and political structures have a sacral foundation and a sacral status. They are essential as providing a dwelling place for humans in history; without them we can neither be nor be human.

In any case, it is clear that according to the Hebrew Scriptures Yahweh established by his creative historical activity not only a religious people or community, a kind of prototype of the Church; he also established a social community, a prototype of the worldly, the secular community; and that, as in modern sociology and anthropology, the two are intertwined and interdependent, the Hebrew religion existing within a social and historical abode and society having a religious center or substance. Surely there can be no doubt that the important later symbols of the New Covenant people, the messianic reign, and even the Kingdom itself repeat and develop, rather than abrogate, this union of the social and the religious, the historical and the ideal, which begins here in the original calling and establishment of the people of God. This interrelation and interdependence of the religious and the social, the individual and the communal—and the providential constitution of both— was re-expressed in classical, Hellenic form in Augustine's *De Civitate Dei,* and variously—and often unfortunately—in the subsequent concepts of Holy Christendom and in the Calvinistic views of the Holy Community. However, later, more "spiritual" (more individualistic and bourgeois?) periods took this union in the Hebrew Scriptures of the socio-historical with the religious as a "material" type of foretaste of the purely spiritual ecclesia and Kingdom of Christ—referred to in the New Testament—and the division between the religious and social we now seek to heal was carried forward.

III

The biblical basis for a religious interpretation of culture which I have just outlined, a view which sees the mythos and the political structures of community established by providence and thus as sacral, has hardly been a popular theme in recent biblical theology. It seems replete with all the wrong vibes: with a divine emperor; with Billy Graham for breakfast; with conservative politics and conservative, if not priestly, religion. As a consequence we think of valid religion, especially ethical religion, as primarily if not exclusively critical in its role in the social order. I would suggest that the Hebrew Scriptures are well aware of these dangers and speak frequently of them without denying our present point, namely the sacral character of social tradition, of law, of mores, and of kingship in Israel's life. After all, how can we understand theologically a retrieval of social symbols unless the latter have also arisen out of the divine providential activity? The point these critics forget is the dialectical character of the Hebrew and Christian understanding of history.

As we all know, in Genesis the good creation neither nullifies nor prevents the demonic misuse by men and women of the gifts of creation; nor does the horror of the fall or of a fallen history negate the reality of the good creation. In the same way, the historical creation through providence of the symbolic meanings and structures of culture does not nullify or prevent their subsequent misuse—nor does it in any way compromise the sharp prophetic critique of the immoral character of Israel's life. Sin enters Israel's life—even the life of the chosen people granted the divine law by grace—as it had once entered an enchanted Eden. In fact, as I have intimated, it was the historical experience of the providential creation of the covenant people in conjunction with their own human misuse of the divine covenant that probably lay back of the dialectic of creation and fall expressed in Genesis 1–3. Here a vivid historical and social experience *coram Deo* of divine creation and of human fall, in this case their own, is universalized into a story explanatory of the same dialectic in all of historical and social life.

In any case, Israel was vividly aware in its historical experience that the gifts of providence to it had been ignored, betrayed, warped, and disfigured; the satanic had appeared in history through it, and with it had come or was to come empirically an historical destruction, breakdown, and nemesis and, theologically, a divine rejection and judgment. This Old Testament theme of the rejection of the covenant and so the rejection of the covenant people is (except for its enactment by the Jews!) notable for its absence in *Christian* self-understanding both in relation to the *ecclesia* on the one hand and to Christendom and the Christian nations on the other. None of these Christian forms of the covenant idea, despite the clear historical evidence, seem ever to have thought that they too might have betrayed their own covenantal gifts!

I will not attempt to give a full account of the view of sin or estrangement in the Hebrew Scriptures. There can be little doubt, however, that this symbol expresses or points to Israel's experiences of its own history from beginning to end. There is hardly a moment in that history when Israel or its kings, despite their sacral gifts and status, are not doing "What is evil in the sight of Yahweh." Surely this is also our own American experience of our own history, replete as it is with vast gifts of nature, freedom, new opportunity, a "new covenant"—but also repeated ambiguity and betrayal. There are two aspects of the Old Testament view of evil which may be helpful to one interested in political theology or theological politics.

The first is what Gerhard von Rad calls the "early view" of evil and its consequences characteristic of the Old Testament. Here a sinful deed is regarded as having objective social consequences, consequences menacing and even fatal not only to the doer of the deed but also to other members of his or her group, to his or her children and the children's children. As you know, this view was regarded by liberal commentators, anxious to show that the mature Old Testament represented nothing but the highest of modern ideals, as itself immoral and therefore "primitive." It well may have been both immoral and primitive; but, unfortunately, it was also true. And in a strange way it represents a most profound and helpful understanding of the processes of social history. In trying to give this view a modern theological interpretation, we shall find another entry, so to speak, into the relation of theology to the political, another base for a gospel that is social.

As I have argued elsewhere, with the obvious help of notions from Kierkegaard, Whitehead, and Tillich, the most illuminating and accurate way to delineate our experience of historical passage is by means of the two fundamental categories of destiny and freedom. By destiny I refer, as did Kierkegaard and Tillich, to what is given to us from the past into our present: not only the world with all its other persons, powers, realities, and forces but also the self with all its own characteristics and powers, or lack of them. Freedom refers to the indubitable fact that while what is given to us is unremovable and unavoidable, what we do with it in the present and for the future remains in part open and up to us. While we must accept, appropriate, affirm, and work with both our own given self, however paltry, and the world about us, however discouraging, nevertheless there are open alternatives. In part we can and do actualize the self that is becoming through our own decisions and our action, and we can in part reshape the world of the next moment of passage. This experience of freedom to choose the self and reshape the world has in our culture been known and expressed by the upper and middle classes; it is still a matter of faith rather than of experience for the oppressed.

Now, deeply implied in Christian experience and symbolism is the affirmation that creation is good and that the continual process of the world is under the divine providence. In terms of the ontological structure of destiny and freedom just suggested, that means that essentially or in possibility each moment is characterized by this union of destiny and freedom that constitutes temporal finitude. That is to say, in essence and so in possibility each moment, in what is given to us and in our own capacities, represents creative opportunities for self-actualization and for enriched experience. This is, I take it, the only genuine meaning the affirmation of the goodness of the creation as historical could have: namely that any person at all (as well as all those of us in the upper middle class!) has a genuine and not a phony chance for realizing his or her own innate capacities and so actualizing possibilities. The radical political implications, uncomfortable as they may be, of such a theological affirmation are obvious.

Our main emphasis at the moment, however, is on Israel's experience of its own estrangement from this essential goodness, as well as, naturally, its experience of the estrangement of others. In its case this was an experience of estrangement in relation to the covenant and so to the explicit presence of Yahweh among them, an experience thematized in the symbols of the fall and of a fallen history. How, then, are we to understand in our own terms the Hebrew insight referred to earlier that each act of sin has objective consequences in the community?

In the whole biblical tradition, sin is regarded as an act of freedom, an inward, spiritual act, an estrangement of the inward, personal center of the self in its relation to God, to others, and to itself. Yet in historical passage what begins in inwardness does not remain there; our actions, gestated in inward freedom, have objective consequences in the world immediately to come. In actualizing our freedom in each moment, we reshape what follows. Thus do we miscreate as well as create; we warp as well as reshape the resulting self and its resulting world. Inward sin, in other words, qualifies, distorts, even obscures and overlays the destiny given the next historical moment, namely the self and the world that are given there and are bequeathed to those who follow us. In personal life this is evident. The self can, through its successive decisions and its accumulating habits, close off gradually and inexorably the creative possibilities for its own continuing future, for its "presents" to come.

In social existence this is even more objectively manifest. Human creativity helps to fashion or to reshape out of what is given to it the social, economic, and political institutions in which subsequent humans live and which, therefore, form the "given world" for others and for generations to come. It is an all too familiar experience how each generation inherits from its fathers and mothers a confused, warped world which it tends to detest and repudiate; and then to its horror and chagrin finds itself thirty years later bequeathing the same sort of mess, in different colors and shapes perhaps, to its own sons and daughters.

On an even deeper level, inward sin is objectively manifest in oppressive social forms. The continuing institutional structures of an entire epoch or culture: of class, property, and privilege; of social rank and authority; of political power and rule; of sexual domination—in short all the familiar forms of institutional injustice—is evidenced objectively in the inward estrangement of men and women from one another. What is evidenced is the turn to the self and for the self against the other, and so the drive to suppress and dominate the other, inward tendencies marvelously and horribly spread before us in the distorted, oppressive forms of these institutions. Sin does have its consequences in community, in the aggressive and imperial policies of each generation and in the warped, oppressive, suffocating institutions of each culture's historical life. This insight is not merely primitive; it is also true.

I would suggest that this fact of social inheritance of the objective consequences of sin—what Rauschenbush perceptively called the inherited Kingdom of Evil—points to a most important aspect of the human experience of a fallen history: the experience of being fated, of being subject to a blind and cruel fate, of an ineluctable power in historical passage that crushes and overwhelms our freedom and closes rather than opens new possibilities for the future. To come to be as the victim of oppressive, exploitative, unjust institutions (for example, slavery or segregation) is to experience the given in one's existence as void of possibility, as radically closed to the chance of creative self-actualization of self or creative reshaping of one's world. It is to be denied one's humanity, to be denied the good creation.

As freedom in historical passage "falls" into estrangement and sin, so created or essential destiny, the goodness of creation and of temporality, fall into fate or threaten to become fate. Thus, and here is the important point, is excluded in the next moment for all those so fated the appearance of genuine self-creative freedom, of real relations to others, of possibilities for the future, of the goodness of being human. In this way the inner reality of the bondage of our human freedom does not remain only inner. It is also manifest in the subsequent outward distortion of historical institutions, in part themselves the creatures of human creativity. Our inner self-concern results in a given for others that is characterized by the estrangement of fate. Social fatedness is thus neither arbitrary nor unintelligible in history—blind, uncaused, and inexplicable. Nor is it, as Marx thought, the cause of inner estrangement. Rather is it the inexorable consequence of estrangement. But fatedness, itself the effect of the sins of others, is the immediate source of untold suffering, of the denial of the human, of the distortion of the possibilities of historical life, of the loss of a future and therefore of hope. It is in the experience of being fated, of being a victim of historical sin and its consequences, as much as in that of being a perpetuator of sin, that evil is undergone, that the goodness of life and its possibilities are obscured, and that bitterness and despair emerge.

The historical situation of fatedness calls, therefore, dramatically—and here the Old Testament is also clear—for political liberation. This is not, let us note, a liberation from sin. But as we have shown, it is a liberation from the dire consequences of sin, from the fate which sin continually creates and recreates for others in and through objective social structures. Political action is directed against fate in this sense, against the continuation or the appearance in the future of a social and historical given that is crushing to self-actualization and to the creative shaping of the world. Creative political action seeks to transform fate or the threat of fate into destiny, into an institutional given in our social world that remains for all persons open to new possibilities and to our own actualization of those possibilities. As is evident, such social action is a direct requirement of any life of faith and of obedience, and also of a theological understanding of history. For the warping of our social world, its fatedness for others, is the direct result of sin and the most immediate cause of the suffering of the children of God.

To change or reshape a political or economic order is not to eradicate sin. The democratic and egalitarian movements of the eighteenth century had real effects but not that effect, as contemporary American life shows! But such change will reduce the scope and so the scourge of sin, and it will liberate sufferers from some of the consequences of sin. To take a current and "homey" example: a cleansed South Africa will, we may be sure, still be characterized by widespread selfishness. But because of institutional changes lives will be freer, more secure, more dignified, more in control of their own futures. Real possibilities for a more authentic humanity and authentic relationships, now closed by fate, will be there. Correspondingly, a University of Chicago divesting itself of economic interests in South Africa will not become an institution suddenly free of administrative or academic self-concern, jealousy, or infighting. But it will be a vastly liberated place, freer from its present onerous responsibility for the fatedness and suffering of others, and freer from bondage in its public statements to one of the weirdest ideologies ever perpetrated by the capitalistic establishment!

A second and related biblical theme about evil in history is what we may call the prophetic mistrust of power, the tipping of the balance in prophetic judgments against those who are mighty or who are considered wise, good, and righteous. This theme is also radically expressed in the weakness and suffering portrayed in the Servant Songs and in the Magnificat. As our preceding remarks have made clear, the problem of sin is universal, characteristic of the weak, the ignorant, the outcast as well as of the strong and the established; being fated does not, unfortunately, of itself necessarily result in an increase of virtue. We all, powerful and weak, male and female, actualize the given present to us in warped and self-destructive ways. This inward estrangement in those who are weak, however, has little effect except on themselves and on their own; it barely touches the wider world of others. On the other hand, the inward estrangement of those who are mighty in any regard both affects others directly because of the power of the mighty and also reshapes the given world of others. It is the powerful and the wise who are creative of and effective within the forms of social life and who are dominant in the continuance of those forms. And, as Marx noted, they shape those forms to serve their own interests. Consequently it is the ruling classes that are primarily responsible for the distorted forms of the social life in both the creativity and the distortion of those forms. Rightly in the day of their glory do they tend to take credit for the creativity, and then rightly are they later blamed by others for the distortion!

The conclusion of this discussion is that the powerful and the affluent are not more sinful than others—as some political theologies have intimated. They are, however, more responsible for the forms of fatedness that any epoch bequeaths to its weak and thus are more responsible for suffering. And they defend with all their power these forms of fatedness and the symbols justifying them that they have helped to create, that support their interests, and that they as a class embody. Thus political liberation from social forms of fatedness generally means liberation from the power and dominance of ruling groups. This seems obvious to everyone except ruling groups! Only thus can there be new possibilities for an oppressed world; only thus can the nemesis, the breakdown, and the destruction so clearly foreseen by the prophets be averted both for Israel and for ourselves.

It is never easy or comfortable, but it is salutary, for our own affluent class and our dominant nation to recognize this biblical bias against the affluent and the powerful. Let us note that while the religious foundations of any culture always tempt organized religion into a conservative and even oppressive role and into an alliance with the establishment, the demonic possibilities of any culture, as of any sacred tradition, correspondingly call for true religion to take a socially critical, a radical, possibly even a revolutionary role, into an alliance with the oppressed and the fated. Consequently acts of political liberation almost always represent acts against the power and dominance of history's ruling elites—another important point for us in our powerful present to recall.

IV

Both Scriptures emphasize the estrangement and fatedness of our common life, the inner bondage of our freedom, the outer bondage of our social fatedness, the judgment of God on the individual and the social results of sin. Nevertheless this is by no means their final word either about our inner personal life or about our historical social existence. For the major theme of both Testaments is of the coming of new possibilities into human life, the freeing from the bondage of freedom and of fate, and in the end from the bondage of death. This theme was first expressed in the symbol of the new covenant; a new relation to the law inside and a new social and historical reality outside, the messianic reign, is the central final promise of the Old Testament. Its proclamation as having come or begun is the central affirmation of the New. In a short summation like this of the political dimensions of theology, we cannot emphasize or even clarify the entirety of this gospel. And my remarks must especially omit those aspects of the gospel relevant to inward, personal liberation, liberation from the inner bondage of our freedom, the redemption from sin, and finally from death, aspects expressed in the Christological symbols of incarnation, atonement, and resurrection, and further elaborated in the themes of justification, sanctification, and the work of the Spirit. Their omission here is due to the limits of space and not to a lack of interest or conviction.

What I do wish to emphasize in these concluding remarks on a theology of politics is that the promise of new possibilities in both Scriptures, and so the important symbols expressive of that promise, have social and historical and therefore political ramifications, as did the creative and providential work of God, our estrangement, and the divine judgment on that estrangement. The later prophets, as we know, are replete with a sense of inexorable nemesis and doom coming to the warped communal existence of the Hebrew people. The social institutions and forms established through the old covenant will, say they, be undone, uncreated so to speak, and an almost primal chaos will result. But—and here sounds the unexpected, astounding, prophetic note— new possibilities are there in the future, new possibilities in the outward, communal structure of life as well as in its inward obedience.

Taking this central theme of the prophets again analogically in order to interpret general history and God's action within it, we can say that confidence in divine providence means confidence in the appearance of creative, new possibilities in social life, even in the hopelessness of an oppressive and unjust situation or in the midst of the evident destruction of still-creative forms and structures given to us from the past. As Tillich said, it is confidence, despite a situation of manifest hopelessness, in the appearance of a new social *kairos* and the possibilities of liberation latent there. Creative political action must take place long before its fruits are empirically or historically visible. It thus requires confidence in the possibilities of the future even when they seem to be in fact impossibilities. Thus is every reform or revolutionary movement dependent on a philosophy or mythology of history. Such confidence is also essential in a time of the disintegration of older orders and the imminent threat of nemesis, a time when the temptations to panic and to destructive selfish action rise. The Old Testament's hope for a new covenant is not just the promise of a new future characterized by religious inwardness, by the appearance of the Christ, and by the establishment of the church community (though it is also that), as the tradition has overwhelmingly interpreted it. As the Old Testament makes clear, it also represents an historical and social hope, a confidence in God's creative action in the political and economic orders of secular history. As the judgment of God signals clearly the imminent destruction of unjust and oppressive orders, so the promise of a new historical covenant signals the coming of new historical possibilities, of new forms of liberation from the fatedness of the present.

To sum up: the work of providence, God's activity in the outward scene of history and of social passage, has three moments crucial for a political theology: the creative activity of providence in the formation of social structures of communal life; the judgment of God on the warped character of these historical gifts; and now the promise and the appearance of new possibilities, of new forms of social existence. The balancing presence in Christian faith of the themes of inward liberation, the themes of sin and grace, atonement and justification, does not remove or replace this promise of outward liberation. Rather that balancing presence reminds us that within the continuing work of providence and so within the appearance of new and less oppressive social orders, in the crucial political conquest of particular forms of fatedness, the problem of sin continues, the need for repentance and grace will be constant, and so the promise of forgiveness remains fundamental for our ultimate hope. This is, sadly, true—even when the new forces are made up of such enlightened and liberated minds as we ourselves represent, the best and the brightest hopes of historical life!

Finally, this union of inner and outer, and of both as dependent on and fulfilled in the presence of God, is most clearly manifest in the central symbol of the New Testament promise, the Kingdom. I need not rehearse here the many ahistorical and nonsocial interpretations that symbol has received both in the tradition and in present exegesis. It seems not to matter whether a supernatural, otherworldly, or a personal existentialist interpretation wins the day; in either case the political relevance of the New Testament is dissolved. Nevertheless, if one traces, as I have sought to do, the fundamental intertwining of individual and social, of personal and historical, of inner and outer in the whole Scripture through the symbols of creation, providence, fall, and the promise of redemption; and thus if one views the symbol of the Kingdom as representing the eschatological culmination of the symbol of the covenant people in all the transformations that that crucial symbol underwent, then these ahistorical interpretations seem very questionable indeed. The Kingdom does express, to be sure, the inward reign of God in the hearts of men and women; it does signal the stark opposition of God's love and justice to the historical world; and it does refer to the final culmination of history and of persons in history in God's eternal reality far beyond the bounds of space and time.

Nevertheless, as its earthly analogue, an actual social kingdom, indicates, this symbol refers not only to redeemed individuals but also to a redeemed social order and ultimately to a redeemed history. For we have seen that there cannot be the one without the other. It is for this reason that the prophetic requirements that the covenant community, and with it all communities, be just and merciful, and the prophetic promise of a messianic community of justice, order, and peace, legitimately fill in or define the outer and social structural content of the promised Kingdom. That Kingdom represents, therefore, the perfected social community that corresponds to the personal and individual perfection of the figure of Jesus, a perfection then realized only in him. The symbol of the Kingdom thus functions in relation to ongoing historical and political life as the individual perfection of Jesus as the Christ functions in relation to the crises, despair, and fragmentary realizations of individual Christian existence. It establishes the ultimate norms, the final bases for critical judgment, for positive policies, and for political and communal action, much as the individual perfection of Jesus' life sets the ultimate norms for our own fragmentary good works. Both—the complete sanctification of our individual existence and that of communal existence —remain eschatological hopes; in both areas our experience is of fragmentary fulfillment at best, and in both we remain dependent in the end on the forgiveness and the promise of God for ultimate fulfillment. But as inner and outer, individual and social cannot be separated at any point in Christian understanding, so individual and social salvation cannot be separated. The Kingdom as a symbol of redeemed community underlines the final social, as well as the clearly personal and individual, character of God's purposes in historical time.

A satisfactory discussion of the political dimension of theology, or the social dimensions of the gospel, has only been initiated at best by these remarks. The implications of the religious dimension of community life for the priestly role of the Church in society; the implications of the estrangement and sin of community life for the prophetic role of the Church in the world; the implications of the resurrection for the hopes of the Church in the future; and the implications of the Kingdom for the constructive politics of the Church—none of these have as yet been drawn.

However, I hope my argument has been clear that when we look closely at the central symbolic content of our faith, and through the spectacles of that witness at the divine activity and purposes in history—as that symbolic content illumines for us that activity—we find an understanding of God, of human beings, and of history that is social and political in form. From beginning to end, through covenant people, betrayal and sin, promise, new covenant to final Kingdom, the inner and the outer, the personal and the communal, the moral and the political are intricately but continuously intertwined. Throughout, the divine redemptive activity is directed not only against inward sin and individual death but also against outward social fate. Throughout, the divine purpose is not only to establish an inner piety but also a just, ordered, and creative outer historical world. Throughout, the divine gift of love involves not only renewed inward motives but also renewed relations between people in actual community. The symbols expressive of the creative, transforming power of God in historical time—creation, providence, redemption, love, and final end—each weave individual and community together into a new fabric, a new world of the inner spirit expressed objectively in and through a community of justice, of reunion, and of love.

Notes

1. I recognize that in this public lecture a host of problems are raised that are not dealt with here. An attempt, however, has been made to clarify these issues in *Reaping the Whirlwind: A Christian Interpretation of History* (New York: Seabury, 1977), where the wider theology of history presupposed by these remarks on political theology is delineated and defended.

7

The Concept of a Theology of Liberation:
Must a Christian Theology Today
Be So Conceived?

Schubert M. Ogden

Schubert Ogden's Faith and Freedom *represents one of the earliest and most detailed responses of a prominent First World theologian to the challenge of liberation theology. Even a summary reading of the other contributions to this collection—particularly those by Schüssler Fiorenza and Soelle—reveal that the assimilation and evaluation of Ogden's book represents a kind of second agenda.*

In the present essay, Ogden first dismisses superficial criticisms of liberation theology, which mistakenly accuse its adherents of reducing Christian faith to the praxis of liberation, and then offers criticism of his own. He concludes that contemporary theology cannot be conceived only as critical reflection on liberating praxis, and accuses liberation theologians of failing to submit their own prior commitments to critical analysis. For Ogden, if theologians can be said to make a prior commitment to any group, it is to the human community in its totality—to all those who ask the question of the meaning of life.

Schubert M. Ogden is Professor of Theology and Director of the Graduate Program in Religious Studies at Southern Methodist University. Author of Christ without Myth: a Study Based on the Theology of Rudolf Bultmann *(New York: Harper & Row, 1961) and* The Reality of God and Other Essays *(New York: Harper & Row, 1966, 1977), he has recently published* Faith and Freedom: Toward a Theology of Liberation *(Nashville: Abingdon, 1979).*

I

The fundamental issue with which I understand us to be concerned here is how Christian theology itself ought now to be conceived. Consequently, in considering the concept of a theology of liberation, I am assuming that the question we are above all concerned to answer is whether Christian theology itself can now be adequately conceived only as just such a theology. A claim to this effect I understand to be the main methodological challenge of the several liberation theologies. But our task, I take it, is to consider whether or to what extent this typical claim is sound and, if or insofar as it is sound, what kinds of reasons may be given to support it.

Obviously, the first thing we must do is to try to clarify just what we are to understand by the term, "a theology of liberation." Granted that it is properly used only to designate a certain concept, or ideal type, of Christian theology, how exactly are we to construct this ideal type? For our purposes here, I propose to construct it simply from some of the methodological reflections of Gustavo Gutiérrez, whose contribution at this point I happen to regard as outstanding. The disadvantages of such a procedure are clear. But, provided we all keep in mind that it is only insofar as particular theologies conform to the type to be thus constructed that they fall subject to the judgments I shall make about them, there should not be any serious difficulty. At any rate, the clear advantage of the procedure is that it allows us to confront the challenge of liberation theology concretely, in at least one of the forms in which it is actually being made.

According to Gutiérrez, Christian theology today, given the present historical situation, is adequately conceived only as "critical reflection on historical praxis, flowing out of that praxis and a confrontation with the word of the Lord that is accepted and lived by faith."[1] I select this formulation because it seems to me both more explicit and more balanced than other formulations where Gutiérrez speaks of theology simply as "reflection in and on faith as a liberating praxis."[2] The difficulty with this second kind of formulation is that, if it is taken simply by itself, out of its proper context, it may lead to either or both of two misunderstandings of Gutiérrez's intention.

On the one hand, it may obscure the distinction he expressly makes between "*historical* praxis" and "*liberating* praxis," the first being the activity essential to human existence as such, by which men and women continually transform the natural and social conditions of their lives, thereby creating themselves and one another, while the second is what such historical praxis does or should become insofar as, under conditions of injustice—social, economic, cultural, or racial—human beings act out of solidarity with the oppressed so as to transform the structures oppressing them.[3] There is no question, of course, that Gutiérrez understands the conditions under which we live today to be so profoundly unjust that our historical praxis certainly ought to assume the form of just such a liberating praxis, even to the point of immersing us in "the political process of revolution."[4] Even so, to ignore the fact that the connection here is contingent is, in effect, to confuse things that he himself is at some pains clearly to distinguish. On the other hand, his meaning is even more seriously misunderstood if faith is taken to be nothing other than human praxis, whether generally historical or specially liberating. As insistent as he is that faith is much more than a theoretical matter of believing certain things *about* God, because it is the eminently practical matter of believing *in* God, he is also emphatic that this practical faith that works through love is "the acceptance of the Father's love and a response to it."[5] In other words, the human praxis of faith has its necessary ground in a divine action prior to it, and hence is lived, as Gutiérrez puts it, as "a confrontation with the word of the Lord."

On this understanding, then, the faith on which theology critically reflects is not merely singly but doubly determined: on the one side, by the historical praxis which, in our situation today, must be the praxis of liberation; and on the other side, by "the mystery of divine adoption and brotherhood that lay hidden from all eternity and was eventually revealed in Jesus Christ," whose gospel "reveals us to be children of our heavenly Father and brothers and sisters of others."[6]

As critical reflection on faith thus doubly determined, theology exhibits the same double determination, albeit as "a second act" of reflection relative to the first act of faith itself.[7] The reason for this is that theology is reflection *in* faith as well as *on* it and is entirely oriented to the communication of faith through the proclamation of the gospel.[8] As a matter of fact, Gutiérrez understands theology and faith to be so closely related that he can say not only that "liberation theology comes only after involvement" but also that it is "a necessary precondition if their work is to be concrete and scientific" that "theologians themselves must be persons involved in the process of liberation."[9]

Here, again, the one-sidedness of Gutiérrez's formulations may only too easily mislead as to what he really means to say. Given his insistence that theology is a process of understanding faith that is based in a prior option for the oppressed and a commitment to their liberation, it may well appear that theology consists simply in "a re-reading of the gospel message from within the context of liberation praxis."[10] But this, I am confident, would be a serious misunderstanding of Gutiérrez's meaning. If he argues that theological reflection "is rooted in a commitment to create a just and communal society," he also maintains that such reflection "in turn should help to make this commitment more radical and complete."[11] Nor can there be any doubt about what he means by this. Just as he understands that "the root of social injustice is sin, which ruptures our friendship with God and our brotherhood with other human beings," so he understands "Christ's liberation" to be "a radical liberation, which necessarily includes liberation of a political nature," although it is "not restricted to political liberation."[12] In short, what Gutiérrez means by theology's making the commitment to social justice more radical and complete—or, as he can also say, "more self-critical"—is precisely its "framing the political commitment to liberation within the context of Christ's gratuitous gift of total liberation."[13] Thus, speaking of the two forms of liberation that remain distinct even though integrally related, he can defend himself and his fellow liberation theologians by protesting that "we are not engaging in facile but denigratory equations, distortions, or simplistic forms of reductionism; instead we are shedding light on both sides and showing how their exigencies complement and fructify one another."[14] In the same vein, he voices the confidence that "the future lies with a kind of faith and ecclesial communion that is not afraid of advances in human thinking and social praxis, that is open to questioning by them and ready to challenge them in turn, that is willing to be enriched but is not uncritical, that knows its own conditioning factors but also its own proper exigencies."[15]

Thus, as Gutiérrez presents it, a liberation theology is like most other types of Christian theology, past and present, in being a critical reflection on Christian faith oriented to the communication of faith through the proclamation of the gospel. What distinguishes it from other types of theology is the prior commitment of faith of which it is the reflection, which is a commitment not only to the gospel as attested by Scripture and tradition but also to fellow human beings insofar as, being victims of structural injustice, they are somehow moved by the question of freedom from their oppression. As such, therefore, a theology of liberation involves a re-reading of the gospel from within the context of the liberating praxis that grows out of this commitment and is directed toward responding to the question of the oppressed by transforming existing conditions.

Negatively, this re-reading takes the form of what I shall call, although, so far as I know, Gutiérrez does not, a deideologizing of the gospel, in that it involves so reinterpreting the gospel's meaning as to disengage it from all interpretations whereby in one way or another it has been made to sanction existing injustice and oppression. Positively, this re-reading of the gospel takes the form of its political, even revolutionary, interpretation, in the sense that the gospel's gift and demand of a faith that works through love is interpreted as necessarily including a praxis of liberation that in our situation today is not only political but must even be subversive of the standing order of injustice. At the same time, a theology of liberation, as Gutiérrez understands it, also involves something like a reverse re-reading of the whole political and revolutionary process to which faith as a liberating praxis is necessarily committed. This it involves because, being a Christian theology in the full and proper sense of the words, it cannot but place the commitment to political liberation in the larger and deeper context of God's gift and demand of total liberation in Christ, thereby rendering the whole praxis of liberation more radical and complete as well as more self-critical.

If we assume now that something like this is what a theology of liberation typically involves, we may say that any such theology must be conceived to have two defining characteristics. Its first and, as we may say, formal defining characteristic is its understanding of the critical reflection in which it itself consists as one particular expression of the faith on which it reflects. More exactly, it understands theological reflection to be not only contingently but necessarily an expression of faith, in that such reflection is not really possible at all unless it arises out of the theologian's own prior commitment as a Christian believer. The second and, by contrast, material defining characteristic of a liberation theology is its understanding of the faith on which it as theology reflects, and of which it itself is necessarily an expression. Specifically, it understands Christian faith to be essentially a loving praxis that, under existing conditions of structural injustice, must necessarily become a commitment to the political, even revolutionary, liberation of the oppressed. Thus, if the first defining characteristic of a theology of liberation allows one to conceive of theological reflection as being of direct service to the proclamation of the gospel, and hence to the praxis of liberation, its second defining characteristic requires one to conceive of theology as necessarily including a deideologizing of the gospel and its political, indeed, revolutionary interpretation.

II

Having constructed the concept or ideal type that the term "a theology of liberation" is properly used to designate, we may proceed to consider the claim, also typical of theologies of liberation, that it is in conformity with just this concept or type that any adequate Christian theology today must be conceived. Clearly, our question whether or not this claim is sound cannot be given a reasoned answer except from some methodological standpoint of our own. Consequently, the next thing I have to do is to try to provoke each of you to reflect on your concept of a Christian theology by offering a summary characterization of my own.

As I conceive it, Christian theology is formally characterized as either the process or the product of a certain kind of critical reflection. As a *process* of reflection, it is the kind constituted as such by the twofold question as to the meaning and truth of the Christian witness of faith. Therefore, insofar as it involves any prior commitment, it is committed simply to understanding the meaning of the Christian witness and to assessing its truth, and, therefore, to any and all human beings insofar as, being human, they are somehow moved by the question of the ultimate meaning of their existence to which this witness presents itself as the answer. As a *product* of this kind of reflection, by contrast, theology is constituted as such, not by a question, but by an answer—specifically, by a reasoned answer to its question of the meaning of the Christian witness and, on that basis, a positive answer to its question of the truth of that witness which is likewise a reasoned answer. Thus, insofar as theology as a product of reflection involves any prior commitment, it is a commitment not only to the truth of the Christian witness, given some understanding of its meaning, but also to giving reasons for the claim that this witness is true. As such, therefore, it is, once again, a commitment to any and all human beings insofar as, being human, they not only ask about the ultimate meaning of their existence but are also bound to seek only the truth in doing so.

On this conception, there are evidently two kinds of reasons that can and must be given for any theological claim, including such methodological claims as theology must make about itself. On the one hand, there is the kind of reasons required by any reasoned answer to its question concerning the meaning of the Christian witness. Insofar as a theological claim is sound, the first thing to be said about it is that it is *appropriate,* in the sense of being congruent in meaning with the witness of faith itself. Clearly, whether a claim is thus congruent can be determined only by first determining the real meaning of the witness of faith, and such reasons as one may give for its congruence all depend on this prior determination. In the final analysis, the real meaning of the Christian witness is the real meaning of the *canonical* Christian witness, and just what is to be understood as constituting the Christian canon has been and remains controversial in theology. But on the principle, which I believe to be sound, that the criterion of canonicity is and must be apostolicity, the real meaning of the Christian witness is the meaning to be discerned in the witness of the apostles as their witness can and must be determined by the best historical methods and knowledge available in the situation. Accordingly, in my view, the first kind of reasons that can and must be given for a theological claim are reasons purporting to establish its appropriateness to the apostolic witness of faith attested by Scripture and tradition.

On the other hand, there is the second kind which comprises the reasons required by any reasoned answer to theology's question about the truth of the Christian witness. If a theological claim is sound, it is so not only because it is appropriate in the sense just explained, but also because it is understandable, or, as I now prefer to say, *credible,* in the sense that it is congruent with the truth disclosed at least implicitly in human existence as such. Of course, any effort to determine this congruence, and to give reasons for it of the kind required, at once becomes involved in even greater controversy. For nothing is more controversial among human beings than just what are to count as the standards or criteria for determining the credibility of their various claims. Even so, if one may say, as I would, that the ultimate criteria for the truth of any claim can only be our common human experience and reason, however hard their verdict may be to determine, then the second kind of reasons that can and must be given for a theological claim are reasons purporting to establish its credibility in terms of what all of us somehow experience and understand, if only implicitly.

The other essential point I must make is that, insofar as theology involves the same human understanding involved in any other kind of critical reflection, it is exactly like everything else human in being thoroughly conditioned both socially and culturally. This means, among other things, that theological reflection always and of necessity takes place in some particular historical situation, in terms of its agenda of problems and of its resources for clarifying and solving them. Consequently, while the demand remains constant that any sound theological claim must be supported by reasons purporting to establish both its appropriateness and its credibility, exactly what this demand requires is also always variable in that it is a function of different historical situations. Because this is so, reasons that would be sufficient to establish the soundness of a claim in one situation may very well not be sufficient to do so in another.

As for the reasons that I should give in our situation today for the soundness of this concept of theology, they, too, as I have indicated, must be the same two kinds of reasons, purporting to show that it is both credible and appropriate. So far as its credibility is concerned, suffice it to say that it seems to be in full compliance with standards of critical reflection that are currently widely accepted. Thus, unlike most other concepts of theology, it requires the theologian neither to make the prior commitment of Christian faith nor to appeal at some point to special criteria of truth other than those given generally in our common human experience and reason. But if this much, at least, can be said for its credibility, there seem good reasons to think that it is also appropriate. This is so, at any rate, if the exegetical argument is sound that in the apostolic witness attested by Scripture it is typically assumed that the claims of the Christian witness are true, in the final analysis, for the same reason that any other claim is true—namely, because they express explicitly and fully what anyone to whom they are addressed at least implicitly understands, and, but for willful suppression of the truth, would also be led to affirm by his or her own experience and reason.

Certainly, this is the assumption when the Johannine Jesus is represented as saying, "My teaching is not mine, but his who sent me; if any man's will is to do his will, he shall know whether the teaching is from God, or whether I am speaking on my own authority" (John 7:16–17); or, again, when Paul represents the method of his own witness of faith by saying that "by the open statement of the truth we would commend ourselves to every man's conscience in the sight of God. And even if our gospel is veiled, it is veiled only to those who are perishing" (2 Cor. 4:2–3).

But if the concept of a Christian theology for which I should thus argue can be established as both credible and appropriate, there is clearly one important respect in which the answer to the question before us must be negative: a Christian theology today must *not* be conceived as a theology of liberation. I refer, of course, to what I distinguished earlier as the formal defining characteristic of the typical liberation theology. Whereas on the concept I have just summarized, a Christian theology is already constituted as a process of critical reflection by asking the twofold question as to the meaning and truth of the Christian witness, and is constituted as a product of such reflection by giving a reasoned answer to this question asserting the truth of the Christian witness, on the concept typical of a theology of liberation, the prior commitment involved in thus asking or answering this reflective question is insufficient to constitute a Christian theology as such. Also necessary is the prior

commitment involved in the actual existence of Christian faith as an historical praxis of love, which, in our situation today, means both an acceptance of
God's prevenient love for us and a praxis of liberating our oppressed brothers
and sisters by political activity directed toward transforming the conditions
oppressing them. Unless and until this commitment of faith is made, liberation theologians contend, there cannot be the kind of critical reflection that is
properly Christian theology, whatever other conditions may also be necessary
in order for it to take place.

From my own methodological standpoint, however, such plausibility as
this contention may claim turns upon mistaking a contingent connection for
a necessary one, thereby confusing two things that should be clearly distinguished—namely, theology as such, as critical reflection on the Christian
witness, and theology undertaken as a Christian vocation. Certainly, insofar
as a theologian is a Christian believer and has assumed theological responsibility for this very reason, he or she may fairly be held accountable for making the same prior commitment that must be made by any other Christian.
But even in that case, it is critical to realize that what makes one a theologian,
insofar as one is such, is not the commitment of faith one shares as a believing
Christian but only reflectively asking and answering the question as to the
meaning and truth of the Christian witness, together with making whatever
prior commitment this kind of reflection involves. So far, then, from being a
necessary precondition of their work's being concrete and scientific, the involvement of theologians in the process of liberation is really necessary to
their work's being and remaining a Christian vocation. On the contrary, what
is really a necessary precondition of their theology's being concrete and scientific is that it go beyond merely assuming the truth of their prior commitment
as Christians to ask and answer the question whether even the claims implied
in that commitment are really true. In fact, unless and until they subject even
the constitutive claims of faith itself to the question of truth, their reflection
must remain bound so closely to the faith on which it is supposed to reflect
that, while it may indeed be a reflection *in* faith, it cannot be a reflection *on*
faith, because the only things of which it can really be critical are the expressions of faith in witness.

At stake, in short, is whether a Christian theology is to be conceived as
critical reflection on witness in the full and proper sense of the words, in
which case its service to witness must be an indirect service only, or whether it
is to be regarded as being of direct service to the proclamation of the gospel
and the praxis of faith only because it is conceived, in effect, as the mere
rationalization of positions already taken. If I am right, the second concept
cannot fairly claim to be either appropriate or credible, given the best insights
of our present situation, while good reasons can be given to show that the
first concept is both in terms of just those insights. Indeed, I am prepared to
argue that it is solely this first concept that can adequately express the legitimate motives of a theology of liberation itself. For this concept alone can do
justice both to the deep aspiration of all human beings to know the truth that

makes them free and to the Christian witness of faith that claims to re-present that liberating truth.

III

Yet, as important as it is to realize what is at stake with respect to this first or formal characteristic of a theology of liberation, we still have to consider its typical claim with respect to its second or material characteristic. Not to recognize this would be to make a double mistake. For not only is the logical connection between the two characteristics contingent rather than necessary, but the formal characteristic alone by no means suffices to distinguish liberation theology as a unique ideal type. On the contrary, it is just this first characteristic that makes it like, rather than different from, most other types of Christian theology. Almost all Christian theologies, historic as well as contemporary, have so understood themselves as to be in effect, if not in intention, instances of rationalization rather than critical reflection, at least when judged by the best current standards of judgment. Consequently, for both of these reasons, we need to carefully consider the material characteristic of a liberation theology in its own right before dismissing its claim to be the only way in which an adequate Christian theology today can be conceived.

What can be said for its claim, then, with respect to its understanding of faith as a liberating praxis? My answer is that quite a bit can be said for it—enough, in fact, to establish it as theologically sound. One reason I speak with some confidence about this is that a theology of liberation may fairly lay claim to all the reasons that have already been given in support of such an understanding of faith by those who have argued, with Rudolf Bultmann, that a Christian theology today must be an existentialist theology. I do not mean by this that there are no important differences between an existentialist theology such as Bultmann's and a liberation theology like Gutiérrez's, or that existentialist theologians have already anticipated the understanding of faith for which liberation theologians are now contending. But I do mean that the understanding of faith that both implies and is implied by an existentialist theology, which proceeds, negatively, by way of demythologizing and, positively, by way of existentialist interpretation, is an understanding of faith precisely as praxis, as a way of existing and acting *in* history rather than merely thinking and believing certain things *about* it, or about some other nonhistorical realm unrelated to it. To this extent, a liberation theology can legitimately claim the support of an existentialist theology for the understanding of faith as liberating praxis which both implies and is implied by the deideologizing and political interpretation that are the negative and positive moments, respectively, of its own theological method.

There is a further reason for my confidence that the claim of a liberation theology can be established as sound as regards its understanding of faith. At the very point where this understanding of faith is different from that of an existentialist theology—and, as I believe, quite rightly different—it is possible to develop an argument for it that point for point parallels Bultmann's earlier argument and is at least comparably sound. Unfortunately, space does not permit me to try to convince you of this by actually developing such an argument. But so that you will have at least some idea of what I have in mind, I want to indicate briefly a few of the points that the argument could very well be made to include.

You may recall that Bultmann argues for the necessity of demythologizing by pointing to the conflict between a mythical picture of the world and the world-picture of modern science, together with our modern understanding of our own existence. Because the two elements on our side of this conflict are simply givens in our historical situation, the credibility of the kerygma as a message addressed to us turns on the possibility of critically interpreting the mythology in terms of which it has traditionally been expressed, and in that sense on demythologizing it. The question Bultmann then presses is whether the demythologizing he has thus shown to be a necessity is really a possibility—or, in other words, whether a procedure that can alone meet the demand for credibility can also meet the demand for appropriateness. To this question, then, he argues for an affirmative answer, for which at this point in his argument he gives two closely related reasons. The first is that it is the very nature of myth in general that, although its terms and categories are those of our ordinary objectifying thinking, its real intention is to express an understanding of our own existence in the world, in relation to its primal source and final end. And the second reason is that the prevailing use of myth in the New Testament in particular is precisely for the sake of thus expressing an understanding of human existence, rather than in any way satisfying the interest in a merely objectifying picture of the world.

Now this whole line of argument can be paralleled point for point to support the procedure of deideologizing that, as we have seen, is an essential moment in the method of a theology of liberation. This is certainly so as regards the necessity of such deideologizing, as is clear from arguments developed by liberation theologians themselves. Gutiérrez, for example, argues that, whereas much contemporary theology seeks to respond to the challenge of the *"non-believer"* who questions our *"religious world"* as Christians, in a continent like Latin America the primary challenge comes to us, rather, from the *"non-person"* who, being excluded from the existing order, questions us about our *"economic, social, political, and cultural world."*[16] What is clearly necessary, then, if the credibility of the gospel is to be maintained in face of this kind of challenge is to deideologize it, in the sense of so reinterpreting its meaning as to disengage it from the economic, social, political, and cultural world whose injustices it is used to sanction. But if this much of a parallel argument has already been developed, I see no reason why one cannot go on to develop the rest of it. On the contrary, it seems clear to me that, having thus argued that deideologizing is necessary, one can give two precisely parallel reasons why it is also possible—or, in the terms we have used here, why it is appropriate as well as credible.

Consider, first, what is properly meant by "ideology." In general, I should say that it means a more or less comprehensive understanding of human existence, of how to be and to act as a human being, that functions to justify the interests of a particular group or individual by representing these interests as the claims of disinterested justice. Thus, by its very nature, an ideology's actual effect, if not its real intention, is to rationalize particular interests, even though it represents these interests in terms of a justice that is universal. But this means that, insofar as the interests an ideology functions to justify are not, in fact, just, it itself provides the criterion for critically interpreting them by its own representation of them as just claims. In this way, the de-ideologizing of the gospel that is clearly necessary if it is to be credible to those who suffer from oppression and injustice can also be said to be possible, in that it is a procedure appropriate to the very nature of ideology itself.

This conclusion can be further supported, then, by considering the prevailing use of ideology in the apostolic witness attested by the writings of the New Testament. I cannot go into the details of what I understand this to involve. But the gist of the matter is effectively set forth by my colleague Victor Furnish in his recent book, *The Moral Teaching of Paul.*[17] Rightly to interpret Paul's teaching on particular moral issues, Furnish argues, one must take pains to avoid two common ways of abstracting his teaching from its actual context: from the social, cultural, and political situation in and for which it was intended; and from the comprehensive theological understanding in which it is grounded and of which it is a necessary part. On the other hand, keeping this context fully in mind permits us to see that the importance of Paul's moral instructions to us, as distinct from those to whom he actually issued them, lies "less in the particular patterns of conduct they promote than in the underlying concerns and commitments they reveal. They show us faith being enacted in love, and love seeking to effect its transforming power in the midst of this present age. . . . In effect, the concrete ethical teaching of Paul requires us to reformulate every question about our life in the world into the question about our common life before God. It requires us to understand that faith is not faith until it is enacted in love. And it requires us to find out what this means concretely, given the realities of our own place and time, and to do it."[18] Assuming, as I do, that Furnish's conclusions about Paul can be generalized to apply to the way ideology tends to be used throughout the New Testament, I cannot but see this use as yet a second reason why the deideologizing called for by a theology of liberation is appropriate as well as credible.

But I should not want to give the impression that I suppose it is on making particular points similar to these that the argument for understanding Christian faith as a praxis of liberation depends. Whatever weight such points may finally carry, the solid foundations of this argument I take to lie elsewhere, and to be all the more secure because they may claim the full support, by clear implication, at least, of an existentialist theology. These foundations, as I see them, are two, and, as you would expect, they have to do with the appropriateness and the credibility of this understanding of faith.

The first foundation is that the faith expressed and implied by the apostolic witness attested by Scripture is precisely a faith that, as Paul puts it, works by love. Given the support for this claim throughout the Christian tradition, especially in the theology of the Reformers and, as we have seen, in the existentialist theology of our own time, few theological claims could be more securely established. Moreover, as we have just noted in the case of Paul, the praxis of love apart from which faith is not faith is understood to be by its very nature unbounded, in that it governs the full scope of human responsibility and is addressed to the full range of human need. This is why it is always seeking to effect its transforming power in the present world, finding expression in concrete acts of service directed toward meeting any and all human needs. To this extent, the faith attested by the New Testament may be said to be a praxis of love that both seeks justice and finds expression in it.

But to infer simply from this that it is also what a theology of liberation means by liberating praxis is clearly unwarranted. For, as we saw earlier, what is properly meant by *"liberating* praxis" is a special form of something more general called *"historical* praxis,"* which means the essential human activity whereby men and women play their proper role as the active subjects of history, and not merely its passive objects, by continually transforming the conditions of their lives, both natural and social. While some mode of this activity is of the essence of human existence, being the very thing that distinguishes us as human, explicit consciousness of ourselves as thus historical is itself a product of our continuing history. As a matter of fact, it is a relatively recent product, in that it has only gradually emerged in the course of the revolutionary transformations, scientific and technological as well as political, that have created the modern world. Just such explicit consciousness, however, is evidently involved in the special form of historical praxis that is properly liberating; for, being the form of praxis that is directed toward transforming the conditions of injustice and oppression, liberating praxis is borne by the consciousness that we ourselves are the agents of history who bear full responsibility for the social and cultural structures of our life together. Consequently, it is plainly anachronistic and, for that reason, unwarranted to infer that the praxis of love and justice attested by Scripture is in the full and proper sense a liberating praxis.

Once given modern historical consciousness, however, the praxis of love and justice that Scripture undoubtedly attests faith to be can be rightly interpreted only as being or essentially including the praxis of liberation. For, as we have already seen, what is striking about the praxis of love attested by the New Testament is that it is unlimited, in that it is coextensive not only with the full range of human need, but also with the full scope of human responsibility. But, of course, the whole effect of historical consciousness must be to extend the scope of our responsiblity to include maintaining and transforming the very structures of society and culture. Insofar as we know that even these basic conditions of our existence are neither divinely appointed nor naturally given but historically created as such by ourselves, we must also know that ours is the responsibility for either maintaining them in the forms in which we have received them from our predecessors or else so transforming them that they more nearly realize the justice that could alone justify maintaining them.

There cannot be the slightest question that this double knowledge is one of the givens of our historical situation as modern Western men and women. Just as this situation is determined by the world-picture of modern science and technology, so the understanding of ourselves by which it is also determined necessarily includes an historical consciousness and the enlarged responsiblity it carries with it. In fact, it is clear that all of these givens of our situation are so profoundly interdependent that any one of them must be as essential to it as all the others. But this can only mean that the historical consciousness necessary to faith's being rightly interpreted as a liberating praxis is most certainly given and that it is, therefore, entirely proper to speak of its being given as the second firm foundation for the material claim of a theology of liberation. Because we now know of our responsibility for the entire social and cultural order of which we are a part, we also know that the praxis of love can no longer be only or even primarily the task of meeting needs arising within that existing order. Rather, the primary, if not the only, task of a loving praxis is precisely the liberating praxis whereby the existing order itself is so transformed as to include all the others who must still suffer the oppression of being excluded from it.

My own conclusion, then, is that the understanding of faith with which a liberation theology typically challenges us is theologically sound. Indeed, if the final defense of an existentialist theology is that it is the contemporary expression with respect to knowledge of the Pauline doctrine that we are justified by faith alone without the works of the law, it seems to me that the final, and comparably sufficient, defense of a theology of liberation is that it is the contemporary expression with respect to action of the equally Pauline doctrine that the only faith that justifies us is the faith that works by love. In this second important respect, then, my own answer to the question of this essay can only be affirmative: a Christian theology today *must* be conceived as a theology of liberation.

Notes

1. Gustavo Gutiérrez, "Liberation Praxis and Christian Faith," in *Frontiers of Theology in Latin America*, ed. Rosino Gibellini (Maryknoll, N.Y.: Orbis Books, 1979), p. 22; "Faith as Freedom: Solidarity with the Alienated and Confidence in the Future," in *Living with Change, Experience, Faith*, ed. Francis A. Eigo (Villanova, Pa.: Villanova University Press, 1976), p. 40.

2. Gutiérrez, "Faith as Freedom," pp. 40–41.

3. Ibid., p. 30.

4. Gutiérrez, "Liberation Praxis and Christian Faith," p. 24.

5. Ibid., p. 20.

6. Ibid., p. 26.

7. Gutiérrez, "Faith as Freedom," p. 42.

8. Ibid., pp. 40–41 and 46.

9. Ibid., p. 42; "Liberation Praxis," p. 33, n. 9.

10. Gutiérrez, "Liberation Praxis," p. 25.

11. Ibid., p. 22.

12. Ibid., pp. 20–21, 23.

13. Ibid., p. 23.

14. Ibid.

15. Ibid., p. 19.

16. Gutiérrez, "Faith as Freedom," p. 37.

17. Victor Paul Furnish, *The Moral Teaching of Paul* (Nashville: Abingdon, 1979).

18. Ibid., pp. 28 and 139.

Index

Advertising, 9
Africa, 1, 32, 41, 54
Afrikaans, 15
Allende, Salvador, 26
Amin, Samir, 42n11, 43n15
Amos, 57
Anabaptists, 77
Anderson, Gerald H., 110n5
apocalyptic movement, 1f.
archetype, 108, 109
Aries, Phillippe, 45n49
Asia, 1, 41, 54
atonement, 123-125
Augustine, 53, 117

"bad faith," 87
Balch, David, 111n21
Barbour, Ian G., 110n13
Barnet, Richard J., 43n16, 46n64, n73, n75
Baron, Harold H., 44n38
Barr, James, 97, 111n16
Barth, Karl, 114
Baum, Gregory, 43n11
Bell, Daniel, 42n2, 43n22, 46n77
Bellah, Robert N., 89n2
Berdyaev, Nicholai, 15
Berger, Peter, 116
Bernstein, Harry, 42n11
Berryman, Phillip E., 43n18
Best, Michael N., 44n25
Bible, 56, 84, 96-104, 133
   and loci of liberation, 93
Black Manifesto, 55, 63n
Black Power, 23, 54, 55
Black Religion and Black Radicalism, 81
Blacks, 30-34, 52-68, 77-90. *See also* theology, black
Black Theology Project, 44n44
Blaxall, Martha, 45n52
Bloch, Ernst, 81
Bodenheimer, Susan J., 42n11

Bonhoeffer, Dietrich, 59, 61, 64n12, 87
Bonino, José Míguez, 43n18, 111n28
Boulding, Elise, 45n52
Braverman, Harry, 44n25
Brecht, Bertolt, 11
Brown, Robert McAfee, 43n18, 93, 110n4
Buber, Martin, 11, 16n1
Bucher, Glenn R., 43n21
Bultmann, Rudolf, 11, 16n4, n5, 100, 127, 135, 136
Bureau of Labor Statistics, 29
Buri, Frank, 11
Burkhardt, Walter, 45n58, 112n41

Cabral, Amilcar, 50, 51, 51n4
Calvin, John, 77
Calvinism, 117
Canada, 41
capitalism, 5, 31-38, 52, 116, 122
Cardenal, Ernesto, 16n7
Carmichael, Stokley, 54, 63n2
Castel, Robert, 46n77
Catholicism, 73, 77, 107
Chagall, Marc, 7
"cheap grace," 87
child labor, 35
China, 115
Chodorow, Nancy, 45n54
Chomsky, Noam, 46n74
Christ, 12, 39, 41, 53, 55-59, 65, 98, 125
   Black, 107
   Feminist, 107
   Johannine, 133
Christ, Carol P., 45n58, 111n32
Christian Faith in Black and White, 78
Christianity, 32, 53, 103, 106, 114. *See also* church; theology, Christian
Christians for Socialism, 43n18
church, 23, 39, 52, 61
   black, 34, 77, 87
classism. *See* oppression

Cleage, Albert, 89n15
Cobb, Jonathan, 44n29
Cockroft, James D., 42n11
Coleman Report, 67
Collins, Joseph, 45n61
Collins, Sheila, D., 45n62
community, 115
Cone, Cecil, 63n1, 64n7
Cone, James H., 3, 44n45, 47n83, 52-68,
    63n1, n4, n5, 64n7, n9, 81, 89n11,
    n14, 90n21, n22
  as a theologian of balance, 89n14, 95,
    100, 107, 110n11, 112n45
Connally, William E., 44n25
Constantine, 53
consumerism, 4, 6, 8-10
consumismo, 6
Cormie, Lee, 24-51, 42n8, 43n11, 47n83,
    110n8

Dante Aligheri, 7
death, 8, 123
death of God. See theology
de Lone, Richard H., 44n42
Deloria, Vine, Jr., 93, 110n5
Denmark, 11
Depression, 22
despair, 62
destiny, 119
Detroit, 55
development
  Decade of, 22
  economic, 39-41
  of faith, 69-75, 80, 81
  human, 5
  moral, 70
  structural, 69, 70
  See also faith, stages of
Dodson, Howard, 44n44
Dos Santos, Theotonio, 42n11
Dowd, Douglas, 46n65
DuPlessis, R. Blau, 112n49
Durken, David, 110n7
Durkheim, Emile, 116

Eagleson, John, 43n18
Easton, Barbara Leslie, 44n47
economy. See capitalism
Edwards, Richard C., 44n38, 46n63

Egypt, 5, 56
Ehrenreich, Barbara, 45n51
Eigo, Francis A., 139n1
Elkind, David, 72
emancipation, 13
Emler, Nicholas P., 47n78
Engels, Friedrich, 64n10
English, Deidre, 45n51
Enlightenment, 77
Enzenberger, Hans Magnus, 14, 16n8
eschatology, 39, 53, 62, 63, 107, 108
ethics, social, 67
Europe, Western, 22, 41
Evans, Sara, 45n55
evil, 86, 119, 121
exile, 5
existentialism, 11, 100
  and immediacy, 11
  and interpretation, 11
  and unconditionality, 7, 8
  See also theology, existential
Exodus, 58, 97

faith
  biblical, 53
  Christian, 52, 53, 55-62, 75, 76
  stages of, 69-83
Faith and Freedom, 17, 127
family, 35, 36
Fascism, 7
Featherstone, Rudolph, 81
feminism, 23. See also theology, femin-
    ist
Feuerbach, Ludwig, 59
Fiorenza, Elisabeth Schüssler. See
    Schüssler Fiorenza, Elisabeth
Fiorenza, Francis. See Schüssler Fior-
    enza, Francis
First World, 5, 9, 10, 21-42
FitzGerald, Frances, 46n67, 47n80
Forman, James, 55, 63n5
Fortune, Marie, 111n38
Fowler, James W., 69-90, 90n1, n3, n9
Frank, Andre Gunder, 42n11
freedom, 60, 61, 107, 109, 119
Freeman, Jo, 45n55
Freire, Paulo, 80, 89n8
French Revolution, 77
Furnish, Victor Paul, 137, 140n17

Gager, John G., 111n20
Gailbraith, John Kenneth, 43n22
Galeano, Eduardo, 12, 16n6
Galilea, Segundo, 43n20
Gandhi, Mahatma, 51
Gans, Herbert J., 44n28, 46n67, 47n80
Garnet, Henry H., 55, 64n6
Geffre, Claude, 43n20
Genesis, 72
George, Susan, 45n62
German Bundestag, 12
Gibellini, Rosino, 43n18, 139n1
Gilkey, Langdon, 46n76, 113-126, 126n1
Gilligan, Carol, 45n58
Ginsberg, Allen, 14
God, 19, 20, 56, 85, 86, 114, 115, 128, 129
    activities of, 124, 125
    as emancipator, 13
    of justice, 54
    as redeemer, 13
Goethe, Johann Wolfgang von, 7
Gordon, David M., 44n38
Gospel According to Matthew, 6
Gottwald, Norman K., 47n83, 111n17, n19
grace, 114, 124, 125
Graham, Billy, 118
Grana, Cesar, 49, 51n2
Greece, 97, 107, 115
Guinea, 51
Gutiérrez, Gustavo, 21, 41, 42n1, n9, 43n18, n20, 46n66, 47n82, 60, 64n15, 105, 110n3, 112n40, 128-131, 135, 136, 140n1f.

Halberstam, David, 46n74
Ham, 58
Hamilton, Charles, 63n2
Hamilton, Roberta, 44n47, 45n48
Harrington, Michael, 43n24
Harrison, Beverly Wildung, 45n58, n61
Harvard, 12
Harvey, Van A., 47n81
Haugerud, Joann, 111n38
Hegel, G.W.F., 11, 60, 115
Heidegger, Martin, 11
Heil, Brad, 44n41
Heinemann, Gustav, 12

Hennelly, Alfred T., 43n18
Herberg, Will, 46n76
Herman, Edward S., 44n30
hermeneutic circle, 100, 101, 109
hermeneutics
    of consent, 99, 101, 106
    of detachment, 100
    of engagement, 100
    feminist biblical, 91-112
    and privilege of the oppressed, 94, 100
    of retrieval, 2
    of suspicion, 2, 91
    of the Woman's Bible, 102-106
    See also paradigm, hermeneutic-contextual
Herzog, Frederick, 111n23
Hispanics, 30, 31, 92
history, 8, 9, 14, 38, 39, 60, 85, 86, 105
Hogan, Robert T., 47n78
Hoge, Dean R., 46n76
Hooker, Isabella Beecher, 103
Howe, Florence, 110n1
Howe, Louise Kapp, 44n34, 45n57
Huber, Joan, 45n50, n55
Hume, David, 18
Hussites, 77

ideology
    and critique, 2
    incarnation, 123
    and theory, 109
Industrial Revolution, 22
    second, 8
Inhelder, Barbel, 89n4
injustice. See oppression
Inkeles, Alex, 42n11
Iran, 15
Iron Curtain, 7
Is God a White Racist? 81
Israel, 57, 98, 106, 118, 120, 123
Italy, 6, 7, 10

Japan, 22, 115
Jeremiah, 87
Jerusalem, 5, 6
Jesus. See Christ
Johnson, Dale L., 42n11
Jones, Major, 81, 84, 89n19
Jones, William R., 81, 88, 89n13, n16

Judges, 117
justice, 9, 53, 55, 60

Kahl, Joseph A., 43n12
kairos, 11, 124
Katznelson, Ira, 44n37
Keck, Leander E., 111n20
Kierkegaard, Soren, 12, 119
King, Martin Luther, Jr., 54, 55, 63n2
Kirk, J.A., 111n17
Knox, John, 77
Kohlberg, Lawrence, 70, 78, 89n5
Kohn, Melvin L., 43n23
Kuhn, Thomas S., 95, 110n13
Kummell, Werner G., 111n18

language, 6-8, 71, 99
    practical-existential, 11, 12
    scientific, 9, 10
    theoretical-objective, 11, 12
Lappé, Frances Moore, 45n62
Lasch, Christopher, 44n32, 45n53
Latin America, 1, 12-14, 54. *See also*
    Third World; theology, Latin
    American
Leghorn, Lisa, 110n2
Lenin, Vladmir Ilych, 11, 16n3
Lerner, Daniel, 42n11
Levellers, 77
Levine, Lawrence, 64n13
LeVine, Robert A., 47n78
Levinson, Andrew, 44n26, n31
Levi's, 4, 8, 14
liberal, 93, 114
liberation, 15, 77, 78
    political, 55, 121, 122
    zones of, 75
    See also theology, liberation
Lindley, Susan Hill, 110n2
Lipset, Seymour Martin, 42n3, n5,
    46n71, n77
Lockheed, D., 110n8
love, 11, 60, 61, 104, 126, 130, 131, 138,
    139
Lovin, Robin, 65-68, 89n1
Lukes, Steven, 46n67
Luther, Martin, 53, 77

Maccoby, Michael, 44n32, 47n79
MacIntyre, Alasdair, 46n77

Macpherson, Crawford Brough, 47n77
Magnificat, 122
Mahan, Brian, 48-51
male, 10, 104
Mann, Michael, 46n67
Mannheim, Karl, 49, 51n1
Mar del Plata, 12
Maritain, Jacques, 27
Marty, Martin E., 46n76
Marx, Karl, 9, 10, 12, 53, 59, 60, 64n10,
    77, 121, 122
Marxen, Willi, 107
Marxism, 6, 11, 55, 66, 81, 94, 97, 102,
    116
McClelland, David C., 42n11
McLaughlin, Eleanor, 111n21
Meaning of Revelation, 81
Meeks, Wayne A., 111n20
memory, 2
Meredith, James 54
Mermelstein, David, 44n43
Metz, Johann Baptist, 81
Míguez Bonino, José, 43n18, 111n28
military, 16
Mills, C. Wright, 46n68, n70
Miranda, José, 97, 111n17
Moltmann, Jürgen, 81
Moral Teaching of Paul, 137
Moses, 27, 58
Müller, Ronald E., 46n64
multinational corporations, 25, 26, 37,
    38, 62

National American Women's Suffrage
    Association, 103
National Committee of Negro Church-
    men, 55, 63n3
National Conference of Black Church-
    men, 63n3
Native American. *See* theology, Native
    American
nature, 14, 15
Neal, Marie Augusta, 43n21
neo-orthodoxy, 99, 114
Newark, 55
New Testament, 57, 59, 98, 125, 136, 137
Niebuhr, H. Richard, 81, 89n3
Nisbet, Robert A., 46n69
Noah, 58
North America, 1, 53, 54, 59, 60, 62

Notre Dame, 102
Nygren, Anders, 47n81

Oakley, Ann, 44n47
obedience, 52, 59, 62, 63, 65
O'Connor, James, 46n65
Oedipus, 71
Ogden, Schubert M., 3, 10, 12, 13, 14, 16n9, 17-20, 20n1f, 94, 95, 107, 110n9, 111n26, 112n43, 127-140
Old Testament, 57, 93, 74, 118, 119
oppression
  classist, 2, 13, 37, 38, 120, 121
  cultural, 2, 13
  economic, 2, 13, 32-39
  political, 2, 13, 53, 54
  racist, 2, 13, 32-34, 52-64
  sexist, 2, 13, 34-37, 102, 103, 108, 120, 121
  spiritual, 5-10
optimism, 21-24

Pannenberg, Wolfhart, 81
paradigm
  doctrinal, 96, 97, 106
  of emancipatory praxis, 109
  feminist interpretive, 106-110
  form and redaction, 98, 99
  hermeneutic-contextual, 98, 99, 101, 106, 109, 110
  historical-critical, 97, 98, 106
  in social sciences, 41, 47n83
Parker, Richard, 43n24
Parsons, Talcott, 42n6, n11
Pasolini, Pier Paolo, 6-8, 16n2
patriarchy, 108
Paul, 14-16, 58, 98, 107, 117, 133, 137-139
Peasants' Revolt, 53
Pedagogy of the Oppressed, 80
Perella, Frederick J., Jr., 44n24
Perrin, Norman, 111n18
Peters, T., 111n23
Petrovic, Gajo, 59, 64n11
Philosophes, 77
Piaget, Jean, 70, 78, 89n4
Piore, Michael J., 44n39
Plaskow, Judith, 45n58, n60, 110n3, 111n32
politics, 103, 124

Politics of God, 84
poor. See oppression
Portes, Alejandro, 42n11
praxis, 3, 12, 52, 54-56, 59-63, 65
  emancipatory, 109
  historical, 128, 129, 138
  liberating, 94, 128-131, 135, 138
  of love, 138
prayer, 6-10, 17, 58
prisoners, 5
prophecy, 2, 50, 58, 97, 122
Protestant ethic, 49
Protestant Ethic and the Spirit of Capitalism, 25
prototype, 108, 109
psychology, 40
  developmental, 81
  structural-developmental, 82

Quakers, 77

racism. See oppression
Radical Monotheism and Western Culture, 81
Raines, John Curtis, 43n24
rationality, 27, 28, 34, 48-51
Rauschenbusch, Walter, 121
Reagen, Barbara, 45n52
redemption, 15
reflection, critical, 3, 10, 17
Reformation, 77
Reich, Michael, 44n38, 46n65
Rembrandt van Rijn, 7
Renaissance, 77
Responsible Self, The, 81
resurrection, 123
revelation, 96, 108
revolution, 6, 53, 131
rhythm of nature, 8
Rich, Adrienne, 110n1
Richard, Pablo, 43n17
Ricks, Willie, 54
Ricoeur, Paul, 74
Roberts, J. Deotis, 44n45, 64n7, 84, 89n18
Roman Catholic Church. See Catholics
Roman Empire, 53
Romans, 14
Roodkowsky, M., 110n2
Rostow, W. W., 42n4, n11, 46n72

Rothman, Sheila M., 45n51
Rubin, Lilian Breslow, 44n27
Ruether, Rosemary Radford, 45n58, n61, 111n21, 112n50
Russel, Diane E. Nichole, 110n2
Russell, Letty, 45n60
Russia, 22
Ryan, T.J., 110n6

Saffioti, Heleieth, I., 45n48
Saiving, Valerie, 45n58
Sallach, David L., 46n67
salvation, 39, 108
São Paulo Justice and Peace Commission, 43n14
Sartre, Jean Paul, 15, 87
Sauter, G., 111n15
Sawers, Larry, 44n43
Schillebeeckx, Edward, 99, 111n24
Schottroff, Luise, 111n22
Schottroff, Willy, 111n20
Schüssler Fiorenza, Elisabeth, 3, 45n59, n60, 91-112, 110n6, n7, n14, 111n21, n32, n48, 112n39, 127
Schüssler Fiorenza, Francis, 43n18, 112n42
science, 116
Segundo, Juan Luis, 43n18, n19, 50, 51n3, 91, 99-102, 107, 111n27, n29
Sennett, Richard, 44n29, n32
Servant Songs, 122
sexism. See oppression
Shakespeare, William, 7
sin, 57, 86, 93, 114, 118, 120, 124, 125, 129, 130
Sinai, 56
Smith, W.C., 89n2
Sobrino, Jon, S.J., 107, 112n46
social gospel, 121
social theory, 52, 65-68
sociology, 56
Soelle, Dorothee, 3, 4-19, 127
Solentiname, 13
South Africa, 62, 122
South America. See Latin America
Soweto, 15
stage theory, 69. See also faith, stages of
Stanton, Elisabeth Cady, 100, 102-106, 111n33, n35, 112n39

Stegemann, Wolfgang, 111n20, n22
Strain, Charles H., 110n12
Stransky, Thomas F., 110n5
Stuhlmacher, Peter, 111n25
suffragists, 102-106
Swidler, Leonard, 111n38

Tabb, William K., 44n43
television, 7-10
Theissen, Gerd, 111n20, n22
theodicies, 88
theologians
   of balance, 83-88
   ideological, 82-88
theology
   academic, 94
   African, 54
   Black, 1, 23, 24, 52-90
   Christian, 1-3, 75, 76, 127-140
   criteria for, 80, 132
   death of God, 81
   definition of, 130, 131, 135
   existentialist, 11, 100, 135, 136, 137
   feminist, 1, 23, 24, 54, 60, 91f, 109, 110
   First World, 1
   foundational, 102, 137, 138
   of freedom, 60
   of hope, 81
   Latin American, 1, 23, 24, 60, 43n18
   liberation, 1-3, 10-14, 23, 24, 43n18, 54, 76-78, 81-84, 91-94, 127-140
   Native American, 93, 95
   of play, 81
   political, 1, 2, 100, 113
   process, 16, 94
   and process of reflection, 17, 131, 132
   as product of reflection, 17, 131
   of relinquishment, 28
   Third World, 1, 23, 24, 43n18, 60
Theology for the Americas, 45n61
theory, 3, 12
Third World, 28, 62. See also theology, Third World
Thomas, Herman, 44n33, n36
Tillich, Paul, 56, 64n8, 89n3, 115, 116, 119
tourists, 7
Tracy, David, 1-3, 42n8, 111n26, 112n44

Traynham, Warner, 78, 84, 89n7, n20
truth, 60, 61, 108, 109

Uncle Silas, 60
unemployment, 38
union, 35
Union for Radical Political Economy, 44n33, n43
United States, 22-39
University of Chicago, 122
Uruguay, 12

Van de Ven, N., 110n2
Vergote, Antoine, 89n1
Victorianism, 35
Vietnam, 15
von Rad, Gerhard, 119

Wachtel, Howard M., 43n13
Walker, David, 64n6
Wallerstein, Immanuel, 42n11, 44n37
Washington, Joseph, 63n1, 84, 89n17
Watts, 55
Waxman, Chaim I., 46n70
Weber, Max, 25, 42n10, 66

Weiner, Myron, 42n11
Weisskopf, Thomas, 46n65
Wellesley Editorial Committee, 45n48
Welter, Barbara, 111n34
West, Cornell, 44n46
West Africa, 81
West Germany, 7
Whitehead, Alfred North, 91, 119
Willard, Frances, 105
Wilmore, Gayraud S., 44n45, 63n1, n4, n5, 81, 89n6, n12
Wilson, William Julius, 44n40
Wink, Walter, 110n14
Winter, Gibson, 46n76
Wire, Antoinette C., 111n17
witness, 3, 10, 17, 131, 132
Woman's Bible, 100, 102-106, 111n33, n35, 112n47
Woman's Work Project, 44n35, 45n56
women, 30-32, 34-37. *See also* theology, feminist
Wright, Erik Olin, 46n65

Zaretsky, Eli, 45n48, 46n68
Zwingli, 77

OTHER ORBIS TITLES

ANDERSON, Gerald H.
ASIAN VOICES IN CHRISTIAN THEOLOGY

"Anderson's book is one of the best resource books on the market that deals with the contemporary status of the Christian church in Asia. After an excellent introduction, nine scholars, all well-known Christian leaders, present original papers assessing the theological situation in (and from the viewpoint of) their individual countries. After presenting a brief historical survey of the development of the Christian church in his country, each author discusses 'what is being done by the theologians there to articulate the Christian message in terms that are faithful to the biblical revelation, meaningful to their cultural traditions, and informed concerning the secular movements and ideologies.' An appendix (over 50 pages) includes confessions, creeds, constitutions of the churches in Asia. Acquaintance with these original documents is imperative for anyone interested in contemporary Asian Christian theology." *Choice*

ISBN 0-88344-017-2   *Cloth $15.00*
ISBN 0-88344-016-4   *Paper $7.95*

APPIAH-KUBI, Kofi & Sergio Torres
AFRICAN THEOLOGY EN ROUTE

Papers from the Pan-African Conference of Third World Theologians, Accra, Ghana.

"If you want to know what 17 Africans are thinking theologically today, here is the book to check." *Evangelical Missions Quarterly*

"Gives us a wonderful insight into the religious problems of Africa and therefore is well worth reading." *Best Sellers*

"This collection of presentations made at the 1977 Conference of Third World Theologians reveals not a finished product but, as the title suggests, a process. . . .On the whole, the book is well written and, where necessary, well translated. It adds to a growing literature on the subject and is recommended for libraries seriously concerned with theology in Africa." *Choice*

ISBN 0-88344-010-5   *184pp. Paper $7.95*

CLAVER, Bishop Francisco F., S.J.

THE STONES WILL CRY OUT
Grassroots Pastorals

"Bishop Claver is the gadfly of the Philippine Catholic hierarchy who persistently buzzes in the ears of President Fernando Marcos and all his toadies. The bishop's book is a collection of fighting pastoral letters to his congregation after martial law closed the diocesan radio station and newspaper." *Occasional Bulletin*
"His gutsy strength has made him a prophet against the repressive regime. Some of his U.S. colleagues could learn from him." *National Catholic Reporter*
ISBN 0-88344-471-2   *196pp. Paper $7.95*

COMBLIN, José

THE CHURCH AND THE NATIONAL SECURITY STATE

"The value of this book is two-fold. It leads the readers to discover the testimony of those Latin American Christians who are striving to be faithful to the gospel in the midst of a most difficult situation characterized by the militarization of society, the consequent suppression of public freedom, and violation of basic human rights. It also invites the readers from other cultural and historical contexts to seek in their own situations the inspiration for a real theology of their own." *Theology Today*
ISBN 0-88344-082-2   *256pp. Paper $8.95*

JESUS OF NAZARETH
Meditations on His Humanity

"This book is not just another pious portrait of Christ. Its deeply religious insights relate the work of Jesus as modern scholarship understands it to the ills of our contemporary world." *Review of Books and Religion*

ISBN 0-88344-239-6   *Paper $4.95*

THE MEANING OF MISSION
Jesus, Christians and the Waytaring Church

"This is a thoughtful and thought-provoking book by a Belgian theologian and social critic, who has lived and taught in Latin America for 20 years. His rich background in evangelization, both in theory and in practice, is evident throughout his book." *Worldmission*
ISBN 0-88344-305-8   *Paper $4.95*

SENT FROM THE FATHER
Meditations on the Fourth Gospel

"In a disarmingly simple and straightforward way that mirrors the Fourth Gospel itself, Comblin leads the reader back to biblical basics and in doing so provides valuable insights for personal and community reflection on what it means to be a disciple of the Lord, to be 'sent' by him." *Sisters Today*
ISBN 0-88344-453-4   *123pp. Paper $3.95*

FABELLA, Virginia, M.M. & Sergio Torres
THE EMERGENT GOSPEL
Theology from the Underside of History

"*The Emergent Gospel*, I believe, is an expression of a powerful and barely noticed movement. It is the report of an ecumenical conference of 22 theologians from Africa, Asia and Latin America, along with one representative of black North America, who met in Dar es Salaam, Tanzania, in August 1976. Their objective was to chart a new course in theology, one that would reflect the view 'from the underside of history,' that is, from the perspective of the poor and marginalized peoples of the world. Precisely this massive shift in Christian consciousness is the key to the historical importance of the meeting. The majority of the essays were written by Africans, a smaller number by Asians and, surprisingly, only three by Latin Americans, who thus far have provided the leadership in theology from the developing world." *America*

ISBN 0-88344-112-8   *Cloth $12.95*

FENTON, Thomas P.
EDUCATION FOR JUSTICE: A RESOURCE MANUAL

"The completeness of the source material on the topic and the adaptability of the methodology—stressing experiential education—to groups at the high school, college, or adult levels make this manual a time and energy saving boon for most anyone having to work up a syllabus on 'justice.' This manual would be a worthwhile addition to any religion and/or social studies curriculum library." *Review for Religious*

"The resource volume is rich in ideas for a methodology of teaching Christian justice, and in identifying the problems. It is also very rich in the quality of the background readings provided. The participant's volume is a catchy workbook with many illustrations. It encourages the student (young or adult) to look at the problems as they are experienced by real live persons." *The Priest*

"Replete with background essays, tested group exercises, course outlines and annotated bibliography, this manual should give any teacher or seminar leader plenty of material to launch a thorough study program—and plenty of strongly stated positions for students to react to." *America*

ISBN 0-88344-154-3   *Resource Manual $7.95*
ISBN 0-88344-120-9   *Participant Workbook $3.95*

GUTIERREZ, Gustavo
A THEOLOGY OF LIBERATION

Selected by the reviewers of *Christian Century* as one of the twelve religious books published in the 1970s which "most deserve to survive."

"Rarely does one find such a happy fusion of gospel content and contemporary relevance." *The Lutheran Standard*

ISBN 0-88344-477-1   *Cloth $7.95*
ISBN 0-88344-478-X   *Paper $4.95*

HENNELLY, Alfred

THEOLOGIES IN CONFLICT
The Challenge of Juan Luis Segundo

"This is another, and a significant, addition to the growing literature on liberation theology. Hennelly's intent is to initiate a dialogue with Latin American theologians and thus foster an indigenous North American liberation theology. After two introductory chapters in which he situates and overviews this new movement, he focuses on Segundo's articulation of some central liberation themes: the relation between history and divine reality, the role of the church, theological method, spirituality, and the significance of Marxism. Throughout, he draws heavily on material not available in English. Hennelly does not write as a critic of but as a spokesperson for Segundo; yet his own convictions are evident when, at the end of each chapter, he extracts challenging questions for North Americans. He voices a growing awareness: the impossibility, the sinfulness, of carrying on theology detached from social-political realities. Definitely for most theology collections." *Library Journal*

"Father Hennelly provides an excellent introduction to Juan Segundo's thought and a helpful guide to the voluminous literature, presenting the theology not as 'systematic' but as 'open': methodological principles allowing for growth and development take precedence over systematic organization of concepts." *Paul Deats, Professor of Social Ethics, Boston University*

ISBN 0-88344-287-6   224pp. *Paper $8.95*

HERZOG, Frederick

JUSTICE CHURCH

The author, Professor of Systematic Theology at Duke Divinity School, continues the pioneering work he began with *Liberation Theology* (1972). *Justice Church* presents the *first* North American methodology of liberation theology while also critically analyzing what is and what should be the function of the Church in contemporary North America.

"Herzog refuses to do an easy or obvious theology, but insists on raising difficult questions which require theology to be done with some anguish. He has seen more clearly than most that we are in a crisis of categories, which must be reshaped in shattering ways." *Walter Brueggemann, Eden Theological Seminary*

"For us in Latin America, the question of how North Americans do theology is critically important. Besides its intrinsic value for the United States and Canada, this book should stimulate theological conversation across the North-South divide." *Jose Miguez Bonino, Dean of the Higher Institute of Theological Studies, Buenos Aires*

ISBN 0-88344-249-3   176pp. *Paper $6.95*